Praise for GodQuest:

"*I highly recommend* GodQuest *for anyone who wants to develop a strong foundation for their faith and be confident about sharing it with others. It's a spiritual journey everyone should take!*"

—**Josh McDowell,** bestselling author of More Than a Carpenter

"*In today's often relativistic culture, the search for truth can be confusing at best and elusive at worst. People are constantly bombarded with contradictory messages of what is real, what is right. But in* GodQuest, *Sean McDowell and Stan Jantz break down the confusion and bring clarity to the reality of Jesus Christ's identity. If you are on a search for what is real, this book lays out the path in ways that challenge, inspire, and ultimately reveal the truth—God's truth.*"

—**Ed Young,** pastor of Fellowship Church and author of Outrageous, Contagious Joy (Berkeley Praise)

"*I am thrilled about* GodQuest *because more than ever Sean and Stan are teaching the critical issues of the day.* GodQuest *does not just give surface answers, but goes into looking at the questions behind the questions out there and exploring worldviews.*"

—**Dan Kimball,** author of They Like Jesus But Not The Church

"All of us are on a journey through life. The journey is often difficult and confusing with many bumps and forks in the road. Many will, therefore, welcome GodQuest as a helpful resource by Sean McDowell and Stan Jantz. The authors aren't merely standing in the road with compasses and pointing journeyers in the right direction. The combination of personal stories, illustrations, and facts make this a fun journey led by warm and trustworthy guides."

–**Michael Licona,** Ph.D., *Apologetics Coordinator, North American Mission Board*

"GodQuest *combines two compelling dynamics: declaration and invitation. It objectively declares the claims of Christianity and its supporting facts. But it also invites people to examine the evidence for themselves and to draw their own conclusions. These two features make* GodQuest *a powerful tool to fortify faith that's factually informed and personally owned."*

–**Pastor Bob Coy,** *Calvary Chapel Fort Lauderdale*

"GodQuest *is a awesome resource to explore life's most important questions in a authentic way. It's filled with practical and useful information for both individuals and groups and encourages taking honest steps on the journey with God. I believe many will read it and discover, or re-discover, the God who is our hope!"*

–**Jud Wilhite,** author of Torn *and senior pastor of Central Christian Church, Las Vegas*

SIGNPOST

THE QUEST

1

WHAT YOU BELIEVE DETERMINES WHERE YOU GO IN LIFE.

This signpost presents an important concept, because our beliefs affect our choices, the paths we take in life, and our ultimate destination. As you choose your path in life, you can decide to seek God and follow after Him, or set off on your own course.

GODQUEST

*Discover the God
Your Heart Is Searching For*

SEAN McDOWELL   STAN JANTZ

GODQUEST

*Discover the God
Your Heart Is Searching For*

SIX SIGNPOSTS
FOR YOUR SPIRITUAL JOURNEY

SEAN McDOWELL   STAN JANTZ

OUTREACH®

ISBN: 978-1-9355-4129-5

Cover and interior design: Tim Downs

Editing: Jennifer Dion and Julia Wallace

Printed in the United States of America

GODQUEST

GODQUEST

CHAPTER 1:

THE JOURNEY OF ULTIMATE DISCOVERY

Going on a quest is one of the most adventurous, important, and significant things you could ever do in your life—if not *the* most important. A quest is a search for something of great value, like a treasure, and going on a quest means embarking on an adventure in pursuit of that treasure. A quest also connects you with the people who are in pursuit of the same treasure. By going on a quest of any kind, especially a quest to find something that enriches your life, you have the opportunity to become part of a community where you develop meaningful and long-lasting relationships.

Great quests are the stuff of legend, and the tales of certain quests are among the most popular stories of all time. You may have heard of one or more of these famous quests. Maybe you've read about them in a book or seen them in a movie or on television:

The Odyssey is an ancient, epic poem that centers on the Greek hero Odysseus (or Ulysses, as he was known in Roman myths) and his long journey home following the fall of Troy. It takes Odysseus ten years to reach his home in Ithaca (Greece, not New York). Because of its twists, turns, and adventures as Odysseus pursues something of great value—in this case *home*—the word *odyssey* has come to refer to an epic voyage. One of the most popular and enduring movies of all time, *The Wizard of Oz*, is based on this classic story structure.

The Quest for the Holy Grail is the classic quest for the cup of Christ, supposedly used by Jesus at the Last Supper before He was crucified. This noble quest to find the cup, which was thought to possess great power, has been told in many forms and with many characters, including King Arthur, Indiana Jones, and Robert Langdon, hero of the blockbuster novel *The DaVinci Code*. For the record, our favorite interpretation of this legendary quest is *Monty Python and the Holy Grail*.

The Lord of the Rings is an epic story written by J. R. R. Tolkien that follows the quest of a hobbit named Frodo Baggins to destroy the one ring that was created to control the other rings held by the leaders of Men, Elves, and Dwarves. The reluctant hero pursues his quest primarily to keep the ring out of the control of the evil Dark Lord Sauron. No doubt you've seen or heard of the marvelous *Lord of the Rings* film trilogy directed by Peter Jackson.

The Chronicles of Narnia follows the adventures of four children— Peter, Susan, Edmund, and Lucy—through a magical wardrobe to the land of Narnia, where animals talk and good battles evil. As brilliantly told by C. S. Lewis, this quest follows Aslan, the mighty lion who asks the children to help him restore Narnia to its rightful line.

Star Wars takes place in "a galaxy far, far away" and chronicles the quest for the Force, an omnipresent energy that can be harnessed by those with that ability. *Star Wars* creator George Lucas describes the Force as "an energy field created by all living things [that] surrounds us, penetrates us, [and] binds the galaxy together." The Force can be used for good or for evil.

And then there's *American Idol*, that annual ritual of culture and music that searches for the best (and most ambitious) singer. What starts as a national talent hunt, culling the truly talented from the delusional fame-seeking hoards, ends up as a contest between ten or twelve young men and women who are on a quest of their own: to claim the treasure of being crowned this year's American Idol.

You'll notice that in all of these grand stories, nobody quests after trivial things. These aren't quests for the perfect burger or the best ice cream. A worthy quest goes after noble causes like home, the Holy

Grail, the ring, the Force, and a recording contract. A meaningful quest involves powerful leaders like Aslan and even reluctant heroes like Frodo Baggins, Luke Skywalker, and Ryan Seacrest as they form relationships and endure trials in the course of their journey.

Of course, at the end of the day, these famous quests may inspire us, they may give us hope and provide a pattern for our own quests, but they aren't real. Only a small number of people will ever seriously compete on *American Idol*. There's no such thing as the ring. Neither Narnia nor Middle Earth exists. Even the cup of Christ, which may have been real at one time, exists now only as a symbol for something else. In fact, that's what all of these legendary symbols are: pointers to something much greater, such as fame and fortune, and a power in the universe that is not available to mere mortals—unless the mere mortals are willing to go on an adventurous journey to find it.

In fact, this power, much more than fame or fortune, is something every person longs for. It's the connection to something that seems unattainable because it offers the promise of an extraordinary life of harmony and peace, above and beyond the evil, suffering, pain, and boredom this ordinary mortal life has to offer. And you know what? It's a longing that God has put in our hearts. As wise King Solomon writes, "He has made everything beautiful in its time. He has also set eternity in the human heart" (Ecclesiastes 3:11).

This is why it's not just the goal of the quest that matters, but the connection our quest gives us to something or someone incredibly meaningful. But in order for the object of any quest to be meaningful, it must be real and it must be attainable. Rings and Grails and the Force don't count. Becoming the next American Idol isn't realistic. But making a connection to and having a relationship with the greatest Force, the greatest Power, and the greatest Person in the universe can be a reality for one very simple reason: God is real and He wants to have a relationship with you.

Don't you find it interesting that some of these famous quests focus on objects that are symbols for God, or at least in some way point to God? That's why some of these quest stories, like *The Odyssey* and The Holy Grail, have endured for centuries, while the others continue to be invented and told in our own time. There is a need in the human heart and the human mind to connect with something bigger than ourselves that provides meaning, a future, and a hope.

WHY A GODQUEST AND WHY NOW?

As interesting and inspiring as all of these quests are, they are ultimately signposts to the greater reality that is God. Why go on a quest for something artificial like the ring or the Holy Grail when you can spend your time searching for the real thing? Why pursue an impersonal Force when the personal God is waiting for you to seek Him? If God is the "something" all the other quests ultimately point to, why not go on a quest for God?

Is that the reason why you picked up this book? Are you longing for something bigger than you, something to give your life meaning and offer you a future and a hope? Maybe you've gone on a quest for meaning in other parts of your life and the world at large and found yourself unfulfilled. Some people look for meaning in the world's material things, hoping fulfillment can be found in riches and wealth. Other people search for meaning in various philosophies and religions, blending them together like a patchwork quilt, desperate for some kind of beauty that enhances their lives. Still others seek after meaning by giving themselves to a cause or political system they hope will make the world a better place, only to find that at the end of every cause and system, no matter how good or how worthwhile, is a host of unmet expectations and a trail of broken relationships.

If you can identify with any of these unfulfilled and unfulfilling quests, then you've come to the right place—not to this book, but to the truth about God and ultimately to God Himself. Because God is the ultimate source of all life, truth, and reality, God is ultimately the only being capable of giving your life meaning. And because God is not some impersonal Force, but a personal, loving Father who loves you deeply, knows you intimately, and wants to have an eternal relationship with you, you can count on Him to have your best interest in mind at all times.

GODQUEST

Of course, you don't need to just take our word for it. As you embark on your GodQuest, you will discover six signposts that will help you discover truth and point you toward a life-changing relationship with God. Or, if you already believe in God, these signposts, will give you a stronger foundation for your belief, and help you draw closer to the God who loves you. The six signposts in *GodQuest* work in about the same way as signposts you would encounter on a hike—they provide direction and then invite you to make a choice. Will you go to the right, or steer to the left?

At each signpost, you will encounter legitimate reasons for believing in God. Along your journey, you will learn about philosophical, historical, scientific, and archaeological evidence for the reality of God, and that evidence will give you confidence in your GodQuest. There are billions of people who have preceded you in history and millions more who live around you right now who have found the truth about God and are living testimonies to His reality.

And here's the best part. You don't need to accept these truths with "blind" faith. You can really believe them. The evidence and the reliable testimonials are there. For our part, our goal is not to convince you that these things are true, or to tell you which way to go. We simply want to show you some signposts that will help you discover these truths for yourself. Besides the overarching signpost that gets you going on your GodQuest, there are five other signposts:

- *The Beginning:* What you believe about creation determines how you view yourself and life.

- *The Word:* What you believe about the Bible determines how you live your life.

- *The Question:* What you believe about God's goodness defines your relationship with Him.

- *The King:* What you believe about Jesus' identity determines your path in life.

- *The Path:* The path you follow in your spiritual journey determines your destination.

WHAT YOU BELIEVE AFFECTS
THE CHOICES YOU MAKE

No doubt you've heard the expression, "ideas have consequences." Well, we're here to share with you that your ideas about God and how He has spoken to you through the natural world, through the Bible, and through His Son, Jesus Christ, have more consequences than any other ideas you can have. How you view God and what you believe about Him will shape your life more than any other belief. What you believe about God is the most important thing about you.

In a way, this book is like one big signpost pointing you to ultimate reality and meaning. This book and the other materials in the *GodQuest* series have been thoughtfully prepared as guides for your life journey. And we can tell you right here at the beginning that there's no better time than right now to go on your GodQuest. We are living in a world and a time in history that is being impacted by dramatic change. Almost everything we have accepted in the past as "normal" is now shifting beneath our feet. Consider these elements of life that you encounter every single day where seismic shifts are taking place.

TECHNOLOGY

We are not making an overstatement when we say the world is experiencing the greatest shift in technology in history. In the 1990s the emergence of the World Wide Web made it possible to instantly access information over the Internet. Google, whose mission is to "organize the world's information and make it universally accessible and useful," became a household name. In the 2000s, social media—epitomized by platforms like YouTube, Facebook and Twitter—became all the rage. Ten percent of the world's population are Facebook users, putting instant communication with people and ideas at their fingertips. Today, it's all about mobility as smartphones and smartpads bring the world to your fingertips— anywhere, anytime. Our ability to communicate digitally is having a wide-ranging impact on civil, social, and religious engagement.

Technology doesn't just give us information and connect us. Technology is a powerful tool that can be harnessed to bring about momentous and meaningful change.

What this means for your GodQuest. No longer do you need to wait for answers to your questions. You can find all the information you need on any given subject. You can connect with other people and other communities around the world, giving you a window into unlimited information and global networks. But there's a danger in all of this instant access. How do you know you're getting the truth? And can you trust the people you are connecting with?

ECONOMY

Most people living today had never experienced an economic meltdown on the scale of the Great Depression until 2008, when a financial tsunami hit the global markets. In a matter of months, trillions of dollars of stock market and real estate value were lost, sending tens of millions of people and companies into a financial crisis unlike anything they had been through before. Suddenly people were questioning the American dream with its promise of upward financial mobility. In fact, if there was a silver lining in the financial meltdown, it was this: Many people were forced to rethink their priorities, to rely less on outward material things and more on inward spiritual values.

What this means for your GodQuest. Putting money in its proper perspective and understanding that material things cannot buy happiness should help you focus on the importance of searching for those things that do have eternal value.

MORALITY

There are still some old television programs shown in syndication that depict a husband and wife in separate beds. Talk about ancient history! Now the media is open about sexual relationships both inside and outside marriage. But don't blame the media for glorifying the kind of sexual freedom on display in movies and on television. It's merely reflecting what's going on in the culture. As a result of the transformational social and moral trends of the last fifty years, there has been a sharp decline in traditional marriage and a rise of new family forms. The Pew Forum reports that in 1960 two-thirds of all twenty-somethings were married. Today just 25 percent are. Overall, less than half of all co-habitating couples are married.

What this means for your GodQuest. There are several factors responsible for the drop in marriage and morality. The economic uncertainty has something to do with it. Many couples figure it's cheaper to live together than to be married. But more than the economy is the reluctance of many people to make covenant commitments. A "covenant" is an agreement between two parties. The Bible talks about God making covenants with His people, and God is all about keeping those promises to us. It's we who break our promises with Him and with each other. If you're serious about going on a GodQuest, you should examine your level of commitment. Are you someone who starts out with good intentions, and then gives up when the going gets tough, or are you willing to make a commitment to the truth and to God no matter what the consequences?

SPIRITUALITY

The last big shift we want to talk about is in the area of spirituality— that part of your life that connects you with spiritual rather than material things. It used to be that almost everybody believed in God, whether they followed Him or not. Atheists were few and far between, and those who didn't believe in God kept their non-belief to themselves. Not any more. The so-called "new atheists" are aggressively promoting their belief that God doesn't exist. (We've always found this rather interesting. We don't believe in unicorns, but we don't go around trying to zealously convince people that unicorns don't exist.)

We'll deal with the new atheists in Signpost 2. Here we just want to make the point that this new emphasis on the non-existence of God, even though it comes from a small minority of the population (less than 5 percent of all people are self-professing atheists), has changed the spiritual landscape. Even for the vast majority of people who believe in God, the impact of aggressive unbelievers has left many of them with doubts about God's goodness and His direct involvement in the world. More and more people (and you may be among them) are asking themselves "Why do I want to have a relationship with a God who isn't good and doesn't care?"

Since most "believers" know very little about what they believe and even less about the God they profess to believe in, they have a hard time answering a question like that. As a result, the spiritual lives of many people have become all about personal preferences and what makes them feel good about themselves and the world rather than what is really true. In the landmark book, *Souls in Transition*, Christian Smith labeled this new kind of spirituality "Moralistic Therapuetic Deism." The core beliefs of this "religion," according to Smith, looks like this:

1. A God exists who created and orders the world and watches over human life on earth.

2. God wants people to be good, nice, and fair to each other.

3. The central goal of life is to be happy and to feel good about oneself.

4. God does not want to be particularly involved in one's life except when God is needed to solve a problem.

5. Good people go to heaven when they die.[1]

This is the reality of spirituality for many people. This is the kind of God most people believe in, and it's the God most people think they have a relationship with.

What this means for your GodQuest. There's a great quote from Patrick Morley that goes something like this: "There is the God who is and the god we want, and they are not the same." Francis Bacon said, "Men prefer to believe what they prefer to be true." As you embark on your GodQuest, you need to ask yourself these questions:

- Are you on a noble search for the god you want, who will make you feel good, not ask too much of you, be there when you need him, but otherwise will leave you alone?

- Or are you searching for the God who is almighty, all-knowing, all-loving, all holy—the God who made you, knows you intimately, wants to have a dynamic daily relationship with you, and who won't leave you where you are but who wants to transform you into someone who reflects His love and mercy in the world?

Quite honestly, it's pointless to search for the god you want, which for many people is the god of Moralistic Therapeutic Deism, because that god doesn't exist. He's a figment of the imaginations of people who want to be comfortable where they are and who live in a story of their own making. On the other hand, if you desire to search for the God who is, then you have a grand adventure ahead of you. It won't necessarily be an easy search, but when you find what you're looking for, a reward is waiting for you. How do we know? Because God has made that promise. The Bible tells us that anyone who searches for God "must believe that he exists and that he rewards those who earnestly seek him" (Hebrews 11:6).

BECOMING A PART OF GOD'S GRAND STORY

As you begin the journey of your own GodQuest, it's important that you know you are getting involved with something much bigger than you are. Rather than staying in a story of your own making, you have the opportunity to become part of God's grand story. We'll cover more of the details about God's grand story in Signpost 3. For now, until we have a chance to talk more about the Bible, we want to give you a glimpse of what that amazing book is about, and why its story should matter to you in your GodQuest.

In *Why the Bible Matters*, author Mike Erre explains the kind of story the Bible offers:

GODQUEST

The Bible offers the truest story of the whole world—all of life, history, experience, culture, and civilization are encompassed in its pages. To see the Bible as the truest story is not to say that the story helps us function well or that it was passed down to us merely as a cultural inheritance. The scriptures must be taken seriously because they claim to tell us the true story from the creation of the universe all the way to its re-creation. Not one moment is left out of its pages. The content of the Bible lies at the very core of reality. This is the way the world really is.[2]

If we don't read the Bible in this way, but instead try to fit its themes into our stories rather than the other way around, "we lose the full reality of God and His work in our world," writes Erre. "Our world shrinks as well. The story of the Bible is the story of enlargement, not reduction …. The scriptures call us into a much larger world, and in so doing, they beckon us beyond the reach of our wills and experiences."[3]

THE HERO'S JOURNEY

By becoming part of God's grand story, you are embarking on what is known in classic storytelling as the Hero's Journey. It's a pattern that goes back to *The Odyssey* and continues in contemporary stories, whether told in a book or portrayed in a film. You can plug virtually every great plot or script into this template, famously articulated by Joseph Campbell. There are several variations of the Hero's Journey. We're going to use three steps to describe your GodQuest where you are the hero.

In our Hero's Journey template, the hero (you) will:

- Depart in response to a Call to Adventure
- Go through an initiation that includes a Road of Trials
- Return home with the Freedom to Live

Now let's break these three steps down one by one.

The Call to Adventure

The call to adventure is the point when the hero realizes everything is going to change. It happened to Odysseus, Frodo Baggins, Luke Skywalker, and the children in Narnia. Heroes may be reluctant at first, but once they commit to the quest, a guide or "magical helper" appears. Each of the characters in the famous stories we have talked about had supernatural help for the journey. Whether or not you realize it, as you embark on your GodQuest, you have a supernatural guide who wants to help you, only this guide is very real, not some character from a book or movie. When you commit to your GodQuest, God is the guide who will reveal truth to you through the wisdom of others (Proverbs 15:22), trustworthy information (2 Timothy 3:16–17) and most importantly, through the inner working of the Holy Spirit in your life (John 14:26).

The Road of Trials

Heroes encounter tests and trials in the course of their quests, and it will be no different for you as you set out in search of the answers to the questions set before you. The tests and trials are different for each person. Some may have to deal with doubts, while others may suffer physical or emotional setbacks. You may have to endure financial difficulties or problems with relationships. These are all part of the normal course of life, but as you go through your GodQuest, you may think you have more than your share. Don't get discouraged! In fact, you can actually be encouraged because of the results that will come from your experience. The Bible tells us:

> Consider it pure joy, my brothers, whenever you face trials of many kinds, because you know that the testing of your faith develops perseverance (James 1:2–3).

So hang in there. The trials you encounter in the course of your GodQuest will only strengthen your faith.

GODQUEST

FREEDOM TO LIVE

Enduring the doubts and trials that will come your way in the course of completing your GodQuest will ultimately lead you to freedom from the fear of death, which will in turn give you the freedom to live both now and forever. This is a classic part of any Hero's Journey and any legendary quest, but for you it is reality. God is inviting you into a life free from fear, no matter what circumstances you may go through and no matter what you have done—not because you are great or worthy, but because God is great and worthy and loves you so very much. As the Bible says:

> "What no eye has seen,
> what no ear has heard,
> and what no human mind has conceived—
> the things God has prepared for those who love him..."
> (1 Corinthians 2:9).

This is the story of God and—no surprise—it's the story of the Bible, which is God's Word, written to show you just how much God loves you and how much He wants to have a relationship with you. "Very simply," writes Mike Erre, "the overall story line goes something like this: God creates the world and everything in it. His creatures rebel, allowing sin and death to mar all that God made. God is rescuing and restoring creation and will renew it completely sometime in the future."[4]

God's story is the story of creation, fall, and redemption, with a rescue plan centered in Jesus Christ. The children of Narnia may have Aslan, but we have Jesus as our Savior. As C. S. Lewis writes, "The story of Christ is simply a true myth: a myth working on us in the same way as the others, but with this tremendous difference that it *really happened*."[5]

WHAT WILL KEEP YOU FROM YOUR GODQUEST?

As we've already said, you are to be congratulated for making a deliberate effort to go on a GodQuest. Many people never cross that threshold from complacency to action. They never embark on the

Hero's Journey. They are content to remain in their own small story rather than enter into God's grand story. They make the choice to go their own way rather than seeking God and going His way. Why do you think that is the case? Why do so many people make a deliberate choice to go their own way? Let us suggest three reasons.

First, some think religious questions are entirely matters of "faith," understood as blindly believing something without evidence. Some religious figures may desire blind allegiance, but not Jesus. He did public miracles so people would have confidence that He was the Son of God, and as a result believe in Him. And as we will see throughout *GodQuest*, the evidence for these miracles can still be investigated today. The Apostle John said it best:

> *Jesus did many other miraculous signs in the presence of his disciples, which are not recorded in this book. But these are written that you may believe that Jesus is the Christ the Son of God, and that by believing you may have life in his name* (John 20:30–31)

Second, some think that truth cannot be known. We're going to devote the next chapter to the topic of truth, but just as a little introduction, think about this. Anyone who says, "You can't know truth," is actually claiming to know something about the world, namely that truth can't be known. But this is hopelessly contradictory. How could someone know that they can't know truth? To those who claim truth can't be known, we'd like to ask them if they have really gone on a deliberate quest for truth? Have they considered the scientific, philosophical, historical, and experiential evidence for Jesus—who claimed to be the truth? Jesus says:

> *"Ask and it will be given to you; seek and you will find; knock and the door will be opened to you. For everyone who asks receives; He who seeks finds; and to him who knocks, the door will be opened"* (Matthew 7:7–8)

Finally, all of us are very busy these days. Despite all of our timesaving devices, our lives are characterized by three words: *busy, busy, busy*. We have work, school, places to go, and people to see. Yet isn't it amazing that Jesus—without question the greatest Hero who ever lived on earth—always found time for what was important, even in the middle of His many responsibilities? He found time to pray, be alone, teach, and to share a meal with people. We make time for what is most important to us. Questions about God are too important not to entertain.

For Blaise Pascal, the influential scientist and philosopher, the ways we constantly divert ourselves by staying busy are a testimony to our fallen state. If we were truly content with ourselves, we would have no need for distraction. But we aren't content, so we escape reality through diversion—busyness. Maybe this uneasiness in the human heart is a sign pointing us to find fulfillment in something beyond this world.

St. Augustine famously said to God in the opening of his book, *The Confessions*, "You have made us for yourself, O Lord, and our hearts are restless until they rest in you." There is a longing for the transcendent—for something bigger than we are—in the human heart. Solomon, the wisest person who ever lived, said God has put this longing in our hearts (Ecclesiastes 3:11). Don't you long for peace, beauty, justice, and for a world where everything is made right? That longing isn't an accident. The God who is, the God who made you and loves you and knows you, put that longing in your heart.

If Jesus is right, this longing can only be fulfilled in a relationship with Him. In Matthew 6:33 Jesus says, "But seek first his kingdom and his righteousness, and all these things will be given to you as well." Your GodQuest is not just about finding truth and the answers to life's most important questions and then moving on with your life. It's about knowing the Creator of the universe, discovering His plan for your life and then entering into a relationship with Him. What could possibly be more exciting and meaningful than that?

Before we bring this first chapter to a conclusion and move on to the truth about truth, we need to give you a warning about your GodQuest. If you're serious and you commit yourself fully to your quest, it's not going to be a stroll in the park. Because going on a GodQuest is unquestionably the most important journey you will ever take, it stands to reason that your journey is not going to be easy. In fact, it could even get a little dangerous.

Now, if you live in North America or Europe, then the kind of danger we're talking about probably does not involved physical danger. However, you need to know, if you don't already, that in many parts of the world—especially in certain regions of Africa, Asia, and the Middle East—seeking after God literally puts you in mortal danger. In particular, converting from Islam to Christianity in some countries can lead to a death sentence, or at the very least expulsion from your family. Yet people willingly choose to give their lives to Jesus Christ anyway, despite the danger, because when they find the truth about God, the Bible, and Jesus, they will pay any price—including their own life—to follow Him.

While you probably won't have to face that kind of persecution, your GodQuest will still present you with challenges. You may disorient your family, who think you are fine just the way you are. You may tick off your friends, who may perceive you as better, kinder, or even smarter than they are. People may call you a prude because you value integrity more than pleasure. Others may see you as a kook or intellectually inferior because you dare to claim that God created the universe, or that Jesus performed miracles. Are you willing to endure that kind of alienation, ridicule, and perhaps even hatred?

Jesus warned his followers that they would be hated because of their belief in Him (Matthew 10:22). But those who search for the truth about God as found in Jesus shouldn't be surprised. Jesus says, "If the world hates you, keep in mind that it hated me first" (John 15:18).

In our safe and comfortable world, where very few of us have ever known anything close to persecution, we want a relationship with God that is safe and comfortable. But that's never the way it's supposed to be. All you have to do is search through the Bible or look around the world, and you'll find that being a serious and committed follower of Jesus is anything but safe.

In C. S. Lewis' book *The Lion, the Witch and the Wardrobe*—the first in the series of Narnia adventures—Lucy asks Mr. Beaver about Aslan, the King and "Lord of the whole wood." Lucy wonders if

Aslan is a man, and when told that he's a great Lion, Lucy worries about meeting him. She asks Mr. Beaver if Aslan is safe.

"Safe?" said Mr. Beaver. "Who said anything about safe? Course he isn't safe. But he's good."[6]

In your GodQuest, there's something very important for you to keep in mind. Your journey isn't going to be "safe" because God isn't safe. But it's going to be incredibly good and satisfying and true, because God is good and satisfying and true.

MORE THAN PIZZA

Recent surveys about trends in church attendance, especially among students, indicate many are leaving the church because they are looking for more meaning, more challenge, and more truth than the church is giving them. A decade ago, most churches could attract big crowds of students with entertainment and pizza. Not any more. Young adults want more than pizza and games. They want the truth. Commenting on this trend, newly-minted youth pastor Jon Nielson writes:

> The gospel—the objective reality that "Christ died for our sins in accordance with the Scriptures, that he was buried, that he was raised on the third day in accordance with the Scriptures," which is received by faith alone—is what students really crave. The amazing (and constantly humbling) thing about continually offering the gospel to students is the response it brings. The response is not: "Wow, Jon, you're cool," or "That music was off the hook!" It's actually a much more biblical response: repentance and faith in Jesus Christ. Students crave the real, true, life-changing, not-watered-down gospel of Jesus Christ. Woe to us if we give them anything less.[7]

How about you? Do you want more than pizza? Are you ready to go on the journey of ultimate discovery? Do you want to go your own way, or are you up for the challenge of a serious GodQuest? If you've made it this far in the book, we think you're ready. The only thing left to do is pack a few things for your journey. Here's what we suggest you bring:

- An open *mind*. It's so easy to rely on preconceived ideas when it comes to God. No doubt you've learned some truth about God in your lifetime, but mixed in with the truth you've probably heard some error. The best tool you have to separate truth from error is your mind, which is capable of understanding God's will (Ephesians 5:17), loving God (Mark 12:30) and praising God (1 Corinthians 14:15). Even more, your mind is capable of being renewed (Romans 12:2). So keep an open mind. It will serve you well on your GodQuest.

- A sincere *heart*. In the Bible as well as all great literature, the heart is viewed as the human control center for emotions and deep desires. Your strongest and deepest longings come from your heart. That's why Solomon tells his son, "Above all else, guard your heart, for it is the wellspring of life" (Proverbs 4:23). Your heart will be a key to your GodQuest.

- A willing *soul*. Heart and soul often go together in music and literature, but there is a distinction between the two. The soul, sometimes referred to as the spirit, is the eternal essence of a person, the part that never dies. Jesus told his disciples not to fear those who "kill the body but cannot kill the soul" (Matthew 10:28). Because the soul is eternal, it is often said that your soul is the real you. The soul is also something that can be lost in a spiritual sense. Jesus talked about forfeiting the eternal soul in exchange for what this temporal world has to offer:

  What good will it be for a man if he gains the whole world, yet forfeit his soul? Or what can a man give in exchange for his soul? (Matthew 16:26).

As you go on your GodQuest, don't exchange anything for your soul. It's the real you.

Moving On

It's no coincidence that Jesus tells His followers that the greatest commandment of all is this: "Love the Lord your God with all your heart and with all your soul and with all your mind" (Matthew

22:37). As you move on to explore the truth about truth, engage every part of you—your mind, your heart, and your soul—in pursuit of God. It's the most you can give, and it's all that God asks.

CHAPTER 2

THE TRUTH ABOUT TRUTH

If you're like most enterprising and curious people, the Internet is your first source of information about any topic. In the old days—oh, say the 1990s—if you wanted to know something about something, you eventually ended up in the library, where you were confronted with the dreaded Dewey Decimal System. Or you called a trusted friend, who may or may not have an answer, but at least you didn't have to go to the library.

Not these days. Now if you want to know something you have the full power of the World Wide Web at your instant disposal, which can come in handy if you want to know something very practical, like how to get gum out of your hair, or something more philosophical, like what is truth. Now, we're not putting gum and truth in the same category in terms of importance. You can always get more gum, and hair grows back. Truth is much more valuable and infinitely more important. Having the truth about something can literally mean the difference between life and death.

In a way, this entire book has to do with "the truth about something," with the "something" being God. When it comes to truth, it doesn't get any bigger than that, but that doesn't make your GodQuest—your search for the truth about God—easy. In fact, just the opposite is true. The bigger the stakes for truth, the bigger the challenge and the bigger the consequences. And there's nothing bigger than God.

That's why people have been searching for the truth about God for as long as, well, for as long as there have been people. It's the world's most important search. By embarking on your own search for the truth about God and the world and everything in it, you are journeying down a path that's been traveled for thousands of years by the world's greatest philosophers, theologians, politicians, artists, scientists, and rulers. Even more significant to our conversation, there are countless everyday people just like you who are hungry to know the truth about God. That's why we've written this book, and we suspect, that's why you're reading it.

In the last chapter we talked about the dangers inherent in your GodQuest. For some people in the world, the dangers are physical. Lives are literally at risk. For you the dangers are more likely psychological, emotional, and spiritual. The same goes for truth. The search for truth isn't necessarily safe, but it is an incredibly important component of your overall GodQuest. You need to do whatever it takes to get to the truth. Gordon Pennington, an international business consultant and a partner in the Burning Media Group in New York, puts it this way:

> The pursuit of truth ultimately necessitates a kind of struggle. The risks of pursuing truth are tremendous, and what could be a greater adventure than to risk everything in pursuit of the one thing that endures. If truth isn't worth all that, then it probably isn't truth at all.[1]

DIGGING AROUND FOR TRUTH

To get to the truth about truth, we need to look at truth itself: What is it, what's it good for and what does it mean to you? Before you can apply truth to any number of things—from gum to God—you have to know what truth is. What are the qualities and the characteristics of truth that make it both valuable for life and practical for living? Maybe you've already thought about truth at this level. After all, you wouldn't have moved on to this chapter in *GodQuest* unless you were interested. So what is truth? As we said, you have the entire Internet at your disposal, so let's do what most people do these days when they want to know something and start with Google.

If you simply Google the word *truth*, here are the first three entries you'll find:

- The most popular website under the category of "truth" is TheTruth.com. You would think this would be a website about Jesus, who claimed to be "the truth" (John 14:6). But no. This most popular truth website is about smoking, as in, don't smoke. No doubt you've seen the ads on television usually showing a large group of young urbanites singing a song or unfurling a flag that shows us in some way the *facts* or the *truth* about smoking, such as how many people die each year from cigarette-related illnesses (answer: 50,000). At the end of the ad is the website address, where you can go and read more facts about smoking.

- The next most popular destination for "truth" on Google is Wikipedia, where you will find this opening paragraph in a very long article:

  Truth has a variety of meanings, such as the state of being in accord with a particular fact or reality, or being in accord with the body of real things, real events or actualities. It can also mean having fidelity to an original or to a standard or ideal. In a common archaic usage it also meant constancy or sincerity in action or character. The direct opposite of truth is "falsehood," which can correspondingly take logical, factual or ethical meanings.[2]

- Third in popularity on Google is Dictionary.com, where you will find this definition of truth:

  1. The true or actual state of a matter: He tried to find out the truth.

  2. Conformity with fact or reality; verity: the truth of a statement.

While these websites in no way exhaust the truth about truth, they do give us a start, and a very helpful start at that. Just from these three sources, here's what we can know about truth:

- Truth corresponds to the facts.
- Truth is in accordance with reality.

- Truth is the opposite of falsehood.
- Truth is the way things really are.

SO WHY DO PEOPLE IGNORE THE TRUTH?

This is an interesting question, because it's something we can all relate to. At various times in the course of our lives we do things even though we know they're not true. For example, we all lie. We do deceitful things. We disregard the facts and do stupid things. And then there are those who smoke, which is about as bold a disregard for the truth as there is in the world.

Thanks to TheTruth.com, we know for a fact that tobacco has the potential to kill, and the statistics are there to prove it. So why do people still smoke? If the facts are right (and no one is disputing them, not even the tobacco industry), why would anybody deliberately put their life in jeopardy—maybe not now but eventually—by ignoring the truth about smoking?

We've thought about this, and we have some ideas that we've put on a scale from -4 (not sure about the truth) to +4 (most open to the truth). You may agree or disagree, which is fine. This isn't the "gospel truth," but it is a way of perhaps answering the question, "Why do people ignore the truth?" And it relates to the truth about God as much as it relates to the truth about smoking.

WHY DO PEOPLE IGNORE THE TRUTH?

Not Sure

-4   They don't believe the truth and don't care.

-3   They have doubts about the truth and have already formed an opinion.

-2   They have questions about the truth but are open to discussion or debate.

-1   They have questions about the truth and are looking for answers.

Indifferent

0   They believe the truth but just don't care.

+1   They believe the truth but don't think it applies to them.

+2   They believe the truth but choose to do something else.

+3   They believe the truth and want to comply but don't know how.

+4   They believe the truth and want to comply and they are asking how.

More Open

WHERE DO YOU FIT?

We're going to assume that you fall into at least one of these categories, probably more on the plus side of being open to the truth. You may even be trying your best to live your life according to God's truth. Of course, there are those occasional nagging doubts about truth that may cause you to doubt God. That's okay! Doubt is a part of any GodQuest, which is why we've devoted an entire section to doubt (see Chapter 10). That's how much we value doubt and how much we respect you for being honest enough to admit you have doubt when it comes to the truth about God and Christianity.

We agree with Mark Driscoll, pastor of Mars Hill Church in Seattle, who wrote this about the value of spiritual honesty:

> Young people are more spiritually honest. The days of feeling some sort of cultural pressure to adhere to historic Christian truths is simply gone. Subsequently, we may not be seeing younger people less devoted to Jesus Christ but simply more people being honest so that those who in the past would have professed faith they did not possess or practice are simply being honest, which is more admirable than being a hypocrite.[3]

Just because the cultural pressure to adhere to historic Christian truths is gone doesn't mean there is no longer any cultural pressure.

The pressure is still there, but it's wrapped in a different message. As the eminent social scientist James Davison Hunter writes:

> In the face of intense religious and cultural pluralism in the past century, the pressures to deny Christianity's exclusive claims to truth have been fantastic.[4]

BE AWARE OF WHAT THE CULTURE IS DOING

Rather than feeling pressure to believe certain truths about God, the culture is now encouraging doubts about truth and God. In their excellent book, *In Search of a Confident Faith*, J. P. Moreland, a professor of philosophy, and theologian Klaus Issler make a compelling case for seven "doubt-inducing background assumptions of our culture" that can easily tip the scales toward unbelief even in the most earnest truth-seeker.[5] Keep in mind that these assumptions aren't necessarily true, but because many people *assume* they are true (that's why they are called *assumptions*) they *appear* to be true.

1. It's smarter to doubt things than to believe them. Smart people question everything, including belief in God. In contrast to these smart people are the people who do believe in God. In general, believers are viewed as simplistic and overly trusting. They aren't well educated, and they don't like to question their faith.

2. University professors don't buy into the truth about God and think that such belief is silly. They don't see Christians as very good at critical thinking.

3. Religion is a matter of private, personal feelings and should be kept out of public life. The separation of church and state doctrine is meant to protect the state from the church.

4. Science is the only way to know reality and it trumps other approaches, especially ones based on faith. Furthermore, the vast majority of scientists aren't Christians because science has made belief in God unnecessary.

5. You can know things only through your five senses. If you can't sense something by seeing, touching, hearing, tasting, or smelling it, it's not really true. What this means is that empirical truth is the only valid truth.

6. If the experts can't agree on the existence and nature of God or on any of the key moral questions of our day, then there must not be a way to discover the truth about these things. To put it another way, science is about knowing, while religion is about feeling.

7. Enlightened people are tolerant, nonjudgmental, and compassionate, whereas unenlightened people (those who think it's possible to know the truth) are intolerant, judgmental, and lacking compassion.

Moreland and Issler are quick to point out that these seven cultural assumptions about God and the nature of truth are rarely stated in such a straightforward way and in so many words, "but we absorb them daily through conversation and largely through the media." Nor are these assumptions part of an intentional conspiracy. "It's far worse than that," the authors write. "With genuine exceptions, these ideas have so permeated our society that media folk govern their work by them without having the slightest idea" that they are operating from this grid.

FIGHT SURROGATE FAITH AND DOUBT YOUR DOUBT

Are you suddenly feeling like a pawn in some grand cosmic scheme? For a long time, there was cultural pressure to adhere to historic Christian truth. These days there is cultural pressure to doubt and even disbelieve these same truths.

What do you do?

Where do you go from here?

As we move forward to consider the nature of truth and how it impacts your GodQuest, we want to make two suggestions. First, when dealing with your own questions about these incredibly important issues, don't settle for a "surrogate" faith. "There are many Christians who are carrying a faith that is not their own," explains Todd Clark, founding pastor of Discovery Church in Simi Valley, California. "Everything they know about God comes from their favorite author, or their pastor and they never spend any time directly with God so it all comes to them in a surrogate way."[6]

In your GodQuest, make it your goal to discover the truth about God for yourself, because ultimately your relationship with God depends on it. Don't just take our word for it—we are merely your guides on this all-important journey. Find the sources, verify them as best you can, and then think through the implications of the scenario you come up with. What you believe about truth and God is going to shape the choices you make, so take it seriously.

Second, don't let your doubts get the best of you. Have the courage to doubt your doubt. Moreland and Issler strongly suggest this in their four-step procedure for dealing with the seven doubt-inducing background cultural assumptions:

Step 1: Be aware of the seven doubt-inducing cultural assumptions. These are not the assumptions of a minority of people in our culture, but represent the beliefs of many people, in particular those who shape the media and guide the educational institutions.

Step 2: Be alert to the sources of these background assumptions: the media, professors, co-workers, etc. Don't just watch a movie or television show (especially the news) or attend a university without reminding yourself that the writers, producers, and professors will probably not reinforce your belief in God.

Step 3: Challenge and question the "truth" of the assumptions. In other words, *doubt your doubt!* Moreland and Issler suggest that you "doubt them, challenge them, call them into question" and ask, "What is the evidence for and against these claims?"

Step 4: Replace the cultural assumptions with *truth*, which Moreland and Issler refer to as "the correct alternate way of seeing reality." Don't buy into the notion that a smart person is someone who questions truth. Moreland and Issler write:

A flourishing life is one that believes more and more truths and fewer and fewer falsehoods as one matures. And a flourishing life can be stopped dead in its tracks by refusing to embrace truths that are available to those who could and should want to know them, every bit as much as believing something false. *The right approach to life is one that hungers to know as many truths as one can and to avoid as many falsehoods as possible.*[7]

SUBJECTIVE AND OBJECTIVE TRUTH

Sometimes you will hear people refer to truth as either "subjective" or "objective" truth. Another way of looking at truth is to say it's either "relative" or "absolute." The common perception today is that objective or absolute truth is binding, restrictive, or at the very least unimaginative. There is also a perception that intolerant people believe in absolute truth, whereas tolerant, non-judgmental people believe in subjective or relative truth. Another way of looking at it is to say that absolute truth is true regardless of the circumstances, while relative truth is "true for you but not for me."

What's interesting is that people tend to think of truth subjectively when the topic is religion or morality, not when it is science or math. You won't hear anybody say, "That's your truth, but I have different truth," when speaking about two plus two. Yet when it comes to the truth about God, it's common to hear people say, "That's fine for you, but I have a different truth."

Before we talk about objective truth, we want to share some thoughts about subjective truth from Peter Kreeft, a professor of philosophy at Boston College. Dr. Kreeft reminds us that truth is essentially "telling it like it is." However, this doesn't mean everyone interprets truth the same way. We all have a tendency to see truth through the lens of our experiences and preferences to the point where it can become "subjective." Since these subjective views are so common in our culture, we need to give you a brief run down of five alternate theories of truth as articulated by Dr. Kreeft.[8]

Truth is what works. The idea here is that truth is what you *think* works or what works *for you*. In other words, truth is whatever is practical. The problem with this theory is that what is true is not always practical. For example, it is true that we all die, but death may not work for you or seem very practical. Likewise, what is practical is not always true. Calling in sick when you want a vacation day might feel practical, but it isn't true.

Truth is what we can sense. This theory rests on the idea that truth is only what you can experience with your five senses. However, this doesn't always work because what you sense about something may not come from what you experience through your five senses. For example, you could sense being in love, but which of your five senses do you use to detect your feelings? Clearly this theory is designed to eliminate anything that can't be physically experienced, which in effect separates the spiritual realm (and therefore, God) from the truth.

Truth is what can be proved by reason. This is exactly what it says: truth is only that which can be proved. But we live with many things that cannot be proved. Using the example in the previous paragraph, how do you "prove" an emotion such as love? You can show the effects of love, but can you absolutely, scientifically prove that love exists?

Truth is the totality of ideas. This theory says that truth is found in the combination of all ideas. So, when it comes to God, you would get to the truth by looking at all the concepts about God and then combining them into one big idea, with the effect that no one idea is wrong. The main problem with this theory is that it is self-contradictory because it claims it is true while holding that the other theories are not true.

Truth is what I feel. No surprise, this is called the Emotivist Theory of Truth. Dr. Kreeft wryly observes that it is held by many teenagers but few philosophers. Feeling something is true may indeed lead to objective truth, but to identify all truth with feeling is absurd since many feelings are false.

Whether we are aware of it or not, all of us slip into one or more of these theories of truth from time to time. When we make a minor decision, such as buying a car or taking a trip, based on emotion the consequences are insignificant. The problem is when we rely on these alternate ways of determining truth for the really important decisions in life, such as the way we view ultimate reality, including our view of God. Like we said, you can play loose and fast with the truth when you're talking about your favorite gum. But when it comes to God, you need to be more certain that what you believe is really true, because what you believe affects the choices you make. And ultimately what you believe will affect the relationships you have, especially your relationship with God.

C. S. Lewis makes this brilliant observation:

> If Truth is objective, if we live in a world we did not create and cannot change merely by thinking, if the world is not really a dream of our own, than the most destructive belief we could possibly believe would be the denial of this primary fact. It would be like closing your eyes while driving, or blissfully ignoring the doctor's warnings.[9]

When taken in their totality, the alternate theories of truth we just talked about can all be classified under the category of the "subjective" or "relative" view of truth. This is more than just a trend in the way people think. In their book, *Relativism: Feet Firmly Planted in Mid-Air*, Francis Beckwith and Greg Koukl refer to this view of truth as a "quiet but desperate revolution of thought—the death of truth." They consider this view as more than the tendency we all have to fall back on personal opinion and preference. Essentially, subjective truth is an assault on "the idea that any particular thing can be known for sure."[10]

The alternate to subjective truth is, of course, objective truth, a view increasingly unpopular in our culture. Why do you think that is? We think the unpopularity of truth has something to do with misconception. Without thinking, most people assume that objective truth is unemotional, detached, impersonal, and oppressive. Those criticisms are based on the notion that truth is itself an emotion or an attitude. But that's simply not true! At its core, truth is simply how and what we know.

Furthermore, objective truth is not necessarily known by all or believed by all. Even if everyone believes a lie, a lie is still a lie, and there are definitely times when simply accepting the majority view of truth can be not only incorrect, but harmful as well. For example, there were times in our history (and even places throughout the world today) that the majority of people believed that women were inferior and not as intelligent or valuable as men.

Objective truth does not mean, "publicly proved." An objective truth could be privately known (such as a buried treasure). An objective truth could also be *known* without being *proved*. For example, you may know you love someone, but you can't prove it scientifically. *Knowing* something is true is one thing, and *proving* something is true is another.

THE BIBLICAL VIEW OF TRUTH

In your GodQuest, you're going to come up against some objections to truth as presented in the Bible. We need to deal with this here before we continue, because more than merely a summary of objective truth, the Bible gives us a view of truth that is consistent with reality, whether or not that truth is believed by all or known by all. It's important to understand that the Bible does not offer a unique view of truth. Rather, the Bible assumes the common sense view of truth that we all use in our everyday lives.

When you get to Signpost 3, you're going to learn more about the Bible and be presented with some reasons why you can trust it to be reliable and true. But for the purposes of this discussion, we want to share with you some things the Bible says about truth. We are grateful to Douglas Groothuis and his book, *Truth Decay*, for some valuable insights.[11]

In both the Old and New Testaments, truth is viewed as something that is rooted in reality and fact. The Hebrew term most often translated as "truth" is *emet*, a word that conveys the idea of conformity to fact. The word can also represent "that which is conformed to reality in contrast to anything which would be erroneous or deceitful."

The Hebrew concept of truth also relates to anything that is authentic, reliable, or simply right, such as "true justice" (Zechariah 7:9).

In the New Testament, the Greek word for "truth" is *aletheia*, which means "conformity to fact." It's often used by John, a biographer of Jesus, to communicate veracity and genuineness and to stand in contrast to that which is false, usually when describing truth as embodied or demonstrated in Jesus (John 7:28, 8:16). In fact, each member of the Trinity—God the Father, God the Son, and God the Holy Spirit—is associated with truth. God is routinely identified with truth (Psalm 31:5). Jesus Christ claimed to be truth when he told his disciples on the night before he was executed, "I am the way and the truth and the life" (John 14:6). And the Holy Spirit, who is called "the Spirit of truth," and specializes in guiding the followers of Jesus "into all truth" (John 16:13).

Roger Nicole gives a nice summary of what all of this means when he writes, "The biblical view of truth *(emet-aletheia)* is like a rope with several intertwined strands"; it "involves factuality, faithfulness, and completeness."[12] Furthermore, this truth is knowable and is not just a matter of "blind faith" or subjective feelings. The truth about God—who has revealed himself as faithful and true—is something you can know and rely on (more about that when you get to Signpost 2).

Douglas Groothuis, a professor of philosophy, lists at least half a dozen qualities of biblical truth that make it well worth your consideration as you embark on your GodQuest:

1. *Truth is revealed by God.* This is a really big deal. For those who think that truth emerged out of the ooze or originated from the human mind, Groothuis reminds us that truth "comes from the disclosure of a personal and moral God who makes himself known." The Apostle Paul writes that even though humans naturally "suppress the truth by their wickedness," they know the truth instinctively "since what may be known about God is plain to them, because God has made it plain to them" (Romans 1:18–19).

2. *Objective truth exists and is knowable.* What this means is that truth doesn't depend on our subjective feelings or beliefs. Neither is truth independent of God's being and revelation. Truth is personal because it comes from a personal God.

3. *Christian truth is absolute in nature.* Before you take offense over the word "absolute," let's look at what absolute truth does not mean in the context of Christianity. First, it doesn't mean that Christians have perfect knowledge about God, and neither does it mean that Christians are infallible in their understanding of their faith. You need to beware of anyone who claims to have the Christian life figured out, or worse, to be an authority on God. Second, believing that there are absolute truths doesn't mean you need to be able to prove them absolutely. For example, nobody can absolutely prove that God exists, yet God's existence is an absolute truth.

4. *Truth is universal.* Dr. Groothuis is right on here: "To be universal means to apply everywhere, to engage everything and to exclude nothing." Another way of looking at the universality of truth is that it isn't bound or restricted in any way and it can't be circumvented by cultural conditions.

5. *The truth of God is eternal, engaging, and momentous, not trendy or superficial.* Don't you love that? If you're like most people, you long to be part of something—a movement, a cause, or even an idea—that's way bigger than you are. Well, it doesn't get any bigger than God. And here's the best part. When you tap into this living truth-giver and the dynamic truth He gives, it will be the most meaningful and fulfilling process you could ever be part of because you are part of what Groothuis calls "the eternal drama." That's what happens when you enter into a relationship with God.

6. *Christian truth is an end, not a means to any other end.* The truth about God is important and vital to your life, not because it is true for you, but because it is true. Period. Even if you didn't exist— even if nothing else existed and there was only God, He would exist and He would be true and He would be the source of truth. God doesn't exist because we made Him up. God exists because God always has been and always will be. The same goes for truth.

TRUTH AND FREEDOM

One of the quickest ways to determine someone's view of truth is to ask how they define freedom. Typically people will answer, "Freedom means being able to do whatever you want without restrictions," or something of that sort. In other words, freedom is having ultimate individual autonomy without being controlled by another. The great philosopher Immanuel Kant said the characteristic feature of modern man is the trust he places in his own reasoning as opposed to some external authority or tradition.

According to this definition, freedom is understood entirely as freedom from something. There is certainly something to be said for being free from tyrannical rulers or oppression. Those who have lived under communism knew the harsh reality of dictatorships. But is this all freedom entails? Ironically, it's actually restriction of our time and talents that leads to genuine freedom. If someone wants to be a good flute player, she must choose to practice for many hours. She must limit herself in order to be free to play the flute. Choosing to practice the flute puts a restriction on other things she may desire to do. If you have the natural aptitude, it takes time and discipline to release that potential. In other words, you cannot freely play the flute without limitations. That means restrictions actually set you free!

This does not mean we all have equal aptitudes. Some are better suited for sports and others for music (or something else). For someone with little athletic skills to spend hours training for basketball may be more restricting than liberating. In *The Reason for God*, Timothy Keller captures this point beautifully:

> Disciplines and restraints, then, liberate us only when they fit with the reality of our nature and capacities. A fish, because it absorbs oxygen from water rather than air, is only free if it is restricted and limited to water. If we put it in the grass, its freedom to move and even live is not enhanced, but destroyed. The fish dies if we do not honor the reality of its nature."[13]

Submitting to reality, then, is the first step in finding freedom. This is why truth is so important! We are free to believe what we want, but we are not free to change reality. The fool bumps his head up against reality, whereas the wise person embraces it. This is why Jesus said, "You will know the truth, and the truth will set you free" (John 8:32).

And this is why the doctrine of creation is so bitterly opposed. If God created us then reality is purposeful. Just as there is a purpose for a pen, a car, or a building, there is a purpose for human beings. And we are only free when we find that purpose and live accordingly. There is a purpose for work, family, marriage, sex, and everything else in creation. We can choose to deny these purposes, but such choices come at a cost—they bring slavery, not freedom. The truly free person understands truth and has the capacity to live it out.

But if there is no God, then *humans* decide their own truth. There is no purpose for the world and we can do whatever we feel like. If God does exist (as the external evidence and our hearts tell us), then we can only be free if we live according to His plan. This seems to be the question that it always boils down to: Is God the authority or are we?

Some of our skeptical friends like to refer to themselves as freethinkers. But, ironically, they are the least free. They reject the very source of their capacity to reason! So, who is truly free? It's those who embrace the right restrictions and have the capacity to live it out. It's those who embrace truth.

KNOW THE TRUTH, BE THE TRUTH, LIVE THE TRUTH

As you continue in your GodQuest, you may be asking yourself, "Who am I to judge what is true and what's not?" Even more, you may be wondering if it's right to judge other people on their view of truth, especially when it comes to morality. Essentially, you're wondering about moral authority, which gets to the heart of many of the issues our culture is dealing with.

In *The Unshakable Truth*, a book I (Sean) co-wrote with my father, Josh McDowell, we answer the question of truth and moral authority. We assert that moral truth is not based on subjective preferences but on objective reality, which is rooted in God. "The basis of everything we call moral and right springs from the truth that resides in the character of the eternal God who is outside us, above us, and beyond us."[14] Knowing what we believe about God forms our belief system, and knowing why we believe these things develops our personal convictions. In other words, what you believe determines the choices you make.

Simply knowing what and why you believe is a great starting point, but it's not in and of itself an adequate framework around which to build your life. According to Josh and Sean, your beliefs must become the core of who you are. "Buying into the Christian faith involves being a living representation of the truth."[15] In other words, it isn't enough to know the truth. You also need to be the truth.

Finally, when it comes to the truth about truth, the way to incorporate it into your life is to live the truth. The truth about God should become so much a part of you that it literally flows out of your life. The Bible tells us, "This then is how we know that we belong to the truth, and how we set our hearts at rest in his presence" (1 John 3:19).

Your GodQuest is just getting started, but already you have a lot to think about in terms of truth and what that means for your life. When we come to Signpost 2 we're going to dig deeper into the person and character of God, where all truth resides, but first we need to deal with some of the other stories in the world that are competing for your attention. That's what the next chapter is all about.

GODQUEST

CHAPTER 3

IN SEARCH OF
THE TRUE STORY

Not long ago Steve Jobs, the co-founder and CEO of Apple, made an announcement that shook the world. For the second time in his career, he was taking a medical leave of absence from his day-to-day role as the chief visionary for what is arguably the most influential and certainly the coolest company on the planet. Commenting on his influence, not just in the realm technology, but in the larger culture, journalist Andy Crouch notes:

> As remarkable as Steve Jobs is in countless ways—as a designer, an innovator, a (ruthless and demanding) leader—his most singular quality has been his ability to articulate a perfectly secular form of hope. Nothing exemplifies that ability more than Apple's early logo, which slapped a rainbow on the very archetype of human fallenness and failure—the bitten fruit—and made it a sign of promise and progress.[1]

Crouch calls Jobs an "evangelist" of this kind of progress, "the perfect evangelist, because he had no competing source of hope." And what kind of hope has Steve Jobs been offering? His own words explain it best. In an excerpt from a commencement address Steve Jobs gave at Stanford University after his initial cancer diagnosis in 2003, here is his take on life, death, and hope:

No one wants to die. Even people who want to go to heaven don't want to die to get there. And yet death is the destination we all share. No one has ever escaped it. And that is as it should be, because death is very likely the single best invention of life. It's life's change agent; it clears out the old to make way for the new. Right now, the new is you. But someday, not too long from now, you will gradually become the old and be cleared away. Sorry to be so dramatic, but it's quite true. Your time is limited, so don't waste it living someone else's life. Don't be trapped by dogma, which is living with the results of other people's thinking. Don't let the noise of others' opinions drown out your own inner voice, heart, and intuition. They somehow already know what you truly want to become.[2]

This is the gospel according to Steve Jobs, and in Crouch's accurate assessment, it's "the gospel of the secular age" as well because it relies neither on an established set of teachings from a religion, nor does it rest in revelation. It's an existentialist message that frequently shows up in movies like *Dead Poet's Society, Yes Man!,* and *The Adjustment Bureau.* Such a view is straight from the heart, responsible to no one and anchored to nothing. If you were to categorize this "truth" in one of the theories we explained in the last chapter, this view would fall squarely in the "truth is what I feel" category.

Yet this is the gospel for millions of people, including many who claim to have a relationship with God personally. In reality, it's not really all that new. You could say Jobs' view on life is a combination of the popular saying, "To thine own self be true" and the ancient adage, "Eat, drink and be merry, for tomorrow we die." So it's not original, but it seems very contemporary and compelling to people raised in a world lacking hope, but having a vast array of technological wonders at their fingertips. The only problem is that today's hot technology is tomorrow's museum piece. Nothing lasts forever, and in the case of the latest gadget, it doesn't even last a year before something better and faster comes along. We don't know about you, but that doesn't sound very hopeful to us.

GODQUEST

THE TRUE STORY AND THE GOSPEL

As you continue searching for truth on your GodQuest, what you're really looking for is a relationship with God and a true story: a story you can live in, a story that provides meaning, not just for this life but for the life to come. "Eat, drink, and be merry, for tomorrow we die" isn't a good enough story for you.

Steve Jobs' story may be "the gospel of the secular age," but it's not the true story. In fact, the true story is related to the gospel, but it's not the kind of gospel you're thinking of. If you're like most people, you equate *gospel* with religion, which most people think has a lot of rules and regulations. So when you hear the term, "preach the gospel," you naturally think of fiery evangelists waving their arms and sweating a lot as they tell people they're going to hell if they don't stop sinning and start following a lot of rules and regulations.

Well, we're here to tell you that interpretation of *gospel* is misleading. At its root, *gospel* means "good news" or "good story." Therefore, preaching the gospel is simply telling a good story, and anyone who thinks they have a good story to tell can become an *evangelist*. In that sense, Steve Jobs is an evangelist for Apple and the larger world of technology, and his good story is that the new is where it's at, so enjoy being new as long as you can, because someday you're going to be old and then you'll die.

By comparison, the Christian story is the good news that God is reaching out to people who have turned their backs on Him, and He's offering a way to have an eternal relationship with Him through the person and work of Jesus Christ. That a holy and perfect God would want to connect with sinful and imperfect people and offer a way to get things right—a way that is available equally to every person, no strings attached—seems too good to be true. There has to be a catch. It can't be that simple.

Oh, but it is that simple, which is probably why so many people overlook the true story of God and try instead to make up a human story, just like Steve Jobs and many others have done. And on the surface it sounds really good because you're at the center and it's all about you living a good life and helping others and feeling good about yourself. You're still spiritual (if you want to be), but you are definitely not religious.

SPIRITUAL BUT NOT RELIGIOUS

In the last few years a number of extensive surveys have been conducted by several reputable polling organizations—including the Barna Research Group, Lifeway Research, and the Pew Forum on Religion and Public Life—on the spiritual condition of young adults. Their findings are pretty much in agreement: Two-thirds of all young adults consider themselves "spiritual but not religious." And just what does that mean? Let the statistics tell the story. Of the people who call themselves spiritual but not religious:

Sixty-five percent rarely or never pray with others, and thirty-eight percent never pray by themselves

- Sixty-five percent never attend church
- Sixty-seven percent don't read the Bible or other sacred texts
- Fifty percent don't believe Jesus is the only way to heaven

So what kind of spirituality is this? It may not include those activities and beliefs that have traditionally been associated with spirituality, but it does embrace faith, which remains a front-and-center topic in our culture. "Politicians, athletes, cultural philosophers, teachers, entertainers, musicians—nearly everyone has something to say about faith," reports Barna. "But as the fundamental values and assumptions of our nation continue to shift, so do our ideas about faith and spirituality. Many of our basic assumptions are no longer firm or predictable."[3]

These are real issues that seriously spiritual people are wrestling with, and you may be one of them. In your GodQuest, you may be wondering if the Christian faith you were taught as a child is still relevant today. A generation ago, there was no other faith in America, but all that has changed in the last twenty years. We live in a multicultural world with pluralistic ideas that come from a wide variety of religions and beliefs, including the belief that God doesn't exist.

Christianity, the belief system named after the historical figure Jesus Christ, doesn't have the appeal it once did, not because of the teachings, but because of the practices. While they don't necessarily have a problem with the Christian story, many young adults view Christianity as aligned with the political right, especially on moral issues like homosexuality. They see Christians as intolerant and hypocritical, and they want no part of it. So they back away from Christianity, leave the church, and do their best to operate within a moral and philosophical framework that is self-satisfying—not unlike the gospel according the Steve Jobs. George Barna puts it this way:

> Ultimately, in a culture where people are busy, distracted, confused and trying to keep it all together, there is less loyalty to a faith brand than to self. The purpose of faith, for most Americans, is not so much to discover truth or to relate to a loving, praiseworthy deity as it is to become happy, successful, comfortable and secure. For a growing percentage of citizens, their sense of spirituality, more than Christianity, facilitates those outcomes."[4]

BEING HONEST ABOUT FAITH

It would be easy to assume that many of these "spiritual but not religious" people are totally self-centered and in danger of losing touch with God. The trends found in this group would seem to back this up, especially when you consider that two-thirds of spiritual but not religious people aren't engaged in those activities that traditionally have marked an "active" Christian. On the other hand, what good are prayer, church attendance, and Bible reading if they are done out of obligation rather than a sincere willingness of the heart? So maybe being spiritual but not religious is less about turning your back on God's true story, and more about being frustrated that the story has been distorted by those who tell it and those who live in it.

We agree with Pastor Mark Driscoll, who believes that spiritual but not religious young adults are simply tired of all the hypocrisy they have seen in the church over the last decade. What they want is an honest faith. Or to put it in the context of this chapter, they want the true story. Driscoll makes these astute observations:[5]

- Many young adults are delaying most major life decisions— from career path, to marriage and having children, to a "set of spiritual beliefs they will adhere to"—until their early thirties. "Subsequently, their ambiguity and lack of certainty about Christian doctrine is not surprising in light of their entire life."

- Young adults are committed to churches not built for them but by them. They may be leaving churches that don't have clear, Bible-based teaching about real-life issues in order to find churches that do. And they are using online social media to talk about the things that really matter to them, such as serving those who are poor and suffering.

- Young adults are being honest about faith. The days of feeling cultural pressure to adhere to historic Christian truths are gone. It isn't that these spiritual but not religious young adults are abandoning Jesus, but that they aren't excited about Christianity.

BURGER KING SPIRITUALITY

Okay, so we can agree that many people who have left the church and historic Christianity have a legitimate reason for their abandonment. They are disillusioned by the hypocrisy they see in traditional Christianity, but they aren't willing to check out entirely. If anything, spiritual but not religious "leavers" are eager to embrace a more vibrant, authentic faith.

If you are disillusioned by Christians and Christianity, but you are searching for a more vibrant, authentic faith—and you long to have a relationship with the true and living God—we applaud you. If you are fed up with the hypocrisy in religion, you're in good company. Jesus condemned hypocritical religious people more than anyone else! But we also need to warn you. It's one thing to abandon the church and historic Christianity, but what do you replace it with? What kind of spiritual experience are you looking for? Don't toss out Christianity because of its fallen followers. The Bible says all people are sinful—Christians are no exception—so we should expect such behavior. Focus on the truth rather than on people.

Unfortunately, many spiritual but not religious people are embracing a kind of Burger King spirituality. You know the Burger King theme: "Have it your way." Rather than accepting what's on the menu, you can custom design your own burger, prepared just the way you like it. The same thing can happen with faith. Why believe in a God whom other people follow when you can have a god just the way you like him (or her)?

Heather Cariou, a New York City-based author who considers herself spiritual but not religious, has adopted a blended spirituality piece together from different faith traditions. "I don't need to define myself to any community by putting myself in a box labeled Baptist, or Catholic, or Muslim," she says. "When I die, I believe all my accounting will be done to God, and that when I enter the eternal realm, I will not walk through a door with a label on it."[6]

Now, you may not identify with Heather's position, but many people do, so we need to hit the pause button and deal with it before we can move on to the final section of this chapter, which is to talk about the authentic Christian story. We need to address the reasons why people abandon Christianity, replacing it with Burger King spirituality, or Moralistic Therapeutic Deism, or the gospel according to Steve Jobs.

REASONS PEOPLE ABANDON CHRISTIANITY

Over the last few years, many people, including an inordinate number of young adults have exited the church and traditional Christianity in favor of a different kind of spiritual experience. Our friend Drew Dyck, a writer for ChristianityToday.com and the author of the excellent book, *Generation Ex-Christian: Why Young Adults Are Leaving the Faith and How to Bring Them Back*, has identified six kinds of ex-Christians and the reasons they leave Christianity:[7]

1. *Postmodern Leavers* reject Christianity's exclusive claims and moral absolutes.

2. *Recoilers* have been hurt by Christians, often ones they regarded as spiritual authorities.

3. *Modern Leavers* have no problem with truth claims and will readily argue their convictions, but any truth beyond the reach of science is dismissed as superstition.

4. *Neo-Pagans* trade Christian faith for earth-based spiritualities such as Wicca.

5. *Rebels* are stubborn and strong-willed. They find it difficult to submit to God's authority and don't want anyone telling them what to do.

6. *Drifters* do not suffer intellectual crises or consciously leave the faith; they simply drift away.

Maybe you can see yourself in one of these six categories, or for you it could be a combination of factors. Or perhaps you identify with the experience of many who have grown up in a home where Christian ideas and values were taught (even if they weren't exactly modeled), but then you experienced a crisis of belief when you left home for college. Some studies have shown that close to three-quarters of all young adults who once went to church and had at least a rudimentary understanding of the Christian faith end up leaving the faith once they go to college. The story of Paul Vitz is typical.

FAITH AND SOCIAL PRESSURE

Paul Vitz is a psychologist who grew up in a "wishy-washy" Christian home in the Midwest, became an atheist in grad school and remained so until his *re*-conversion back to Christianity in his late thirties. While he would have denied it at the time, Vitz now realizes his reasons for becoming an atheist for nearly twenty years were "intellectually superficial and largely without a deep thought basis."[8] Rather than reasoning his way to his atheistic beliefs, he was simply socialized into them. He cites three reasons for his initial conversion.

First, he had a degree of social unease coming from the Midwest. It seemed terribly dull, provincial, middle class, and narrow. He wanted to be part of the glamorous secular world at the University of Michigan when he arrived on campus as an undergrad. Just think about all the young people arriving in New York, Los Angeles, Chicago, or other big cities or campuses who are embarrassed by their fundamental upbringing. This kind of socialization, says Vitz, has pushed many people away from God.

Second, he wanted to be accepted by the powerful and influential people in his field of psychology. His professors at Stanford had two things in common—their intense ambition and their rejection of religion. Vitz concludes, "In this environment, just as I had learned how to dress like a college student by putting on the right clothes, I also learned to think like a proper psychologist by putting on the right, that is, atheistic or skeptical, ideas and attitudes."[9]

The third factor was personal convenience. Vitz explains, "The fact is, it is quite inconvenient to be a serious believer in today's neo-pagan world. I would have to give up many pleasures, some money, and a good deal of time. I didn't have enough pleasures, I didn't have enough time, and I didn't have enough money to do any of that as far as I was concerned".[10] After initially believing in God, people often experience doubts once they realize how inconvenient Christianity can really be.

Taking these three factors into account, we can see why many young adults leave the faith. When someone goes off to college there is no accountability structure, and the separation from family often creates an even deeper desire to fit in with the crowd. Given that we are like sheep, prone to wander (Isaiah 53:6), there's no wonder so many people abandon their faith in the midst of social pressure, whether that pressure happens in college or later in life.

The Main Reason People Abandon Christianity

As we said, these are all common reasons why people leave the Christian faith, and as you continue your GodQuest, you may find yourself identifying with one or more of them. But there may be an even bigger reason why people either a) leave the Christian faith, or b) refuse to accept it in the first place. In fact, in our view this is the *main* reason. Are you ready for it? Here it is: *The main reason people leave or stay away from Christianity is because it claims to have the only true story.* Tim Keller, senior pastor of Redeemer Presbyterian Church in New York City, goes even farther and says the exclusive truth claims of Christianity are the biggest reason people are skeptical about God.[11]

It isn't that Christians don't believe their story. They do. But many of them, especially young adults, are uncomfortable saying that their beliefs are the only valid ones. They will say something like, "I think Christianity is true, but God is much too loving to condemn people whose beliefs are different than mine." They want God to be generous and non-judgmental, so they come to the conclusion that all religions basically teach the same thing.

In this view, God lives at the top of a very big mountain, and all the religions and belief systems in the world are like different trails that lead to the top. Just like every trail eventually reaches the summit, so the reasoning goes, every religion eventually reaches God. Christians may even think they are doing non-Christians a favor by saying that they can be saved, as long as they believe in God.

There's only one problem with this thinking. All religions can't be true because all religions are different and mutually exclusive at various points, especially as you climb higher on the mountain. For example, at the base of the mountain, Christianity and Islam agree that there is one God. But as you begin to compare the characterstics of the God of the Qur'an (Allah) with the God of the Bible (Jehovah), we soon find clear distinctions.

Religion scholar Stephen Prothero, a Boston University professor, puts it even more bluntly. The notion of "pretend pluralism"—that all religions are essentially the same—may be well intentioned, but it is "dangerous, disrespectful, and untrue." Prothero writes, "Christians who think they're doing non-Christians a favor by saying they too can be 'saved' ignore the fact that Jews, Muslims, Buddhists, and Confucians either don't believe in sin or don't focus on salvation from it."[12]

The reality is that every religion makes exclusive truth claims. All believe they have the correct view of truth as it relates to God (or gods or karma or whatever it is a particular religion teaches). So why does Christianity get criticized the most when it comes to its exclusive truth claims? Why does our culture seem to give a free pass to other religions, but comes down hard on Christians for their belief that in order to be saved, you have to believe in Jesus?

Bingo. There's the reason: *Jesus*. There are many things about Christianity that make it unique among world religions, but this one is the biggie. All religions include Jesus in one way or another, but only Christianity says Jesus is the only way to God. Furthermore, Jesus is the only religious figure who made the incredible claim: *I am God.* There's no getting around that fact, and that's what makes people uncomfortable. This is why many popular movies that have a Christian message—*The Blind Side* and *The Book of Eli* are two recent examples—talk about God, but not Jesus.

We're going to deal with this claim in much more detail when we get to Signpost 5, but for the purposes of this chapter, we want to review with you how the culture has attempted to deal with the exclusive truth claims of Christianity. We think this will help you sort out your own views and feelings as you continue on your GodQuest.

DEALING WITH EXCLUSIVE TRUTH CLAIMS

We are grateful for Tim Keller's perceptive analysis of the cultural response to Christianity's exclusive truth claims. In his book, *The*

Reason for God, and in a talk he gave at the University of Chicago in 2008, Keller shows four ways people deal with the idea that just one religion, belief system, or story is true.

- *By hoping there's another way.* We've pretty much already made this point, but Keller does a much better job of it. He says that most people just want to get along with everyone else, including those they disagree with, so they hope that someday everybody will come to an agreement about God and how we get to heaven. Basically, they want a belief system—it can be Christianity, but it doesn't have to be—where they just live a good life and make the world a better place (sound familiar?). They don't need to believe in miracles or that a person has to be "born again." And all this talk about sin has just got to go. We need to find those things we agree on and leave it at that.

The problem with this way of thinking is that it just doesn't work. People may live like this for a while. They may think Moralistic Therapeutic Deism provides a workable framework for life, but at the end of the day it ends up being totally unsatisfying. Why? Because God won't let them live this way. If you've tried watering down your beliefs like this, you know what we mean. It's impossible to be fulfilled when you live with a wishy-washy faith. Jesus put it this way:

> *I know your deeds, that you are neither cold nor hot. I wish you were either one or the other! So, because you are lukewarm—neither hot nor cold—I am about to spit you out of my mouth. (Revelation 3:15-16).*

- *By making it illegal.* This is actually an old tactic, and despite it's dismal track record, there are a few people today who honestly think outlawing religion is the way to restore peace in the world. In truth, it's the way governments—from the Soviet Union to China—have historically attempted to suppress and control people, and it's never worked. If anything, outlawing religion only leads to a flourishing of belief. In the first century, Christianity was against the law, and believers were executed for putting their faith in Christ. Yet the Christian church grew incredibly fast despite (or maybe even because of) the persecution, and ultimately it toppled the oppressive regime that was against it.

In our own time, we only have to look at China, where Christianity was suppressed for decades until the underground church began to grow at an astounding rate, to the point that there are probably more Christians in China right now than there are in America.

- *By explaining it away.* This tactic has been used with great success by the so-called "new atheists" of which Richard Dawkins, Christopher Hitchens, and Daniel Dennett are the most prominent and vocal examples. Their goal is to explain away the exclusive truth claims of all religions—in particular Christianity—by offering an alternative explanation for belief in God. Keller puts it this way: "They say that if you believe in God, it's not because there is a God out there, but because you're hard-wired to believe in God. You kind of can't help it.[13]

The problem with this argument is that it's self-refuting. Keller wisely points out that if we can't trust our "belief-forming faculties" that tell us God exists, then we can't trust those same faculties when they tell us God doesn't exist. But we know from experience—and you do, too—that our internal beliefs and inner convictions that God exists are much stronger than our beliefs that He doesn't exist. We may have doubts about how God works in the world, and we may have questions about His character, but the vast majority of us—if we're being honest with ourselves—cannot deny that God is out there.

- *By keeping your beliefs to yourself.* A lot of people believe religion and discussions about God are strictly personal matters and should never be a subject for public debate, least of all in a political forum. But this is absurd when you consider what religion really is. "It is a set of beliefs that explain what life is all about, who we are, and the most important things that human beings should spend their time doing," says Keller.[14] When any of us enters into the "public square," whether that's politics or public education or the arts—basically, anything that has to do with the way we operate as a culture—we can't help but be influenced by our beliefs and convictions about the way things ought to be.

GETTING TO THE TRUE STORY

You have now come to an extremely important signpost in your GodQuest journey; Signpost 1 is the understanding that what you believe determines where you go in life. In other words, your belief in some view of the world—how it got here, how it operates, and how you fit into it—will affect everything you do. *What you believe affects the choices you make.* Tim Keller puts it this way: "Everyone lives and operates out of some narrative identity, whether it is thought out and reflected upon or not."[15] In other words, everyone lives in a story, whether it's a story of their own making or a much grander story.

So the next big question is this: How do you know your "narrative identity"—your story—is the one that will give you the most meaning, and how do you find out? Or to put it more in the language of your GodQuest, the question might be, "Where do you start your quest for meaning?" We've already established that there are differences in the various religions and belief systems in the world, so it's not really practical or advisable to piece together a worldview framework that includes a little of everything. In order for your life to have coherence and meaning, you have to get a coherent and meaningful story that is also the *true* story. That's not to say there isn't truth in other belief systems. But there's only one that is true through and through. The question is, which one?

Recently Sean had the opportunity to speak to a group of students at the University of California at Berkeley. Rather than trying to convince them that Christianity is true, he simply wanted to persuade them that any religious quest should begin with Christianity. Sean was motivated in this approach by a creative novel written by Dr. Craig Hazen called *The Five Sacred Crossings*. In this novel, Hazen, who is an expert in comparative religions, lists four reasons why a thoughtful person should begin with Christianity.[16]

1. *Christianity is testable.* There is no other religion or belief system entirely based on a testable, historic event: the resurrection of Jesus Christ. In his letter to the Corinthian church, the

Apostle Paul writes that without the resurrection, there is no Christian faith (1 Corinthians 15:14, 17). That's a huge claim that Paul would never make unless he was absolutely certain the resurrection of Jesus actually took place and was testable. In fact, throughout his life on earth, Jesus gave public evidence that He was the Son of God, and we can test these claims through historical investigation. Christianity alone invites people to weigh the evidence about the identity of Jesus, the miracles he performed, and the miracle of his resurrection, and to come to an informed decision (John 20:30–31).

By comparison, Mohammed refused to do miracles. According to reports, he received the Qur'an in a cave and gave no external proof that his revelation was divine. Likewise, Mormonism talks about events as if they are historical, but as soon as we go to investigate these claims they are nowhere to be found.

Mormons often point to Moroni 10:4, a verse from the Book of Mormon, as a test to use for Mormonism. This verse promises that if you pray with a contrite spirit the Holy Ghost will reveal to you the truth of Mormonism. But for this promise to be valid one has to already believe in the book of Mormon. But if someone doesn't already believe in the book of Mormon, why would they trust the promise from Moroni 10:4? Rather than providing external, testable evidence for the book of Mormon, Mormons often simply *assume* it is true.

Zen Buddhism focuses on emptying the mind. For example, Buddhists are encouraged to focus on the sound of one hand clapping in the forest. Buddha allegedly said, "By this you shall know that a man is *not* my disciple—that he tries to work a miracle."

2. *Salvation is offered as a free gift.* When buying a car, we have different criteria that help us decide, such as color, safety record, appearance, company reliability, and so on. One of the most important criteria is *cost*. If we were evaluating cars with similar features, the cheapest one would certainly get our attention first. The same applies to choosing a religion. Shouldn't we begin with the religion that costs the least to "buy" into?

Christianity is unique in that salvation is free. Ephesians 2:8–9 says, "For it is by grace you have been saved, through faith—and this is not from yourselves, it is the gift of God—not by works, so that no one can boast." By contrast, consider these requirements from two other sacred texts:

- *The Qur'an*, Surah 17:13: "And we have made every man's actions to cling to his neck, and we will bring forth to him on the resurrection day a book which he will find wide open."

- *The Book of Mormon*, 2 Nephi 25:23: "For we labor diligently to write, to persuade our children, and also our brethren, to believe in Christ, and to be reconciled to God; for we know that it is by grace that we are saved, after all we can do."[17]

Every other religion is about man trying to get to God; Christianity is uniquely about God coming to us.

3. *Christianity is completely true to the way things really are.* What we mean by this is that Christianity gives reasonable explanations for the way things are in the natural world. First, the truths of Christianity are consistent with *history*. The Bible is filled with facts about real people and real events in real time in ways that can be verified. Second, the truths of Christianity are consistent with *science*. The Bible is not a scientific book, but the explanations it gives for how the universe got here are compatible with what science tells us.

Finally, the truths of Christianity are consistent with *reason*. This means that rational beings can objectively evaluate the Christian belief system and find that it is reasonable and noncontradictory in its approach to the human condition.

Furthermore, Christianity acknowledges the existence of a spiritual dimension in each of us that does not change and in fact grounds our human identity (remember what we said about your heart and soul being the "real" you). Buddhism maintains there is no soul. The human being is like a flame that is constantly changing. Life is transitory and every natural object is perpetually perishing. Thus, humans are constantly changing and do not literally remain the same over time. Likewise, naturalism says a human being is simply a collection of physical particles that make up the human body and are replaced every seven years. Both the Buddhist and the naturalist confront the same problem: what grounds human identity through time?

4. *Christianity alone has Jesus at the center.* Jesus is the most sought after religious figure in the entire world. His influence is unparalleled. He wrote no books, had no military power, no political position, traveled less than two hundred miles from his hometown, and publicly ministered for only three years. Yet Jesus is the figure virtually every other religion wants to claim as their own:

- Islam says Jesus was a great prophet who was sinless, virgin-born, and a miracle worker.

- Buddhists claim Jesus is an enlightened one.

- New Age followers claim that Jesus tapped into the cosmic consciousness.

- Hindus say Jesus is an avatar (incarnated god).

- Many Jews say Jesus was a good teacher.

However, only Christianity has Jesus at the center as the self-proclaimed Son of God who is equal to God in every way. As the Bible says:

He is the image of the invisible God, the firstborn over all creation. For in him all things were created: things in heaven and on earth, visible and invisible, whether thrones or powers or rulers or authorities; all things have been created through him and for him. He is before all things, and in him all things hold together. And he is the head of the body, the church; he is the beginning and the firstborn from among the dead, so that in everything he might have the supremacy. For God was pleased to have all his fullness dwell in him, and through him to reconcile to himself all things, whether things on earth or things in heaven, by making peace through his blood, shed on the cross (Colossians 1:15–20).

With all of this in mind, let's move on to Signpost 2, where we take a closer look at the God of Christianity.

THE BEGINNING

WHAT YOU BELIEVE ABOUT CREATION DETERMINES HOW YOU VIEW YOURSELF AND LIFE.

Have you been taught that your life is the chance product of a vast and purposeless universe? Or, have you gazed at the beauty of the star-filled sky and believed that an intelligent Creator designed the universe and then gave you life? Depending on what you believe, you will seek to know your Creator, or decide there is no creator and go your own way.

GODQUEST

CHAPTER 4

THE SEARCH FOR GOD

It's the nature of human beings to search. We can't help it. If we lose something, especially something of great value, we will pretty much stop everything else we're doing and look for it. Obviously, there are some things we search for because we need them immediately—our car keys, for example. Other things, like a credit card or wedding ring, require a search because there are bound to be consequences if we can't find them. And then there are those lost items we search for in a panic because they bring our lives meaning and we can't imagine our lives without them; a missing child or even a lost dog can create this feeling of desperation.

So where does your search for God rank on this informal scale, with car keys being least valuable and a child being most valuable? In order to sound like you're a deep thinker, you might say the search for God is the most important search you can ever undertake. But would that be an honest answer? It's okay, you can admit it. The search for God may seem like a lofty and worthwhile pursuit, but there are a lot more important and tangible searches you would probably make first, if by "important" you mean "drop everything and start searching."

If you're like most people, your search for God isn't at the top of your priority list. You look to God when it's convenient, when you have time, when you have a problem, when you're in a contemplative kind of mood, or maybe after you check a bunch of other things off your list—like finishing school, getting a job, finding that perfect soul mate, getting married, and having kids. And even after getting through all of that life stuff, there may not be any urgency to your search. Oh, you may go to church or even make an attempt to read the Bible, but it's not a matter of life and death. Searching for God is more like enhancing your quality of life, like joining a health club.

If we sound a little cynical, we don't mean to be. You may already be on a serious GodQuest, and for that we applaud you. On the other hand, we completely understand what it's like to work your GodQuest into your life when it's convenient, because that's where most people are (assuming they are engaged in the search at all). But just because we understand doesn't mean we want to leave you where you are. For us, and for many other people just like you who are genuinely interested in discovering the truth about life, the search for God is not just another pursuit. It's *the* most important pursuit because it deals with the most important topic in the world: the true story of the true God and what it means to be part of that story and to have a relationship with Him.

WHAT IF ALL OF THIS IS TRUE?

In the beginning of this book we talked about some famous quests for things that don't exist. We compared these romantic quests to the quest for God, which is the most noble and worthwhile quest of all because God really does exist. Now, we realize we're getting a little ahead of ourselves because in the next chapter we're going to look at some compelling reasons why you can truly *know* that God exists as opposed to *feeling* that God exists. However, for the purposes of our present discussion on the search for God, we're going to assume that you have at least a basic belief in God, even if you have a few questions and doubts.

What we are *not* going to assume, however, is that your belief directly affects the choices you make (at least not yet), or that you believe you can relate to God in a dynamic way that makes your life different and more meaningful every day. More likely, if you're similar to most people who claim to believe in God, your belief doesn't go much beyond your desire to live a good life, be happy, and have God around when you need Him. The reality is that most of your choices in life are the result of your own desires independent of God. That doesn't mean you don't believe in God; it simply means you live as if He doesn't really matter that much. Or, as Craig Groeschel says in his book *The Christian Atheist*, you believe in God but live as if He doesn't exist.

But what if all of this is true? What if God really does exist; and what if everything you know about God from the universe and from the Bible is true? How will that change the way you live? Will your search for God take on more urgency? Rather than pursuing your GodQuest in a casual manner, will it suddenly become the most important thing you can ever do?

TWO COMPETING REALITIES

We can't answer those questions for you, but we can give you two scenarios that go to the heart of your GodQuest. These scenarios contain the elements of two competing realities about the way things are. This first reality is that God exists, and the second is that God doesn't exist. Notice how these two different realities—or worldviews—affect the choices you make and the paths you take in life.

THE FIRST REALITY: GOD EXISTS

- God is the most powerful, intelligent, loving, perfect, and awesome being in the universe.

- God created the universe and everything in it, including you. You're here on earth for a reason; your life has a purpose.

- Because of His perfect and complete knowledge, God knows everything about you down to your innermost thoughts. In fact, He knows what you're going to do or think even before it happens.

- God created you with a free will; therefore, you have choices. And even though God knows the choices you're going to make, they are your choices to make—for good or bad.

- Just about every choice you make is a choice between what God wants you to do—God's will—and what you want to do. Sometimes your choices line up with God's will, and sometimes they don't.

- When your free-will choices go in the opposite direction of God's will, things usually turn out bad—maybe not at first, but eventually your life may be characterized by frustration and needless worry.

- When your free-will choices line up with God's choices, you are within God's will—whether your circumstances are positive or not. And even when you experience trials, you will still have an attitude of joy (James 1:2).

THE SECOND REALITY: GOD DOESN'T EXIST

God didn't create the world, which means you are the product of natural selection and random mutation. There's no reason or purpose for your existence, except to survive and reproduce.

- Nobody knows more about you than you do; you are the final authority for your choices.

- There's no ultimate standard for your morality and behavior, so most of the choices you make are based on the standards you set for yourself. If you need to move them around to get more out of life, that's fine, as long as nobody gets hurt.

- In the end, your goal is to just be happy and fulfilled.

Again, we want to make it clear that you don't have to be an atheist to live in the framework of the second reality. In fact, many believers live and make choices as if God doesn't exist. And if we're being honest with ourselves, every one of us would admit that we have lived this way at one time or another in our lives. You may be living like that now. There's only one problem with living this way—there can't be two realities. Either God exists or He doesn't. You can't have it both ways. So the only question you have to ask yourself is this: Which reality is true?

GODQUEST

SEAN'S STORY

My story is very different than most people I've met. Even though I grew up in a Christian home, I hit a point in my life where certain questions came crashing down on me like never before:

- How do I really know Christianity is true?
- What would I believe if I had been raised in a different family?
- Is Jesus really the only way to God?
- What is going to bring real happiness and meaning to my life?
- What about other religions?

Before this period in my life, my faith was simply something I took for granted. I have fond memories of attending Christian conferences, going on mission trips, and listening to my father as he taught the Bible. My parents raised me in the Christian faith. In fact, as a child growing up, I can never remember not believing in the Christian story of the world.

Yet as a college student, the answers I had based my faith on were no longer enough. Nagging doubts about my faith simply wouldn't go away. Rather than basing my faith on the opinions of others, I wanted a faith based on fact. I had to know with confidence that what I believed was really true. At times, these questions led me to feel the despair that existentialist writers such as Albert Camus and Jean Paul Sartre said comes from believing God does not exist. I remember staying up late at night reading the psalms of David as he wondered why God seemed so absent in his time of need.

As I began to wrestle with the big questions of life, I realized there was one person I needed to be honest with—my father. To understand how difficult this was for me, it's necessary to understand my dad's story as well.

If you haven't figured it out by now, my father is the well-known Christian apologist Josh McDowell (that means he is a defender of the Christian faith—see 1 Peter 3:15). He's the author of more than one hundred books and is probably best known for his book *Evidence that Demands a Verdict*, in which he documents the historical evidence that persuaded him to seriously consider the claims of Christ. He grew up in a small Michigan town in a deeply dysfunctional family. In fact, my father can never remember his father being sober until he was in his twenties. His older brother sued his father for everything, just out of spite. And one of his older sisters committed suicide. In the recently updated version of *More Than a Carpenter*, my dad shared an even more devastating truth about this childhood—he was sexually abused for about eight years.

As you can imagine, my father was desperate for a life of happiness and meaning. He excelled in school, was elected to student government, made a lot of money, and yet nothing seemed to fill the void in his heart. After meeting some Christian students whose lives were genuinely different, he decided to write a book disproving the Christian faith. While he records his story in more depth in *More Than a Carpenter*, the bottom line is that he became intellectually convinced that Christianity was in fact true. He has since committed his entire life to defending and telling the truth of Christianity.

This is why my conversation with my father was so tough. How would he react to his own son questioning the faith he so deeply cherished? As we sat at a small café in the mountains of Breckenridge, Colorado, I told my dad about my doubts. His response completely took me by surprise. "I think it's great that you want to find truth," he said. "It's wise not to simply accept things just because you were told them. You need to find out if Christianity is true. You know that your mom and I love you regardless of what you conclude. Seek after truth and take to heart the things your mom and I have taught you. And let me know if I can help along the way."

That is exactly what I did. I started reading books by Christian apologists such as J. P. Moreland and William Lane Craig. And I also read skeptics such as Michael Martin (*The Case Against Christianity*) and Dan Barker (*Losing Faith*). I read as much of both sides as possible. After a lot of thought, deliberation, and soul-searching, I came to the conclusion that my faith was well grounded. We will talk more about this in the rest of GodQuest, but I wanted you to glimpse what has helped to shape my worldview. Very briefly, here is what persuaded me.

While there is plenty of compelling evidence for Christianity , I just couldn't explain away Jesus of Nazareth. His public ministry was only three years. He never wrote a book. He had no political or military power. And He had little money. Yet He turned the world upside down through His teachings. The claims Jesus made struck me as utterly profound. He didn't just claim to know how to get to God—He claimed to be God. He didn't claim simply to know truth—He claimed to be the truth (John 14:6). Jesus asked His disciples, "Who do you say I am?" I realized that how I answered this question would define my life.. The evidence was compelling that Jesus really was who He claimed to be.

And yet it wasn't solely the historical evidence that I found persuasive. It was also Jesus' prescription of the human condition that humbled me. Jesus said:

> For it is from within, out of a person's heart, come evil thoughts, sexual immorality, theft, murder, adultery, greed, malice, deceit, lewdness, envy, slander, arrogance and folly. All these evils come from inside and make a man "unclean" (Mark 7:21–23).

The core problem with the world, according to Jesus, is not economic inequality (Marxism), our forgetfulness that we are divine (New Age), but the wickedness of the human heart. As Frank Sinatra observed, we want to do it our way. Even though I was a pretty good kid growing up (i.e., I didn't do any of the "big" sins), I began to realize the depths of my own pride and rebellion against God. I, too, needed a savior.

NOW IS THE TIME

If God doesn't exist and the story of God as found in the Bible is false, then you may as well put this book down and get back to your life, because a search for something that doesn't exist doesn't make sense. On the other hand, if you have come to the place where Sean ended up—aware of your own pride and rebellion, ready to believe that the story of God as found in the Bible is true—now is the time to earnestly and eagerly search for Him. Whatever else you are doing, whatever cares and concerns and priorities you now have, your search for the true God and the true story needs to become the most important priority of your life. This doesn't mean you have to stop everything else in your life, but you need put your GodQuest at the top of your list—it's that important.

Don't just take our word for it. God Himself—the creator of the universe, the one who knows you intimately and loves you unconditionally—wants you to search for Him. Here is what God is saying to you right now:

> Seek the LORD while he may be found; call on him while he is near (Isaiah 55:6).

Now is the time to begin your search. God is nearby, ready to reward those who believe He exists and who are earnestly searching for Him (Hebrews 11:6). Even more, the gracious and loving God who isn't a human invention but the greatest reality you can ever know is looking for you! The Bible says:

> For the eyes of the LORD range throughout the earth to strengthen those whose hearts are fully committed to him (2 Chronicles 16:9).

What an amazing reality! If you commit your heart, soul, mind, and strength to your GodQuest, God will strengthen you. He will give you the courage and perseverance you need in order to truly find Him and live in the reality of His love and care. That's not to say your search for God will be easy or quick, though. To the contrary, your GodQuest is going to require courage and perseverance, and you have to go about your search in the right way. You need to think about where you're going. If you don't, you're going to end up expending a lot of energy going in circles.

I (Sean) have a friend who was out golfing with his wife. He shanked the ball and hit his wife right in the temple. She immediately collapsed, blood pouring down the side of her head. My friend picked her up, ran to the car and took off driving as quickly as he could. A few minutes down the road he realized that he had absolutely no idea where he was headed. He was in such a rush to get somewhere that he didn't even have a particular destination in mind. Yogi Berra once said that if you don't know where you are going, you will probably end up somewhere else. For your GodQuest, it's important to go about your search in the right way. Urgency and passion are essential, but without having the right path to follow, you may end up right back where you started.

As we see it, your path to searching for and finding the true story and the true God begins with knowledge, which is simply a matter of being conversant in or having an acquaintance with the truth. Specifically, here are three things to know that will help you in your GodQuest:

- Know the correct perspective
- Know the unique challenges
- Know that God can be known

KNOW THE CORRECT PERSPECTIVE

The Swiss theologian Karl Barth identified two perspectives with which we can begin a search for God: our perspective and God's perspective. Our perspective begins with us and reasons upward, while God's perspective begins with God and accepts His revelation to us.

On the surface, our perspective sounds really good. Why wouldn't we start from a human perspective since that's the only one we have? In fact, beginning with us is the starting point for every human-centered religion and belief system. It's where the gospel of Steve Jobs and Moralistic Therapeutic Deism start. Our perspective is bringing God down to our level, having God on our terms, turning God into a Goldilocks "just right" kind of God. A. W. Tozer puts it this way: "Left to ourselves we tend immediately to reduce God to manageable terms. We want to get Him where we can use Him, or at least know where He is when we need Him."[1]

Erwin Lutzer is more direct. He says this "bottom up" approach to God leads us to idolatry:

Whenever we begin with man and reason upward, we manufacture an idol. Our temptation is to invite ideas of God into our minds that are either just wrong or are notions that diminish Him. Idolatry is more than dancing around a statue of silver or gold; it is constructing a mental idea of a deity that bears little resemblance to the God who actually exists. Idolatry is giving respectability to our own opinions of God, formed after our likeness. Idolatry is fashioning an idea of God according to our inclinations and preferences. It is to pare God down to more manageable proportions.[2]

This whole notion of idolatry is really important, so let's think about it a bit more. Where does idolatry come from? Lutzer gives us two sources:

1. We get impatient with God's silence. When God doesn't answer our prayers as soon as we would like, we tend to get impatient and lose hope. When God is silent on the problem of evil and suffering, we rush to discredit God or give him a "pass," saying he is disinterested in the human condition or incapable of helping us. What we have left is a God we can manage and manipulate. But this isn't the real God. This is an idol.

2. We want God to be more tolerant of us. We don't like the idea of a demanding, judgmental God, so we cast him as a God who judges no one, turns a blind eye on sin, and tolerates everything in the name of love. But this isn't the real God. This is an idol.

Both of these idols—the manageable God and the tolerant God—stand in stark contrast to the true and living God described in the Bible. The psalmist captures the difference with poetic beauty:

> Our God is in heaven;
> he does whatever pleases him.
>
> But their idols are silver and gold,
> made by the hands of men.
>
> They have mouths, but cannot speak,
> eyes, but cannot see.
>
> They have ears, but cannot hear,
> noses, but cannot smell;
> They have hands, but cannot feel,
> feet, but cannot walk;

nor can they utter a sound with their throats.

Those who make them will be like them,
and so will all who trust in them (Psalm 115:3–8).

The last line is a stinging indictment on what happens when we start with us and reason upward: We idolize the God we want, and He ends up being just like us. Not content to merely construct our own ideas about God, we humans have another way of dealing with God, one that's been around for as long as idolatry: We invent new religions. There are literally thousands of religions and belief systems in the world, but all are based on seven different ways of relating to God. Here's a quick summary:

- *Theism:* The belief in the existence of a divine being. Theists believe that God created the world, is separate from the world, but is very involved with the world. Christianity, Islam, and Judaism are examples of monotheistic religions, or religions that believe in just one God.

- *Deism:* The view that God exists but is not involved in the world. The deist believes that God does not perform miracles. God made the world, but He removed Himself after creation and is letting it run on its own.

- *Pantheism:* The view that all is God. Most Eastern religions—Hinduism, Taoism, and some forms of Buddhism are pantheistic—along with Western religions such as Christian Science. To a pantheist, God is the absolute being that unites all things. The world was not created by God, but comes from Him. Two of the most popular movies ever made, *Star Wars* and *Avatar,* feature a pantheistic worldview.

- *Panentheism:* The view that the universe is the body of God. Every person is part of the universe, so every person is a part of God. Just as the world is changing, God is changing as well.

- *Finite Godism:* The view that God exists but is limited in power. There is no major religion that follows this view, but many people subscribe to its main idea that because there is evil in the world, God is unable to stop it and therefore isn't all-powerful.

- *Polytheism:* The view that many finite gods rule over the various realms of the universe. The gods of ancient Greece and Rome were constructed from a polytheistic worldview. Different gods perform different functions, and not one is personal.

- *Atheism:* The view that there is no God. The atheist denies the existence of any supernatural beings. There is no form of transcendent order of meaning in the universe. In practice, atheism denotes a way of life conducted in disregard of any alleged supernatural reality.

With the exception of theism, all of the religions and belief systems that emanate from these worldviews begin with us and reason upward. Theism alone sees the world from God's perspective, and only Christian theism holds the view that God has reached down to humanity through the person of Jesus Christ.

KNOW THE UNIQUE CHALLENGES

We've already said that your search for God requires courage, strength, and perseverance. One reason you need these qualities has to do with the abundance of false idols and competing worldviews and religions that are all around you. Not everyone is going to agree with your conclusions about God and the way He works in the world, and you may even be criticized for your "narrow-minded" beliefs.

The other reason your search for God requires courage, strength, and perseverance has to do with God Himself. The bottom line is that God isn't easy to understand, which is what you would expect from an infinite, invisible, independent, incomprehensible God. If God were easily understood, as St. Augustine once remarked that He would be an idol. But God is not an idol. He is God and above Him there is no other. God is so vast, so powerful, and so far beyond us that it isn't possible to fully grasp Him.

Theologians call this the incomprehensibility of God. Because God is infinite and we are finite, we don't have the ability to understand God completely. But that doesn't mean we can't know anything about God. It simply means our knowledge is limited and partial. As R. C. Sproul says, "The finite can 'grasp' the infinite, but the finite can never hold the infinite within its grasp. There is always more to God than we apprehend."[3] Consequently, any search for God is not going to uncover everything about God. Zophar, a friend of the suffering Job, makes this observation:

> Can you fathom the mysteries of God?
> Can you probe the limits of the Almighty?
> They are higher than the heavens above—what can you do?
> They are deeper than the depths of the grave—what can you know?
> Their measure is longer than the earth
> and wider than the sea (Job 11:7–9).

And God Himself tells us:

> "For my thoughts are not your thoughts,
> neither are your ways my ways,"
> declares the LORD.
> "As the heavens are higher than the earth,
> so are my ways higher than your ways
> and my thoughts than your thoughts" (Isaiah 55:8–9).

Embedded in these immortal words of the one true God is the idea that God is not only incomprehensible, but He is also transcendent and self-sufficient. That is, God exists outside of His creation and doesn't depend on the universe or anything in it for His existence. Furthermore, God is self-existent, which is to say God has no origins and is answerable to no one.

For inquisitive humans, especially those inclined to philosophy and science, these qualities of God present tremendous challenges. James Boyce, former pastor of Tenth Presbyterian Church in Philadelphia, sums it up this way:

> Philosophers and scientists will admit that there is much they don't know. But it is another thing to admit that there is something they can never know completely and which, in fact, they don't even have techniques for discovering. To discover God, scientists may attempt to bring God down to their level, defining him as "natural law," "evolution" or some such principle. But still

God eludes them. There is more to God than any such concepts can delineate.[4]

As you continue in your GodQuest, you need to comprehend as best you can that God is … well … incomprehensible. He is unlike anything else in your experience. There's nothing that compares to God and nothing that you can measure Him against. This fact alone should cause you to stand in awe at God's awesomeness. Rather than criticizing Him for not showing Himself more clearly, you should wonder why, as the psalmist David once did, this majestic God pays attention to you at all (Psalm 8:1–5). Rather than getting frustrated that you can't know more about God, be thankful that you can know something.

KNOW THAT GOD CAN BE KNOWN

The correct perspective for beginning your search for God is to have God's perspective. But how is that possible since God is incomprehensible? Thankfully, God in His wisdom and love has made Himself known to anyone who sincerely seeks Him (Hebrews 11:6). In other words, you can add this quality to the incomprehensible, transcendent, self-existent, and self-sufficient God: He is self-revealing.

Theologians refer to this quality of God as divine revelation, which Albert Mohler calls the "starting point for all genuinely Christian thinking." God's self-revelation is His gift to us, for not only does God give us information about Himself, but He also gives us the capacity to grasp it. "The fact of God's existence sets the Christian worldview apart from all others," writes Mohler. "From the very beginning we must affirm that our knowledge of God is entirely dependent upon the gift of divine revelation."[5]

Divine revelation is critical to your GodQuest, for it gives you the knowledge you need to make an informed decision about who God is and how you can relate to Him. Of course, with any thing or person that you can know, there are two kinds of knowledge. First, there is knowledge based on what you can actually *know*. For example, if you were getting to know someone you just met, you would find out certain facts about that person—where they live, what kinds of activities they are involved with, where they work, what kinds of movies they like, etc. This kind of information is useful, but it doesn't give you a complete picture.

That's where the other kind of knowledge comes into play, which is knowledge based on emotional experience, or how you *feel* about the other person. Simply knowing about someone isn't enough to make a true connection. Your emotions need to be involved so you can decide whether or not you want to spend more time with a person. Sometimes the emotional connection is immediate, and other times your emotions need time to develop.

The process of knowing God is no different. In order to even begin a relationship with God, we need to know certain objective things about Him. But in order for that relationship to develop and deepen, we need to know God on a deeper and more experiential level. Truth is, you need both kinds of knowledge. Just as knowing God through facts and reason alone will not satisfy what your heart and soul want to *feel*, knowing God through your emotions and feelings alone will not satisfy what your mind needs to *know*.

How God Has Revealed Himself

God is so smart. In order for us to make a true and satisfying connection with Him, God knows we need head knowledge, which gives us a wide appreciation for what God does, and heart knowledge, which gives us a deep appreciation for who God is. So in His self-revelation, He has given us both kinds of knowledge.

God reveals Himself to your mind. There are two vehicles God uses to give you head knowledge about Himself: the natural world and His written word. The natural world is the created world, which tells us so much about God. And it's there for everyone to observe. As the psalmist David writes:

> *The heavens declare the glory of God;*
> *the skies proclaim the work of his hands.*

Day after day they pour forth speech;
  night after night they display knowledge.
They have no speech or language
  where their voice is not heard.
Their voice goes out into all the earth,
  their words to the ends of the world (Psalm 19:1–4).

In his letter to the Romans, the Apostle Paul amplifies God's self-revelation through the natural world and makes it a personal matter: "For since the creation of the world God's invisible qualities—his eternal power and divine nature—have been clearly seen, being understood from what has been made, so that men are without excuse" (Romans 1:20). Whenever we are exposed to the natural world with all of its splendor and order and majesty, we are in touch with divine revelation.

A second way God reveals Himself to your mind is through His Word—the Bible, God's written revelation of Himself—His creation, and His desire to have a relationship with you. We're are devoting an entire Signpost of GodQuest to the Bible, but for now we want to make the point that the Bible is a book rooted in history and facts that also contains incredible wisdom for living. It can be read objectively with great benefit, as people have done for nearly two thousand years.

At the same time, there is something about God's created world and God's written Word that go beyond facts and head knowledge. When you find yourself watching a brilliant sunset or gazing up at millions of stars, you can't help but feel there's more to these natural things than pure reason and science. Your mind may be informed by what you see, but your heart and your soul are lifted by the beauty and wonder of what you are experiencing.

Similarly, when you read a passage of Scripture, it engages your heart as well as your mind, because you realize that when you read the Bible, you are connecting with its author on a personal level.

God reveals Himself to your heart. There are two ways God connects to your heart. The first is through the inner conviction you have that there is something more to life than what you can experience with your five senses. People may try to deny with their head that God exists, but their heart tells them a different story. As Solomon explains, that's because their Creator has put a longing for something beyond themselves and their finite experience in their hearts:

> He has made everything beautiful in its time. He has also set eternity in the hearts of men; yet they cannot fathom what God has done from beginning to end (Ecclesiastes 3:11).

The other heart connection God has made with us is through His Son, Jesus Christ. Because we can't connect with God on a visual level, God has given us a visible image of Himself through the person of Jesus, who is God in the flesh (John 1:14, Colossians 1:15). When Jesus lived on the earth, people were invited to make an emotional connection to Him. He touched people, healed them, prayed for them, and grieved for them. And now, nearly two thousand years later, we have the same opportunity to connect with God emotionally through the person and work of Christ.

At the same time, having an inner conviction that God is real, and experiencing God through Jesus, are things you can truly know with your mind. There is mounting scientific evidence that we are "hard wired" for God, so your inner feelings are there for a reason. Similarly, you don't have to just believe in Jesus with your heart. You can know that He truly lived and died and was raised from the dead through eyewitness accounts and the historical records, something we're going to deal with more fully in Signpost 5.

MOVING FORWARD WITH AN OPEN MIND AND HEART

We hope your GodQuest is beginning to take on a bit more urgency and importance. Knowing that you can truly know God with both your mind and your heart should give you the motivation you need to open them both to the exciting and life-changing truths of God. In the next chapter of GodQuest, we're going to give you some reasons why you can truly know that God exists, and in knowing you can believe with your heart that God loves you and wants a relationship with you.

GODQUEST

CHAPTER 5

HOW DO YOU KNOW
GOD EXISTS?

Don't you sometimes wish that knowing whether or not God exists were a simple matter? Why hasn't God made it so clear and so obvious that anybody would believe in Him without question? On the other hand, what if the evidence for God's existence were so obvious that nobody had a choice except to believe in Him? Would that automatically mean that everybody would believe, or would there still be some holdouts?

As we see it, the truth about God's existence lies somewhere between absolute proof and no proof at all. It's a continuum of belief with no definite point of demarcation, with belief in God on one side and unbelief on the other. For some people, belief in God comes easy, and to others the idea that God exists is filled with problems. That doesn't make the person who needs minimal reinforcement for his or her beliefs any better than the person who needs a lot. In fact, we know from experience and from the Bible that God pays close attention to doubters. Rather than send them away, He invites them to get closer and examine the evidence.

To get a sense of how God does this, we want to tell you a true story about a dramatic incident that occurred around AD 30 in the city of Jerusalem. Think about what it would have been like to actually be there. Try to put yourself in the sandals of the person history calls Doubting Thomas. In doing so, try to feel the emotions that Thomas must have felt when God in the flesh met him at his unbelief.

THE STORY OF THOMAS

Behind the locked doors of a small house in Jerusalem, ten men gathered and wondered: Would they ever see Jesus again? Eight days earlier, the authorities had put Jesus to death following a trial that was a mockery of justice. Even the Governor had declared Him innocent, but His enemies wanted Him dead, and so it happened in a public execution. For those ten frightened, grieving men there was no question about the outcome. Their master was dead.

The authorities had taken great pains to bury Jesus in a secure location, in a tomb donated by a respected religious leader. Concerned that Jesus' followers would steal the body and say He had come back from the dead—something Jesus said would happen— the authorities had rolled a huge stone in front of the tomb, put the Governor's seal on it, posted twenty-four-hour guards, and threatened them with death if the body of Jesus disappeared.

Then the unthinkable and unimaginable happened. Jesus did rise from the dead, just as He said He would. Only it wasn't in full view of any of these ten men huddled in secrecy because they feared retribution from the authorities. In fact, earlier that morning, on the third day following the execution of Jesus and His burial in the guarded tomb, Jesus had appeared, not to any of these devoted disciples, but to two women—Mary Magdalene and Mary the mother of Jesus. Two of their group, Peter and John, had run to the tomb, only to find it empty. Still, they had not seen Jesus with their own eyes.

Then, without warning and without fanfare, Jesus stood there with them. The doors had not been opened, yet He was there, in the flesh, telling them, "Peace be with you." Instantly their troubled hearts collectively skipped a joyful beat as they realized this was truly Jesus. He showed them the physical evidence of His execution: His wounded hands and side, pierced with nails and a sword. Then, as quickly as He had appeared, Jesus blessed them and was gone.

The eleventh member of their little group, the one called Thomas, came later, after the miraculous appearance of their Master. Excitedly, ten voices smothered Thomas with the single refrain, "We have seen the Lord!" But Thomas, one skeptic among ten believers, refused to acknowledge what they knew to be true, telling them, "Unless I see the nail marks in his hands and put my finger where the nails were, and put my hand into his side, I will not believe."

Now, eight days later, the followers of Jesus are once again meeting in the same house behind locked doors and Thomas is among them. For the second time, Jesus silently and suddenly stands among them, greeting them with peace. Then, without hesitation, Jesus turns to Thomas, the one who for centuries has been known as the Doubter, and invites him to place his finger into the wounds of His hands, and his hand into the awful gash in His side.

"Stop doubting and believe," Jesus tells him. All Thomas can do is answer with those immortal words that accurately describe Jesus for who He is: "My Lord and My God!"

It's hard to believe that the eyewitness account of ten trustworthy people wouldn't be enough to convince a skeptic like Thomas of certain reality—in this case the reality of the resurrected Son of God—but such is the nature of belief. Sometimes it's not enough to take the word of others. Like Thomas, some people refuse to believe until they can see it with their own eyes. It's the way it was in the first century, and it's the way it is in the twenty-first century. The names of the skeptics may be different, but the dynamics of their doubt are the same.

PROOF AND THE EXISTENCE OF GOD

Many of the so-called "new atheists" today (the most well-known are Richard Dawkins, Christopher Hitchens, Daniel Dennett, and Sam Harris), whose bestselling books and public displays of opposition to the existence of God have become part of popular culture, insist that the reality of God should be subject to "rational demonstration."[1] They refuse to believe in God until it can be demonstrated scientifically that God truly exists. In other words, they want proof in the form of testable data.[2] At first glance such a demand appears perfectly reasonable, but when you look below the surface, you quickly discover two problems. First, there's no guarantee these professing atheists or any skeptic would believe in God even if presented with irrefutable scientific proof. I (Sean) have seen this happen time and again as I take my high school students on apologetics mission trips throughout the country.

Recently we went to the University of California, Berkeley and had the opportunity to interact with an organized group of skeptical students whose purpose is to rid the world of religion. Needless to say, the evening was quite lively. The last question we were able to ask them is what it would take for them to be convinced of the existence of God. One graduate student said he would need an obvious supernatural miracle that he personally witnessed along with multiple people to verify his experience. But then he said he probably still would not believe because it is more likely that he was on drugs than really seeing a miracle. In other words, *nothing* would convince him of the existence of God, even if he witnessed a miracle.

Truth is, God has revealed Himself to humankind in several remarkable ways. The trouble is that none of those ways stand up to the type of strict scientific proof skeptics demand. But is it fair to subject any kind of belief to such a test? Not really, and herein lies the second problem with the demand for scientific proof. Not even scientists use such a test in all cases! Tim Keller points out that scientists prefer to use the word *theory* (as in the theory of relativity, or Darwin's theory) when talking about a particular proposition, and they are very reluctant to ever say that a theory is "proved."[3]

If you are a Christian who already believes that God is real, but you're looking for an irrefutable "smoking gun" that will finally "prove" once and for all that God exists—maybe not so much to reinforce your belief, but to show your skeptical friend that he's wrong and you're right—we've got news for you. There's no such thing. There's no smoking gun. There's no bombproof evidence for

God's existence. There is no proof so strong that any rational person would automatically believe it. But you know what? That's okay because there's no such thing as complete objectivity when it comes to believing anything. As J. P. Moreland says:

> Asking whether or not it is possible to prove there is a God is the wrong question because the notion of a proof sets such a high standard. Very few beliefs in the world are bombproof—that is, beyond dispute of disagreement. One exception may be a mathematical equation, but even then there may be people who take exception with "2+2=4." About the best we can do with 99.9 percent of the beliefs in the world—whether we're talking about belief in the aerodynamics of an airplane or belief in God—is to say, "It's reasonable to believe that," or "A reasonable person would accept that as truth."[4]

Just because God can't be detected by any of the five senses doesn't mean He isn't real. There are many things in life we accept as real even though we can't prove them scientifically—love, for example. How do you scientifically prove that love exists? You can show the effects of love, but trying to prove that love exists from a series of experiments? Not possible. But does that keep you from believing that love exists? Of course not. You may not be able to *prove* love, but you know it exists because you can *feel* it and you can see the effects of love, both in yourself and in others. As C. S. Lewis observes about the Christian faith:

> I believe in Christianity as I believe that the Sun has risen, not only because I see it, but because by it I see everything else.[5]

As we're going to soon show you, it is reasonable to believe in God because there are reasons for belief. There is a rational component to faith. On the other hand, it's inappropriate to use "rational demonstration" in order to show that God exists. What is appropriate, not because it's the easy way out but because it is reasonable, is to identify certain "clues of God" that can lead us to conclusions that a reasonable person would consider.[6] To dismiss these clues outright because they don't meet the scientific test is unreasonable. In fact, not even atheists can live within the boundaries of such absolutes.

WHO HAS THE BURDEN OF PROOF?

Bruce Bickel is a lawyer and also the co-author (with Stan Jantz) of several books on Christian apologetics and belief. As a lawyer, he is keenly aware of the concept of burden of proof in the criminal justice system. In any trial, the burden of proof is on the prosecutor (the District Attorney) to convince the jury that the defendant is guilty. If the prosecutor doesn't present enough convincing evidence, the defendant is declared not guilty.

"It is the declared intention of atheists to put the burden of proof for the existence of God on the theists," writes Bruce. "They don't want to be put in the position of having to prove the nonexistence of God. They know it can't be done."[7] What's interesting in recent years is that atheists like Richard Dawkins and Christopher Hitchens have tried to have it both ways. They want to take the strong position that God doesn't exist, but they also want to shift the burden of proof to the theists. But that's not possible, because it's impossible to prove a negative existential claim—that is a claim that something does *not* exist. Perhaps that is why there has been such a backlash to these aggressive strong-position atheists. In his evaluation of *The God Delusion*, New York University professor of philosophy Thomas Nagel, an atheist, found Dawkins' attempts at philosophical argument "particularly weak" and the work of an "amateur."[8]

So where does the burden of proof lie when it comes to God and His existence? Here is how *Positive Atheism Magazine* describes the ideal sequence when a theist talks to an atheist about the existence of God:

- It must be realized that we are dealing entirely with claims— claims that various deities exist.

- In discussing such claims, it is always the person making the claim [the theist] who is responsible for providing evidence and strong argument.

- The person listening to the claim [the atheist] need not make any argument at all.

- The listener [the atheist] does not need to disprove a claim in order to reject it.

- If the person making the claim [the theist] fails to make a convincing case, the listener rightly rejects the claim as falsehood (or suspends judgment, based upon the strength of the claim). In either event, the listener ends up lacking a belief in the object of the claim.

- It is never the atheist's responsibility to prove or disprove anything. That job belongs to the person making the claims, which is the theist.[9]

We don't disagree that theists have a responsibility to justify their positive claims about the existence of God, but we definitely think atheists have a responsibility to justify their claims as well. For example, atheists believe the universe is either eternal or came from nothing. They also believe life can come from non-life, morality can come from nature, and consciousness can come from matter. These are all knowledge claims that need to be justified.

The bottom line is that whoever makes a knowledge claim—theist or atheist—must back it up. Atheism is not the default position. In fact, given that over 95 percent of the people in the world believe in God, maybe the atheists have the heavier burden of proof than the theists! However, since you are continuing your GodQuest with the most basic claim of theism—that God exists—we are going to continue to provide good reasons for that claim. But first we need to finish the story of Thomas.

THOMAS AND JESUS: THE REST OF THE STORY

When we left Thomas and Jesus in that little room in Jerusalem, Jesus had proven to Thomas through the physical evidence of His body and the scars of His execution that He had risen from the dead.

Thomas responded with his affirming declaration that he believed. But Jesus wasn't finished. He had more to say:

> *"Because you have seen me, you have believed; blessed are those who have not seen and yet have believed"* (John 20:29).

Here's the deal. Thomas and his fellow disciples had the unique advantage of seeing Jesus, who was the visible image of the invisible God (Colossians 1:15). But everyone living since Jesus left the earth and His original disciples died have not had the privilege of seeing Jesus with their own two eyes. But that doesn't mean we can't believe in the same way the original eyewitnesses believed. That's what Jesus meant when He said, "Blessed are those who have not seen and yet have believed."

Because there's no record in the Bible that Thomas responded to this statement about belief, we don't know if he "got it" at that moment. Thomas probably felt satisfied that his faith in Jesus was based on first-hand knowledge, but it should not have taken such a dramatic "up close and personal" demonstration for Thomas to believe. On many occasions prior to this incident, Jesus had told His disciples He would rise from the dead, and then He demonstrated His supernatural power by performing many miracles during His three-year ministry. Given these "proofs," Thomas should not have been surprised when Jesus miraculously showed up that night in Jerusalem. But even if he had not remembered those declarations and forgotten all about the miracles, the eyewitness accounts by people he trusted should have convinced Thomas that Jesus had indeed risen. Yet he still refused to believe.

Perhaps that's why Jesus told Thomas that faith must go beyond what we can personally know and experience with our senses. He knew that even in the face of objective proof, sometimes we humans have a hard time believing. That's because true belief in God needs to go beyond the *facts* of faith to something even deeper—trust. When Jesus said, "Blessed are those who have not seen and yet have believed," He was getting to that *trust* part of faith.

This is what the writer of Hebrews means by this definition of faith: "Faith is being sure of what we hope for and certain of what do not see" (Hebrews 11:1). Hope and certainty are the basis of trust. This is what the Apostle Paul means when he writes, "We live by faith, not by sight" (2 Corinthians 5:7). This is the part of faith that moves from your head to your heart, from merely believing in the existence of God to believing that God desires to have a relationship with you. This kind of belief doesn't come because you can *see* that it's true, which is not possible; rather, it comes because you *trust* by faith that it's true.

THE DIFFERENCE BETWEEN KNOWING AND SHOWING

William Lane Craig, one of the world's most respected Christian thinkers, makes a distinction between *knowing* that the Christian faith is true and *showing* that it is true. If you are a Christian, you *know* God is real and His word is true even if you don't know everything about God and the Bible. But you trust God and the Bible because you have God's presence in your life, giving you what Dr. Craig calls a "self-authenticating witness."[10] At the same time, as you grow in the knowledge of what you believe, you can *show* the truth and substance of your belief by pointing to the evidence that points to God.

If you aren't quite there yet, don't stop your GodQuest. As long as you continue your quest with an open mind and heart, allowing the reality of God to become real to you through reasonable evidence "that it is systematically consistent,"[11] you can reach the point where you trust God completely and know the truth about Him. Let's get started.

SIGNS POINTING TO GOD

Rather than offering you proof for God's existence, our intention is to suggest some clues we hope will provoke some thoughts about the big question: *How do you know God exists?* After all, you are on a journey we're calling a GodQuest, and we're using Signposts to point you in a particular direction. As with any set of hiking trails, in addition to the signposts telling you about path markers, intersections, and the distance to your destination, there are signs along the side of the path containing information that may be useful for your journey, such as why you should stay on the trail in order to avoid poison ivy and snakes.

We aren't going to be so presumptive as to suggest that the information on any one of these signs is compelling enough on its own to demonstrate the reality of God. In fact, what may be persuasive to one person may be rather ho-hum to another. You need to decide which of the three signs offers the best reason to believe that God does indeed exist. However, at the end of this particular segment of your GodQuest, we do hope the accumulated weight of each sign—containing "the clues of God"—will add up to a reasonable case for His existence. To get back to our burden-of-proof analogy, each sign—or each clue—doesn't have to bear the burden of proof on its own. Instead, the preponderance of the evidence from all three signs will show the case to be true. At least that's what we think. You need to decide for yourself.

Here are the signs, identified by a single word, followed by an important question.

SIGN #1
CONTINGENCY
QUESTION—WHY IS THERE SOMETHING RATHER THAN NOTHING?

Seems like a pretty obvious question, doesn't it? Maybe so, but the answer will have some serious implications, especially when you're talking about the universe. Even with objects you see around you—a chair, your iPhone, your car—you can ask why they exist. And when you really think about the answer, it doesn't take long to trace a certain object backward to a store, a manufacturer, an engineer, a designer, some basic materials, and eventually to the earth itself. In other words, you would conclude that the object you're thinking about came from something else. It didn't just appear out of nowhere.

This logical sequence preceding any object that you can think about relates to the idea of *contingency*, which basically means this: Anything that exists is dependent (or contingent) upon something else. A corollary to this principle is that nothing that exists is *necessary*. In other words, a chair or your iPhone or your car doesn't *have* to exist. Neither do you for that matter—or the universe. Everything that exists is contingent upon something else, and therefore is not necessary.

But this idea of contingency has a big problem. You can't have an endless series of contingent things. At some point, the process has to start with something that isn't contingent. If not, you would never arrive at the present moment where the chair, your iPhone, your car, or you exist. This is known as "the impossibility of crossing infinity." Put in the language of mathematics, it means "infinite regression is impossible." You can't keep going backward in a series of infinite causes and events for the simple reason that you can't get from minus infinity to zero. Mathematically, it's not possible. To get to a *present* thing, you must have a *first* thing. To get to a present event, you must have a first event.

The only way to overcome the impossibility of infinite regression is to propose a source for all contingent objects and events that in itself is not contingent. Philosophers call this a *necessary being*. By definition, for the universe and everything in it to exist, this being *must* exist. Or to put it in the double negative, it cannot *not* exist.

So what or who is this necessary being? Well, you have a couple of choices. First, you could believe that something that had a beginning just popped into being from nothing. Call it an entity or a force. Call it whatever you want. But you still have a problem: who or what caused the entity? As we've already established, things don't just pop into being. The other option is to believe the existence of a necessary being that is by definition self-existent, eternal, and uncaused. This brings us to our second sign.

SIGN #2

CAUSATION

QUESTION—WHAT IS THE FIRST CAUSE THAT STARTED ALL THE OTHER CAUSES?

This clue relates closely to the contingency argument. But rather than showing how the existence of contingent things requires a necessary source, this sign points to the beginning of the universe as good reason to believe there must be a cause outside of the universe, namely God. Furthermore, because the universe must have a beginning, it must have a cause. There are three components to this clue:[12]

1. *Whatever begins to exist has a cause.* Although there are some ways that people challenge this premise, it seems to be self-evidently true. As the philosopher Peter Kreeft writes, "Most people—outside of asylums and graduate schools—would consider it not only true, but certainly obviously true."[13]

2. *The universe began to exist.* Once upon a time scientists believed the universe was infinite. Then came the twentieth century and a series of discoveries that persuaded the vast majority of scientists to believe a new theory: The universe had a beginning. In fact, the two main components of this series of discoveries—the expansion of the universe and background cosmic radiation— are the primary features of the Big Bang theory, now widely accepted by scientists as a way of accounting for the beginning of the universe. The esteemed astronomer Robert Jastrow, a self-professed agnostic, writes this:

The astronomical evidence proves that the Universe was created fifteen billion years ago in a fiery explosion … the seeds of everything that has happened in the Universe since were planted in that first instant; every star, every planet and every living creature in the Universe owes its physical origins to events that were set into motion in the moment of the cosmic explosion. In a purely physical sense, it was the moment of creation.[14]

3. *Therefore, the universe has a cause.* This is the logical conclusion: If the universe had a beginning, then the beginning had a cause. The only question that remains is whether this first cause is an impersonal event, like the Big Bang, or a personal agent. But it can't be an event, because the Big Bang creation event was the first contingent event in the history of the universe. The only

other option is that the beginning was caused by a personal agent, or "a personal being, acting with powers and intentions suitable for such an act."[15]

Is this personal agent God? Based on what we've talked about so far, we can't say the evidence points to the Christian God. But it does get us to a timeless, powerful, intelligent, changeless, personal being. The next question (one that we will address later in this chapter and in the next) is what this God is like and has He revealed Himself through His creation? In the meantime, you can be confident that we are going in the right direction. We like the way Tim Keller puts it: "The theory that there is a God who made the world accounts for the evidence we see better than the theory that there is no God."[16]

SIGN #3
CHARACTER

QUESTION—WHY DO WE HAVE A MORAL OBLIGATION?

It happens every time you learn about an injustice being done, especially if it's done to you or someone you know, you get upset. You may even become outraged, particularly if the people who did the wrong thing got away with it. There's even a sense of moral outrage when injustice happens to people you know nothing about. Human rights abuses can and should infuriate you.

Then there's the matter of animals being abused. Remember the Michael Vick saga, when the professional football star was caught running a dog fighting ring? Almost everyone was outraged. Vick was tried, convicted, and sentenced to eighteen months in federal prison, but there were those who felt they should have thrown away the key. The point is that even though people disagreed on the punishment he deserved, everyone agreed that what he did was objectively wrong.

Where does this sense of moral obligation and outrage come from? And why does virtually everyone—with the exception of psychotic criminals and sociopaths—have it? It can't be a law made by humans that produces this inner compass. Laws simply point out the wrongdoing and give us a way of holding wrongdoers accountable, but laws don't produce moral obligation. In fact, there are some laws that allow behavior that we would consider immoral. Just think of slavery, the mistreatment of women, and Nazism. Regardless of what kinds of laws are in place, the vast majority of people know when wrong is being done. We don't need laws to tell us to do the right thing, and we don't need laws to produce moral outrage. The sense of right and wrong is just in us. Here's how C. S. Lewis explains this innate moral sense that all of us possess:

> This Rule of Right and Wrong, or Law of Human Nature, or whatever you call it, must somehow or other be a real thing—a thing that is really there, not made up by ourselves. And yet it is not a fact in the ordinary sense, in the same way as our actual behavior is a fact. It begins to look as if we shall have to admit that there is more than one kind of reality; that, in this particular case, there is something above and beyond the ordinary facts of men's behavior, and yet quite definitely real—a real law, which none of us made, but which we find pressing on us.[17]

So if we didn't make this "Rule of Right and Wrong," who did? Call it what you want—your inner moral compass or your conscience—it's an inner obligation to do the right thing, even if you don't always do it. Where does it come from? It couldn't come from something *less* than us or something *equal* to us. And it couldn't come from just us. The only viable option is that our sense of moral obligation comes from something *greater* than us, which is God. Peter Kreeft writes:

> Thus God, or something like God, is the only adequate source and ground for the absolute moral obligation we all feel to obey our conscience. Conscience is thus explainable only as the voice of God in the soul.[18]

The Apostle Paul says exactly the same thing in his letter to the Roman church:

> For it is not those who hear the law who are righteous in God's sight, but it is those who obey the law who will be declared righteous. (Indeed, when Gentiles, who do not have the law, do by nature things required by the law, they are a law for

themselves, even though they do not have the law, since they show that the requirements of the law are written on their hearts, their consciences also bearing witness, and their thoughts now accusing, even defending them) (Romans 2:13–15).

If you were to frame this argument in a basic logical sequence, here's what it would look like:

If objective moral values exist, an objective moral lawgiver (God) must exist.

Objective moral values exist.

Therefore, God must exist.

We know objective moral values exist. We don't need to be persuaded that torturing babies for fun is wrong. All reasonable people know this intuitively. Therefore, since moral values do exist, then God must as well.

IF GOD EXISTS, WHERE DID HE COME FROM?

We are suggesting that the answer to the questions posted on the three signs—is God.

1. Why is there something rather than nothing?

2. What is the first cause that started all the other causes?

3. Why do we have a moral obligation?

But if that's the case, there's an even more important question to ask and answer: *If God exists, where did He come from?* This is a variant on the question virtually every child asks a parent at one time or another: *Who made God?* You probably asked it when you were a kid. Maybe you're still asking it. That's okay, because it's a great question. In fact, it's a *necessary* question. Remember a few pages ago when we proposed that in order for contingent things to exist, there must be a necessary being that cannot not exist? Here are three other characteristics of this necessary being:

• *Uncaused:* The being had no cause and no beginning.

- *Self-existent:* The being depends on nothing else for its existence.
- *Eternal:* The being has always existed and always will exist.

If this seems like a pretty narrow job description, you're right. It's so narrow that there's only one like it and only one being that fits. There has never been a being like this before, and there will never be anything like it again. The being that fits this set of characteristics is totally unique, the one and only. That being, by definition—uncaused, self-sufficient, and eternal—is God.

If you're still thinking that God needs a cause, here's another way of looking at this. We can only ask for the source of things (What made it?) that in principle can be made. God is more like the laws of logic. They cannot be caused because they are necessary. God is by definition unmakable! In fact, to ask what caused God is a category fallacy, like asking what does the color red smell like. Colors don't have smells. Similarly, to ask what caused God is like asking, "What caused the uncaused eternal creator of the universe?"

IF GOD EXISTS, WHAT IS HE LIKE?

The three signs and three questions in this chapter may not appear to tell you very much about God, but we hope they tell you enough to continue your GodQuest. The characteristics suggested by these signs—that God is a necessary being, the first cause of everything, and the ultimate moral lawgiver—may not be warm-and-fuzzy qualities that would endear God to you , but they are incredibly important "first steps" to know that God exists and wants to have a relationship with you. Indeed, when you look below the surface of these qualities and really think about what they tell you about God, a more compelling picture of a personal God—not just a universal force—emerges.

That God is the only *necessary being* and the one and only self-existent, self-sufficient, eternal God with no beginning and no end tells us that God depends on nothing, owes nothing to any creature, and has no needs. To put it in more personal terms, the God who wants to have a relationship with you isn't seeking you out because He *needs* you. He wants a relationship with you because He wants you to share in His life. As the Apostle Paul says to the philosophers in the city of Athens:

> *"The God who made the world and everything in it is the Lord of heaven and earth and does not live in temples built by hands. And he is not served by human hands, as if he needed anything, because he himself gives all men life and breath and everything else"* (Acts 17:24–25).

That God is the *first cause* of everything tells us that God is the beginning of everything. The Bible starts out with this truth: "In the beginning God created the heavens and the earth" (Genesis 1:1). God didn't need to create the universe, but He did. God didn't need to create humankind, but He did. As we will see in the next chapter, God was extravagant in all He created, investing in the world with unfathomably creative energy and variety. Even more, when it came to His crowning achievement in all of creation, God stamped human beings with His own divine imprint, making it possible for us to have a personal relationship with Him.

That God is the ultimate *moral lawgiver* means He has hard wired in each one of us His own divine sense of right and wrong. This divine gift shows that He values order and opposes chaos. It demonstrates God's love for holiness and justice over and against sin and injustice. And it means that human beings have the ability to live together in relative harmony, as much as can be expected in a sinful world, and they also have the capacity to show compassion and offer help to those who are suffering.

So you see, God is not some impersonal force. He is the independent, personal creator whose perfect character fills the universe and brings order and goodness to our lives. God is generous, creative, loving, forgiving, and absolutely good—not because He chooses to be—but because He simply is. God cannot *not* be God. And because He is, we are here, thinking about Him, talking about Him, and marveling at these qualities that make Him God.

GOD MADE EVERYTHING THAT ISN'T GOD

In his excellent book, *The God Who Is There*, D. A. Carson makes this somewhat obvious, but no less important, observation about the God who simply is:

> If someone were to ask, "Yes, but where did God come from?" the answer the Bible gives is that his existence is not dependent on anything or anyone else. *My* existence is dependent, finally, on him; *his* existence is self-existence. God has no cause; he just is. He always has been. By contrast, everything else in the universe began somewhere, whether in a big bang or in human conception—somewhere. God made it all.[19]

That's where going next in our GodQuest: origins—as in the origin of the universe, the origin of the earth, and the origin of you. How we answer the question, "How did everything get here?" opens the door to more clues or reasons to believe that God not only exists, but also is intensely interested in having a relationship with us. The clues in the next chapter center on the extreme care and precision God took to make a home for His created beings.

GODQUEST

CHAPTER 6

IN THE BEGINNING
GOD CREATED

What comes to mind when you think about God? Do you think about the all-powerful, all-knowing, far-beyond-your comprehension God who doesn't need you but loves you anyway? Or do you think about a God who desperately needs your approval and is not very powerful and maybe not all that good, at least not when it comes to the big issues in our world; otherwise why wouldn't He do something about them?.

Do you think about God as the awesome Creator of the universe, who made everything and gives life to all things down to the smallest detail, and who would very much like to be involved in the details of your life if you would just invite Him to do so? Or do you think about a God who stands off to the side, not interfering with your life unless you really need Him, and then it's hit-and-miss whether you may or may not improve?

Or to put it like we did a few chapters ago: Do you think about the God who *really* is, or do you think about the God you want?

If you think about the God who is, you have a big view of God. You see God for who He is and you are immediately transformed from a place of helplessness when confronted with problems to a place of courage and strength—not because you're so good and great, but because God is good and great. On the other hand, if you think about the God you want, you have a small view of God. Your everyday problems never seem to go away because you view God as being either unable or unwilling to help you.

In the classic book, *The Knowledge of the Holy*, A. W. Tozer writes about the consequences of having a small view of God. Even though these words were written more than a half-century ago, they could easily apply to our situation today:

> It is my opinion that the Christian conception of God current in these middle years of the twentieth century is so decadent as to be utterly beneath the dignity of the Most High God and actually to constitute for professed believers something amounting to a moral calamity.[1]

As you continue your GodQuest, gathering more clues about God, it might be a good idea to stop and think about the way you think about God. As we've been saying from the beginning, the way you think about God influences the choices you make in life. And now as we continue on the trail past "Signpost 2: The Beginning," it might be a good idea to review what that Signpost actually says:

*What you believe about creation
determines how you view yourself and life.*

THE CREATOR GOD

When you started this particular segment of your GodQuest, "Signpost 2: The Beginning" may have been little more than an abstract idea. Now, two-thirds of the way to "Signpost 3: The Word," things are starting to move from abstract to substance. More than a force, you're starting to see that God is a personal being. This is incredibly important because it's impossible to have a relationship with a force. If God were not personal, you couldn't have a relationship with Him. But He is, so you can!

The other important truth you're discovering is this: It's possible to know that this personal God really does exist, independent of us, yet very much involved with us and our world. There are clues that give us a clear and accurate picture of who God is. God is not an idea made up by humans to make them feel better about themselves and to help them cope with the problems of this world. You have learned that unlike the gods of other religions, the Christian God is not capricious or arbitrary. He has given us a sense of moral obligations and justice, reflecting His own holiness and just nature.

These are the clues we have so far, none of which may be convincing on their own, but collectively they are starting to gain strength, so that you can have more confidence that God really does exist. Think of these clues as strands in a rope: the more strands you have, the stronger the rope. Unlike a chain, which comes apart when just one link is broken, a rope doesn't break when one strand comes unraveled.

In this chapter, we want to add more strands to the rope of belief. Specifically, we're going to expand the truth about God as the Creator, which takes us to Genesis 1:1: "In the beginning God created the heavens and the earth." This is where the story of God, as told in the Bible, begins. This is where Christianity begins, telling us how the universe came to be. If God really doesn't exist, there's no sense talking about any of this. But if God is real, and Christianity is the belief system that tells the truth about God and His desire to have a relationship with us, then we need to pay attention to what it says. As C. S. Lewis puts it:

> Christianity is not patent medicine. Christianity claims to give an account of facts—to tell you what the real universe is like. Its account of the universe may be true, or it may not, and once the question is really before you, then your natural inquisitiveness must make you want to know the answer. If Christianity is untrue, then no honest man will want to believe it, however helpful it may be: if it is true, every honest man will want to believe it, even if it gives him no help at all.[2]

If Christianity correctly explains how the universe got here, then it's worth our time and attention and ultimately our belief. If it's false, then let's move on to something else and not waste another minute talking about this version of reality. Of course, where you are concerned, the only reason you are on this GodQuest is to find out if this version of reality is true, and whether or not it's possible to have a relationship with the living God who's at the center of that reality.

BEGINNING AT THE BEGINNING WITH SCIENCE AND FAITH

We're going to go to the beginning of the universe and attempt to provide more information so we can better answer the question: Why is there something rather than nothing? Naturalism—the view that the universe came about by natural means—answers the question one way, while creationism—the view that God created the universe—answers the question in a much different way. Yet it would be false to conclude that science and faith are incompatible.

In fact, throughout this chapter, we're going to be talking about clues, or evidence, for God that come from science. These include a number of different concepts and terms such as *evolution, creation,* and *intelligent design.* No doubt you've heard most if not all of these terms; and you may have your own ideas about their meanings. You may or may not agree 100 percent with the way we define these terms. Tthat's a good thing, by the way; we would get really nervous if people agreed with us all the time. But we do hope you see that our goal is not to convince you to see things our way. We simply want to clear away some of the baggage these terms often carry with them, and as a result show that science and faith—rather than being in conflict—are actually quite compatible.

SCIENCE

Science is neither good nor evil. It's not a replacement for God, but neither is it evil. Science is neutral. The word *science—scientia—* simply means "knowledge." Dr. Jay Richards, a senior fellow at the Discovery Institute, says this about science:

> The essence of natural science is the search for knowledge of the natural world.

Knowledge is an intrinsic good. If we are properly scientific, then we will seek to be open to the natural world and not decide beforehand what it's allowed to reveal.[3]

What Dr. Richards is saying is important for our culture. We should be able to have an ongoing and mutually beneficial discussion about origins that seeks the best explanation for how the universe got here. In an ideal world, those who believe the universe came about through purely natural means—naturalists—would explain their reasons for excluding God, and those who believe God created the universe—creationists—would explain their perspective. Then, people who are processing this very important question—Why is there something rather than nothing?—would be able to make an informed and intelligent decision based on a combination of science and faith.

But that's not the way things are in the world today. Rarely do such productive conversations take place, mainly because creationists are effectively excluded from the public square, especially public schools. In fact, many "enlightened and intelligent" educators and scientists consider the supernatural view to be the product of superstitious and unintelligent people. The only publicly (or socially?) accepted view of how the universe got here is naturalism.

But the door on this issue swings both ways. Just as naturalists typically belittle creationists for believing in a God that created the universe, many creationists criticize naturalists for leaving God out of the picture, often referring to them as atheists and godless, even if those labels are categorically untrue. The myth on both sides of the debate is that naturalists only use reason to build their case, while creationists have to rely on faith alone.

The fact of the matter is that both sides in this ongoing origins conversation employ elements of both reason and faith to build their case. Because nobody was there at the moment of creation—whether that moment had a natural or supernatural cause—all arguments have to rely on reason, inferring from the evidence the best explanation and then by faith accepting that the conclusion is true. The only question that remains to be asked is: Which view is most reasonable?

NATURALISM

Okay, we've already started to use this term, so let's make sure we understand its meaning. *Naturalism*, also known as *scientific naturalism*, is the view that "nature, understood as a purely physical system, is all that exists." This means, according to philosopher Norman Geisler, that "there is no supernatural realm and/or intervention in the world. In the strict sense, all forms of nontheisms are naturalistic, including atheism, pantheism, deism, and agnosticism." [4]

EVOLUTION

The term *evolution* can mean different things depending on who is using the term. For some, it can mean simply "change over time." Nobody disagrees with this simple definition of evolution. In other cases, it can mean "common ancestry"—the idea that if you go back far enough, all living organisms descended from one single organism. According to this view, both you and the fungus growing in your gym locker are related.

While common descent is controversial, there's a third meaning of evolution that is even more controversial. The modern theory of Darwinian evolution holds that evolution is an unplanned and undirected process that combines random mutation and unguided natural selection.

It is also important to distinguish between two degrees of evolution:

- *Microevolution* is "evolution at and below the species level." It generally refers to relatively minor variations that occur in a group over time. No one on either side of the origins debate disputes the reality of microevolution. This is a form of horizontal evolution because organisms stay within their kind.

- *Macroevolution* is "evolution above the species level." It generally refers to major innovations such as new organs, structures, or body plans that produces completely new species. Macroevolution is a key feature of Darwinism. This is a form of vertical evolution because organisms transform into different kinds.

When most people say "evolution," they don't mean the weaker definitions like mere microevolution or change over time, but rather they mean full-blown macroevolution, universal common ancestry among all organisms, and an unguided process of natural selection acting upon random mutation.

Some evolutionists believe in *theistic evolution*, which according to Geisler holds that "God used evolution as his means of producing the various forms of physical life on this planet, including human life."[5] Christians who desire to reconcile evolution and Christianity believe in theistic evolution, but many scholars have raised serious theological, philosophical, and scientific challenges to the concept (or theory?).[6]

DARWINISM

Also known as neo-Darwinism and evolutionism, Darwinism is the belief that undirected mechanistic processes—primarily random mutation and natural selection—can account for both microevolution and macroevolution, and thus for all complex living organisms that exist. In a book he co-authored with William Dembski, Sean writes that Darwinism makes two big controversial claims:[7]

- All organisms, life forms, are related back through time to a common ancestor. This is typically called *common descent* or *universal common ancestry.*

- The process that brought all organisms into existence from a common ancestor is *natural selection* acting on *random variations.* This process operates by chance and necessity, apart from any evident intention or direct design.

The whole point of Darwinism is to explain the world in a way that excludes any role for a supernatural Creator. It's a completely naturalistic way of understanding reality. This is why Darwinism is the focal point of naturalists and new atheists who have tried very hard since the nineteenth century, when Charles Darwin published his seminal book *On the Origin of Species*, to equate science with naturalism.

Theistic evolutionists think they can reconcile Darwinism and Christianity, but Darwinism is by definition an unguided and random process. Does it make sense to say God guided an unguided and random process to create life? But there's an even bigger problem with the theistic evolution position—the scientific evidence.

Because science has become so intertwined with naturalism, evolution, and Darwinism, you may wonder if these theories of how the universe came into existence have effectively put God out of a job. This may have been the case in the twentieth century, when creationists didn't have much to offer as a reasonable scientific rebuttal to naturalism. However, all that has changed in the past decade or so with several formidable challenges offered by scientists, philosophers, and theologians working in the emerging field of intelligent design—an exciting area of study we will soon deal with in more detail.

CREATIONISM

The term *creationism* refers to God creating the universe and everything within it. There are two major views within theistic creationism:

- *Young Earth Creationism:* This is the view that God created the universe approximately ten thousand years ago in a period of six literal twenty-four-hour days.[8] The reason the earth looks much older than it is can be explained primarily by Noah's global flood (Genesis 6–8), which dramatically changed the geology of the earth. Young earth creationists interpret the Creation account in Genesis 1 and 2 literally. They prefer a *probable* reading of the Bible. That means take the Bible for what it says, even if it contradicts a more *plausible* scientific picture of an old earth.

- *Old Earth Creationism:* Also known as *progressive creationism*, this view says that God created the universe ten to fifteen billion years ago. Some old earth creationists believe the *days* of Creation in Genesis 1 and 2 are long periods of time (this is the day-age view), while others believe that each *day* of Creation was a literal twenty-four-hour day separated by long periods of time (this is the gap or intermittent-day view). Many old earth creationists believe that even a literal interpretation of Genesis allows one to believe in an old earth.

Both views of creationism hold to the view of *Creation ex Nihilo*. This comes from a Latin term meaning "from nothing." The theistic view of origins maintains that God—who alone is self-existent, self-sufficient, and eternal—brought the universe into existence without using pre-existing material. Neither did God make the universe out of "pieces" from His own being. God literally made the universe from nothing.

In addition, both Creation views agree that humans are created in the image of God (Genesis 1:26–27). This is incredibly important because having God's divine imprint (*imago dei*) distinguishes us from all other living creatures and means we have a unique relationship with our Creator, as well as very special responsibilities for caring for God's creation. Because humans are created in the image of God, it also means that all people have fundamental worth and value. Both young and old earth creationists also agree that God created Adam and Eve, the first humans made in God's image, between ten thousand and forty thousand years ago.

INTELLIGENT DESIGN

Also known as the design argument, this relatively new field of scientific inquiry has taken root for a couple of reasons. First, Darwinism, despite its serious scientific flaws, has become as much of a belief system—or for some, a religion—as theism. In his recent book *What's So Great About Christianity*, Dinesh D'Souza writes, "We have Darwinism but not Keplerism; we encounter Darwinists but no one describes himself as an Einsteinian. Darwinism has become an ideology."[9] As I (Sean) and Bill Dembski explain in *Understanding Intelligent Design*, "an ideology is an all-encompassing worldview that attempts to explain everything, often on the basis of a single principle such as natural selection. Moreover, it demands complete obedience from our hearts and minds."[10] That's what Darwinism has become, and it has made a lot of people, some naturalists included, very uncomfortable.

The second reason intelligent design has gained credibility hinges on science itself. The more science discovers about the universe, from the outer reaches of space to the inner world of microscopic organisms, the more scientists and non-scientists alike have come to believe that life is too complicated and intricate to have arisen by natural forces alone. Instead, the complexity and order we find in nature can only come from an intelligent agent.

As you would expect, naturalists are very opposed to intelligent design, often calling it "junk science." But that's a false claim. In other fields of science, such as forensics, archaeology, and cryptology, we use design theory without question. We don't tell a crime-scene investigator that she should forego the evidence and simply believe that the knife stuck itself into the victim's back through a series of undirected, mechanistic events. However, that's exactly what naturalists do when it comes to explaining biological complexity, not to mention the origin of the universe.

In truth, as the Princeton trained philosopher and mathematician David Berlinski points out, the theory of evolution "is unique among scientific instruments in being cherished not for what it contains but for what it lacks."[11] By contrast, when the theory of intelligent design is applied to the question of origins, it can be applauded not for what it lacks but for what it contains. William Dembski, a major voice in the intelligent design movement, explains the design argument this way:

> The design argument begins with features of the physical world that exhibit evidence of purpose. From such features, the design argument then attempts to establish the existence and attributes of an intelligent cause responsible for those features.[12]

Dembski emphasizes that the primary purpose of the design argument is not intelligent causes *per se* but information produced by intelligent causes. "ID," as it is often called, doesn't force God as the answer, but is instead "theologically minimalist."[13] If you were to frame the basic premise of intelligent design theory in a logical sequence, it would look like this:

Certain phenomena in nature have feature F.

Intelligent agents are capable of, and regularly associated with, causing this feature.

There are no known plausible natural explanations for this feature.

Therefore, intelligent design is the best explanation for such phenomena.

Next, we're going to look at three of the features—or clues—found in these phenomena—going from the largest to the smallest, from the telescope to the microscope. These three features are:

- Design Parameters of the Universe
- Irreducible complexity
- DNA and Biological Information

DESIGN PARAMETERS OF THE UNIVERSE

Just in the past forty to fifty years, as technology has advanced, scientists have been able to measure the universe's limits and characteristics, known as design parameters—in greater detail. Consequently, as the noted astrophysicist Hugh Ross points out, the indications of exquisite design are becoming irrefutable.

Astronomers and physicists, even the few who still hesitate to call themselves theists, widely acknowledge that the only reasonable explanation for the intricately harmonious features of the universe, our solar system, our planet—all ingeniously focused on the requirements for life—is the action and ongoing involvement of a personal, intelligent designer.[14]

Let's take a look at some of these design parameters from the natural world that make life possible.[15]

A Fine-Tuned Universe

Scientists have discovered several parameters in the universe that must be fine-tuned if life is to exist on earth. Here are just a few:

- *The gravitational force.* If it were stronger than it is, the stars would be too hot, and they would burn up quickly and unevenly. If gravity were weaker than it is, stars would remain so cool that nuclear fusion would never ignite.

- *The expansion rate of the universe.* If it expanded at a faster rate, no galaxies would be able to form. If the rate were slower, the universe would have collapsed prior to star formation.

- *The velocity of light.* If light traveled faster, the stars would be too luminous for us to tolerate. If light traveled slower, the stars would not be luminous enough.

- *The electromagnetic force.* With a force either stronger or weaker, there would be insufficient chemical bonding, which means no basic building blocks for all organic life.

There isn't a lot of wiggle room in these parameters. For example, just in the expansion rate, scientists have determined that life would not be possible in a universe that had an expansion rate different than ours by more than one part out of ten to the fifty-fifth power.

A Special Solar System

As we narrow our focus from the universe itself to those elements in the universe that are closer to home, the fine-tuning continues. Our own solar system, the Milky Way, demonstrates certain features needed to allow and sustain life on earth. Here a sampling of them:

- *Only one star.* If this planet we call home had more than one star—the sun—the tidal interactions would throw earth's orbit out of whack.

- *The age of the sun.* When stars are newly formed, their burning rate and temperature are not stable. They begin to maintain a stable burning phrase only after they have matured a bit. If our sun were too old or too young, its luminosity would change too quickly to allow life.

- *The size of the sun.* If the mass of the sun were too large, its luminosity would change too quickly, and it would burn too rapidly. If the sun were too small, the range of distances necessary for life would be too narrow. For example, there wouldn't be enough ultraviolet radiation for plants to make sugars and oxygen.

- *The sun's distance from earth.* If our sun were too far away from us, the temperature would be too cool to permit a stable water evaporation cycle. The oceans would freeze, killing most life. If the sun were too close, the climate would be too warm, boiling the oceans off into water vapor. If the distance from earth to the sun differed by just two percent, no plant life would be possible.

A JUST-RIGHT EARTH

Here's where the fine-tuning gets very personal. A change in any of the following parameters would make life on earth extremely unpleasant, if not downright impossible:

- *The orbital pattern around the sun.* A change would produce extreme temperature changes that would make life impossible.

- *The tilt of earth's axis.* The precise angle keeps the differential in the surface temperature from becoming too extreme.

- *The speed of earth's rotation.* This keeps temperature changes and wind velocities from becoming too great.

- *Earth's age.* The earth would rotate too fast if it were too young or too slow if it were too old.

Looking at physical constants like these, plus the phenomena of the first Big Bang creation event, the prominent scientist Francis Collins makes this observation: "The chance that all of these constants would take on the values necessary to result in a stable universe capable of sustaining complex life forms is almost infinitesimal. And yet those are exactly the parameters that we observe. In sum, our universe is wildly improbable."[16]

IRREDUCIBLE COMPLEXITY

Arguments in favor of an intelligent designer aren't new. Ancient Greek philosophers like Plato and Aristotle made arguments that nature showed evidence of design. In the thirteenth century Thomas Aquinas articulated what is known as the teleological argument for the existence of God. *Teleology* is the "study of final causes." Arguably the most famous teleological argument was advanced by William Paley in his book *Natural Theology*, published in 1802. Here's where Paley came up with the analogy of the watch and the watchmaker. Paley asked his readers to imagine they were walking through a field and found a watch, whose specific function is to tell time. A reasonable person would conclude that the watch didn't just appear as the result of an undirected natural process, but was the product of an intelligence—a watchmaker. The watch, with all of its intricate, delicate parts, didn't just fall into place by itself.

This concept, now known as irreducible complexity, lies at the heart of intelligent design theory. An irreducibly complex system is one that cannot be reproduced directly by gradual, successive modifications or refinements. In the case of Paley's watch, all the parts have to be in place at the same time in order for the watch to work. The same principle applies to life.

In his groundbreaking book, *Darwin's Black Box*, biochemist Michael Behe introduced the concept of irreducible complexity to explain biological machines that characterize life at the molecular level. Our cells are full of hundreds, if not thousands of microscopic molecular machines that perform a myriad of functions in the cell. According to Behe, it is in these molecular machines that design can be most clearly seen. Behe defines *irreducible complexity* as "a single system that is necessarily composed of several well-matched, interacting parts that contribute to the basic function, and where the removal of any one of the parts causes the system to effectively cease functioning."[17]

Charles Darwin actually saw this concept as a test for his theory of evolution. "If it could be demonstrated that any complex organ existed, which could not possibly have been formed by numerous, successive, slight modifications, my theory would absolutely break down," he wrote in *On the Origin of Species*. Of course, the technology did not exist in Darwin's time to observe these complex organs. Now it does, and science now knows there are irreducibly complex biological systems that have to arise as a completed unit, or else they couldn't function or even exist in the first place. The best explanation for such systems is that they are the result of intelligent causes.[18]

DNA AND BIOLOGICAL INFORMATION

A third component of the design argument has to do with biological information, specifically the information contained in deoxyribonucleic acid, or DNA. In 1953, Francis Crick and James Watson discovered the now-famous double helix of DNA, which contains the genetic information unique to each human being. DNA is formed by pairing up two of the four nucleotides found in DNA. In order for DNA to work, the nucleotides must be arranged in a precise and incredibly complex way so that the information contained in DNA is meaningful.

The purpose of DNA is to store information for the processing of proteins throughout the body. Much like a computer programming language, your DNA contains thousands upon thousands of commands and codes that instruct your cells how to build proteins, when to build them, how many to build, and what to do with them. It is these computer-like instructions that make all living organisms possible.

Amazingly, the average human body contains one hundred trillion cells. If you unravel the DNA in just *one* of those cells, it would be an average of nine feet in length. And if you aligned all the DNA in your body it would go from here to the sun and back seventy times! As for the information DNA stores, the DNA in one cell has the equivalent of eight billion letters, or five hundred million words, or eight thousand books.

From a naturalist perspective, the only explanation for how DNA generates and stores such a massive amount of information is through a series of physical occurrences and chemical reactions. There's a major problem with this explanation. It may explain the information contained in DNA, but not the way this information is organized. In my (Sean) book *Understanding Intelligent Design*, I tell the story of biology professor Dean Kenyon, who once believed that the information in DNA organized itself. The more he learned about his area of expertise, however, he came to see that naturalism was not an adequate explanation for the information content in proteins and DNA. As I state in my book, "Kenyon became convinced that the information content in biological systems could not have arisen through natural processes. He decided that the most sensible explanation was an intelligent designer."[19]

The argument for design based upon cutting-edge discoveries in biology is extremely compelling. In the twentieth and twenty-first centuries, biologists have learned that life is fundamentally built upon a language-based code filled with information. This code is similar to computer programming, and instruct your cells to build structures. These structures then turn out to be micromolecular machines whose efficiencies and complexities make the best human technology look like sticks and stones.

But where in our experience does language, information, programming code, and machines come from? In our experience, they come only from intelligence.

MORE THAN INFORMATION

Speaking of information, you've had to wade through a lot of it in this chapter, and we've given you just the bare minimum on a very complex topic. You could go a lot deeper, and if this stuff interests you, we encourage you to do just that.[20] Just keep in mind that information can take you only so far in your GodQuest. At some point you will need to decide if what you know about God is enough to convince you that you need and want a relationship with Him.

At the same time, the design clues presented in this chapter should move you along in your quest for truth and for God. Even more, they should encourage you to respond in some way. Just on the basis of the fine-tuned universe argument, Francis Collins lists three possible responses:

1. There may be an infinite number of universes out there with their own sets of physical constants and laws. We'll never know if these other universes exist, however, because all we know are our own universe's physical constants and laws, which work together to make life possible.

2. There is just one universe, and we're living in it. That our universe has all the properties essential to intelligent life is a product of chance.

3. There is only one universe, and the fine-tuning of all the physical constants that make life possible is not an accident, but "reflects the action of the one who created the universe in the first place."[21]

How you respond to the information presented in this chapter will have a significant impact on your GodQuest. If you favor the first response, that our universe is one of any number of other universes that could exist "far, far away" beyond the scope of our knowledge and understanding, then it may be difficult to think that this universe and everything in it—including you—are special. It would be like discovering that your father, who you thought was yours alone, had secretly fathered another family in another part of the world. How would you feel about that? Betrayed? Confused? Heartbroken? Of course, there's absolutely no evidence for this "many universe" theory, so in a way it's counterproductive to even entertain this option. And besides, even if there were more universes out there, it would not discount design.

You could also favor the second response, that the universe and everything in it are an accident and the result of chance. But where's the meaning in that? If there's no purpose or design in your creation, how can there be purpose and design in your life? Even the renowned atheist Bertrand Russell acknowledged, "Unless you assume a God, the question of life's purpose is meaningless." The difficult thing about choosing this response is that you actually need more faith to believe that undirected mechanistic causes produced the grand universe, the galaxy, and the planet we call home—not to mention the DNA in your body that appears so specifically and purposefully designed for *your* life.

At the end of the day, after weighing all of the evidence, after searching your own heart for the feeling and the meaning that's in there, you could come to the reasonable conclusion that there is a purpose and a design, and yes, even a designer, behind it all. Even more, you could have this longing to somehow connect with God, the only being who fits the description of the designer, who has enough power to create something out of nothing, and yet enough love to make it possible for you to have a meaningful life in relationship with Him.

God has revealed Himself to those who want to know Him. From the tiniest DNA strand to the vast structures of the universe, creation reveals the glory of God. Perhaps you're at a place in your GodQuest where you're ready to consider that this designer is God, and not just any God, but the Creator God who has revealed Himself to you in creation and beyond. You are not a cosmic fluke. You are made in the image of a God who loves you, who values you, who knows the number of hairs on your head, and who now desires a relationship with you.

This is a view worthy of the God who is. It is a big view of God that will carry you from "Signpost 2: The Beginning" to "Signpost 3: The Word," from the God who speaks through His creation to the God who speaks through His Word, with a message that could literally save your life.

SIGNPOST

③

THE WORD
WHAT YOU BELIEVE ABOUT
THE BIBLE DETERMINES
HOW YOU LIVE YOUR LIFE.

If you believe the Bible is true, then you have an inspired, flawless, incredibly wise guidebook that will keep you on the right path in life. If you don't believe the Bible is true, then you need to decide on your own rules and your own map for life.

GODQUEST

THE STORY OF GOD'S WORD

Every quest needs a guide, a map, or a set of instructions. Frodo the Hobbit had Gandolf to guide him in his quest for the ring. Indiana Jones used his father's notebook as a map pointing him to the Holy Grail. Dorothy followed the yellow brick road in her quest to go home.

For your GodQuest, the guide, the map, and the instructions—everything you need for your journey—are found in one source, the Bible. There's nothing sacred about the word *Bible*. It actually means "book." What is sacred about the Bible is that it comes directly from God. That's why you always see the word *Holy* in front of Bible. The Bible is God's book, or more appropriately, God's Word. Just as God is holy, so is His Word.

Here's what a few of the Bible's writers have to say about this Word that has influenced and affected the course of humanity more than any other book in history:

Moses, the great deliverer and author of the first five books in the Bible, declares:

These are the commands, decrees and laws the LORD your God directed me to teach you to observe in the land that you are crossing the Jordan to possess, so that you, your children and their children after them may fear the LORD your God as long as you live by keeping all his decrees and commands that I give you, and so that you may enjoy long life (Deuteronomy 6:1–2).

- David, the mighty King of Israel and the world's greatest poet, writes:

- *Your word is a lamp for my feet and a light for my path* (Psalm 119:105).

- Jesus, the Son of God sent to earth to show us God, says:

  "It is written: 'Man shall not live on bread alone, but on every word that comes from the mouth of God'" (Matthew 4:4).

- The Apostle Paul, the greatest missionary in history, writes:

  All Scripture is God-breathed and is useful for teaching, rebuking, correcting and training in righteousness, so that the servant of God may be thoroughly equipped for every good work (2 Timothy 3:16–17).

- The Apostle Peter, the leader of the early church, observes:

  For prophecy never had its origin in the will of man, but men spoke from God as they were carried along by the Holy Spirit (2 Peter 1:21).

Clearly the writers of the Bible and Jesus Himself acknowledge that the word of God bears the authority of God because it comes from God. But how is this possible? How could a mere book contain such divine authority and power? And how do we know that something you can buy from Wal-Mart or instantly download to your phone actually is the Word of God?

GOD WANTS TO KNOW YOU PERSONALLY

These are important questions, especially at this stage of your GodQuest. It's one thing to know that your search for Truth (*Signpost 1*) will eventually lead you to a search for God (*Signpost 2*), but how can you truly know God personally? Even if you are convinced by the clues about God that He exists and created the universe, what good does that do if God is unknowable? And even if He's knowable, how do you know God really wants a relationship with you? Who's to say He isn't "out there" someplace paying no attention whatsoever to you?

That's where God's Word comes in. Not only has God made Himself known through creation and the human conscience (Romans 1–2), He has also revealed His character and desires for the world in His holy book. The Bible is more than a book containing ancient history and unpronounceable names. The Bible isn't just a collection of wise sayings and instructions. The Bible is unlike any book you have every read or ever will read. The Bible is God's personal message for humankind that lays out His desires for each one of our lives. That's why we're devoting an entire Signpost to the Word of God.

There's a reason why the Bible contains messages like these:

> *For the eyes of the LORD range throughout the earth to strengthen those whose hearts are fully committed to him* (2 Chronicles 16:9).

> *But these are written that you may believe that Jesus is the Christ, the Son of God, and that by believing you may have life in his name* (John 20:31).

> *And without faith it is impossible to please God, because anyone who comes to him must believe that he exists and that he rewards those who earnestly seek him* (Hebrews 11:6).

God wants to connect with you personally. He wants to have a relationship with you. And the primary way He is telling you about His plans and His love for you is through His Word, which contains the greatest story ever told.

THE STORY OF GOD

Imagine for a moment that a big New York publishing company wanted you to tell your life story in a book. There are two ways you could do this. One way would be for you tell your own story in your own words from front to back. This is what an autobiography does. It's quite literally the account of your life told by you. Of course, an autobiography can be a little biased since you're the one telling the story. You might just have a tendency to minimize the negative parts of your life while emphasizing just the good things. That's why on the whole, autobiographies, while interesting, aren't as reliable as biographies.

That's the other way of telling your story is through a biography. A biography of your life would be your story as written by someone else. Biographies can be told about dead people, but in your case let's say the biography would be written while you are still alive. You would probably want to choose your biographer based on his or her writing and research skills, personality, integrity, commitment to the project and, above all, the ability to tell your story accurately and truthfully. Your biographer would interview you and people who know you to get the complete picture. In addition to including lots of background information about your life, your biography would have quotes from you and others explaining how you do things, what your philosophy of life is, and details about the various relationships you have.

If you can picture all of that, you have an idea of what the Bible is about. Essentially it is God's biography. The Bible is God's story, told not to just one writer but forty writers (God is a big personality, so it takes a lot of writers to tell His story). The Bible tells the sweeping story of God from eternity past to eternity future, including His own words as well as the words of others about Him. God's story is told through historical records, poetry, prophecy, eyewitness accounts, and letters. It includes His interactions with people of different times, nations, and ethnicities. Many of the people in God's story know Him well, others not at all.

Most of all, the Bible reveals God's plan and God's intention to have a personal relationship with us, His human creation, those He made uniquely in His image. Because the Bible reveals that God always has our best interest in mind at all times, the Bible contains God's proven philosophy of life and His instructions for how we should live our lives in order to flourish, not just exist. And because the Bible is the story of the one who set everything into place and who continues to be closely involved with all that happens, the Bible is an accurate compass for reality. As Mike Erre says in his excellent book *Why the Bible Matters*, "The Bible presents itself to us as a story that describes the way things really are."[11]

GODQUEST

WHAT IS GOD'S WORD ABOUT?

In the next chapter we're going to talk about how God's biography was written, but before we get to the mechanics, we need to know the plot. We like the way Henrietta Mears puts it in her classic book, *What the Bible Is All About*:

> The Bible is one book, one history, one story. His story. Behind 10,000 events stands God, the builder of history, the maker of the ages. Eternity bounds the one side, eternity bounds the other side, and time is in between: Genesis—origins, Revelation—endings, and all the way between, God is working things out. You can go down into the minutest detail everywhere and see that there is one great purpose moving through the ages: the eternal design of Almighty God to redeem a wrecked and ruined world.[2]

In telling God's story, the Bible tells us the true story about the world and ourselves. As Mike Erre writes:

> The Bible offers the truest story of the whole world—all of life, history, experience, culture, and civilization are encompassed in its pages. To see the Bible as the truest story is not to say that the story helps us function well or that it was passed down to us merely as a cultural inheritance. The scriptures must be taken seriously because they claim to tell us the true story from the creation of the universe all the way to its re-creation. Not one moment is left out of its pages. The content of the Bible lies at the very core of reality. This is the way the world really is.[3]

Are these descriptions a little lofty, a bit too grand? Okay, how about this four-act summary of God's story:

Act 1: Creation

Act 2: The Fall

Act 3: Redemption (of which Israel, Jesus, and the church are all parts)

Act 4: Restoration (the renewal of all creation)

If that sounds kind of familiar, this four-part structure is the basis for all great stories. It's the plot line for all classic quests. Even love stories use this framework:

Act 1: Boy meets girl

Act 2: Boy loses girl

Act 3: Boy gets girl

Act 4: Boy and girl live happily ever after

In a very real sense, God's story is your story too. It's God's love story written for humankind, describing the incredible lengths God has gone to in order to have a relationship with you:

Act 1: God creates humanity, and it's very good

Act 2: Humanity disobeys God, bringing sin and death into God's perfect creation

Act 3: God demonstrates His love by sending Jesus to save us from our sins

Act 4: All who accept God's redemption plan live forever

GOD'S STORY UNFOLDS

Most stories begin at the beginning, and that's exactly what the Bible does. There it is on the first line of the first page: "In the beginning God created the heavens and the earth." Those are the words that set the tone for everything that follows. In fact, in just this one phrase the stage is set for the entire world and all of reality. These words tell us three things about God: that He exists, that He existed before the beginning, and that He created all things.

Of course, there are those who believe the Bible is a work of fiction, or at least the part about creation. But to believe this denies the immense reality and trustworthiness of God's Word (something we're going to cover in some detail in Chapter 8). For the purposes of your GodQuest, we are moving forward with the assumption that the Bible is a work of nonfiction—a trustworthy story that describes the way the world really is. In fact, your GodQuest is going to fall flat unless you believe the Bible is a true story. As Tim Keller says, "The Christian faith requires belief in the Bible."[4] If the Bible is fiction, your GodQuest is an exercise in futility. But if the story of God as found in the Bible is true, your GodQuest is not just meaningful but life altering.

So let's begin with the assumption, to paraphrase the famous opening line from the 1950s television drama *Dragnet*, "The story you are about to read is true."

ACT 1: GOD CREATES HUMANITY, AND IT IS VERY GOOD

The Bible contains 66 individual books and 1,189 chapters; Act 1 occupies just the first two chapters of the first book. Here is where the miraculous story of God creating the universe is told in elegant fashion. Is this a scientific account of how the universe came to be? No, but neither is it antiscientific. Just because the universe was brought into existence by a supernatural act, something you would expect from a supernatural being, the process doesn't contradict science. It simply explains that creation was done *above* the natural world that science observes (*super* means "above"), and that it was brought into existence by the power of God's Word. When God said, "Let there be light," an unfathomable amount of pure energy was unleashed, planting "every star, every planet, and every living creature" in what even secular scientists describe as "the moment of creation."[5] The Bible states this fact with classic elegance:

> By faith we understand that the universe was created by the word of God, so that what is seen was not made out of things that are visible (Hebrews 11:3, ESV).

The Bible then describes the sequence of what happened next. Again, Genesis doesn't give us a scientific account, but neither does the description contradict science. Notice how God's creative activity on each day corresponds with the general sequence science has outlined for the beginning and early formation of the universe.

Day	Biblical Sequence	Scientific Sequence
1	Heavens and earth are created	The Big Bang
2	The waters separate	Earth's atmosphere changes
3	Dry land appears; plant life begins	Bacteria and algae grow
4	Sun, moon and stars are visible	Earth's atmosphere becomes transparent
5	First animal life in water and air	Multicellular life appears in water; winged insects appear
6	Land animals and humans appear later	Land animals appear; human life appears

How long did all of this take? The old earth creation theory seems to be compatible with scientific theory, but let's be careful not to restrict God by any timeframe. God is eternal and He is also infinite, which means He stands above creation and apart from time. Speaking of God's relationship to time, Moses, the author of Genesis and a pretty good poet, gives us this mind-bending observation about God:

> For a thousand years in your sight
> are like a day that has just gone by,
>   or like a watch in the night (Psalm 90:4).

And yet, though God stands apart from time and is separate from His creation, God is also involved in it. On the final creation day, this vast, and at times incomprehensible God becomes very near and very involved in the crowning achievement of His creative work when He personally forms man from the dust of the ground. Everything else God made came into existence by God speaking— showing His *transcendence* or distinction from the created world. With our first human father, God showed His *imminence* or nearness to the created world, when He formed man "from the dust of the ground and breathed into his nostrils the breath of life" (Genesis 2:7). Furthermore, God made woman from man's own body, showing that male and female are created not just in the image of God (Genesis

1:26–27), but also in relationship with one another (Genesis 2:21–25). And they are made to be in relationship with God, who communes with them and tasks them to be caretakers of His magnificent natural world.

And God said it was all very good.

Act 2: Humanity disobeys God, bringing sin and death into God's perfect creation.

Why is there evil in the world? How could a good and loving God allow pain and suffering to afflict His magnificent world? We're going to address these big issues in some detail in "Signpost 4: The Question," but the origin of evil, pain, and suffering starts right here in Genesis. We may not know exactly why God allows these negative qualities in His world, but we can discover how they got there.

Being the all-wise and loving being that He is, God created humans with the capacity to freely love and obey Him. Adam and Eve weren't automatons, programmed to perform in a pre-scripted play. They were, as we are, people with the capacity to freely choose between right and wrong. God gave Adam and Eve unlimited freedom to inhabit and enjoy paradise, start a family, manage the natural world, and eat anything except for the fruit of one tree—the tree of the knowledge of good and evil (Genesis 2:16–17). Seems like a pretty fair deal.

SATAN'S LIES, HUMANITY'S FALL

Then Satan, a fallen angel who freely rebelled against God sometime in eternity past and who now inhabits the earth, comes into the perfect garden and targets God's human creatures. The conversation between Satan, embodied in the serpent, and the woman tells us all we need to know about his strategy and struggle to ruin humankind. When you read Genesis 3:1–5, you can see the progression of lies Satan tells in order to undermine God's goodness, starting with, "Did God really say" that? See if these lies don't sound kind of familiar—because Satan still uses them today.

Lie #1: God is placing an unreasonable restriction on you.

Lie #2: Restriction is bad because you would be better off without it.

Lie #3: God's rule is bad.

Lie #4: You'd be better off if you didn't pay attention to the restriction.

Did God allow this temptation as a test? Sure looks like it. But ultimately it's not a test to see if Adam and Eve were going to break God's rule. Breaking God's rule is merely the doorway to something much more sinister. "We should not think that the serpent's temptation is nothing more than an invitation to break a rule, arbitrary or otherwise," notes Don Carson, research professor of New Testament at Trinity Evangelical Divinity School. "What is at stake here is something deeper, bigger, sadder, uglier, more heinous. It is a revolution. It makes me god and thus de-gods God."[6]

Suddenly the happy days are over. Life in God's new world gets tragically messed up. Evil is now present in the world, and it's not just the evil that people do to each other. As bad as it was in the beginning when only a few people inhabited the earth (it didn't take long for the first murder), and as horribly bad as things are now with nearly seven billion people on the planet, we must never forget that God is the one who is most offended by sin and rebellion. Put yourself in God's position for a minute. He lovingly and with great care and precision creates a world that works perfectly. And in that world He personally places people made in His own image. He wants nothing greater than for His children to enjoy everything He has given them and to love Him in return, and what do they do? They throw everything back in His face because they buy into the lie that God wants to restrict them. They aren't content to glorify God and enjoy Him forever; they want to be like God.

The consequences of this rebellion are severe. The marvelous fellowship Adam and Eve have enjoyed with God is broken, as is their harmonious fellowship with each other. They are declared guilty, as is every member of the human race thereafter. And they are banished from the Garden of Eden, destined to lives of hardship and toil instead of the bliss they have previously experienced. And to top it all off, they would experience physical death. It seems as if the story of humankind is over almost as soon as it has begun.

But God isn't about to give up. Although the human race is alienated from God, there is hope. Referencing Genesis 3:15, the first indication that there will be some good news amidst all the bad, a glimpse of redemption immediately after the fall, Mike Erre explains the essence of God's plan to bring His rebellious human creation back to Himself:

God does not give up on His purposes for His creation and kingdom. Though Adam and Eve flee, God pursues. Though they are exposed and naked, He clothes them. Though judged and driven from the garden, God promises to provide help (3:15): The woman's offspring will be at war with the serpent and will ultimately crush his head. God promises to destroy the forces of darkness that Adam and Eve unleashed. This is the first promise of redemption—Christ is the seed of the woman, and He will defeat Satan, though at great cost to Himself (His heel will be wounded).[7]

Act 3: God demonstrates His love by sending Jesus to save us from our sins.

God's promise of a Savior who would mediate between Himself and sinful humanity, who are God's enemies in every respect, is given in Genesis 3:15. But it will be thousands of years before Jesus appears on earth. So what happens in the meantime? We know that Adam and Eve get serious about God's command to "be fruitful and multiply." But Adam and Eve and their descendants aren't the only ones who are busy. As the centuries pass and the human race increases in number, it also increases in wickedness. The people of the world aren't atheists—they believe in gods—they just don't believe in the real God. Idolatry is rampant. By the time of Noah, only one decent family remains on earth. In anger and disappointment, God causes an awful flood to clean the slate. But the flood solution doesn't seem to wash either. The slate of the human heart just doesn't come clean.

GOD'S COVENANT WITH ABRAHAM

God still intends to implement His plan to provide a means of redemption, not just for the sinful Adam and Eve, but for the sins of all humankind. As part of that plan, God selects a certain group of people to be His "chosen nation" for the purpose of bringing a redemptive blessing to the whole world (Genesis 12:1–3). God makes a covenant, or agreement, with His people, that through this nation God will dramatically and personally reveal Himself to the entire world.

Abraham does have incredible faith, but the sin virus continues to plague his descendants, the nation of Israel, to the point that four hundred years after Genesis comes to a close, Abraham's family— now numbering in excess of two million people—is in Egypt, trapped under the tyranny of an oppressive regime. Israel's enslavement to the Pharaoh and his oppression is a vivid picture of our enslavement to Satan and sin. And just as God raises up a deliverer for the nation of Israel in the person of Moses, God promises to raise up a deliverer for us in the person of Jesus so we can become slaves of God.

> When you were slaves to sin, you were free from the control of righteousness. What benefit did you reap at that time from the things you are now ashamed of? Those things result in death! But now that you have been set free from sin and have become slaves to God, the benefit you reap leads to holiness, and the result is eternal life. For the wages of sin is death, but the gift of God is eternal life in Christ Jesus our Lord (Romans 6:20–23).

Shortly after Israel's exodus from Egypt, God makes another agreement with His people and reveals His purposes for them: They are to be set apart to be His "treasured possession." God gives Israel the Ten Commandments in order to show them the conditions of the agreement (Exodus 20). "They reflect God's purposes for humanity and show Israel how to live in ways that mirror God's character."[8] Despite this expression of personal love and care for them, God's people refuse to be bound by God's rules. For the next forty years they wander in the desert until an entire generation passes from the scene. During this long sojourn, God miraculously provides His children with food and water every day. Still, they complain.

GODQUEST

Under the direction of Joshua in roughly 1400 BC, the Israelites cross the Jordan River into the Promised Land with God's mandate to drive out the godless people there. This period of conquest should end quickly, but God's people frequently lose faith in His provision and protection. Rather than drive out the pagans, they choose to live with them and marry them, leading Israel into an era of violence, lawlessness, and immorality—a time when "everyone did as he saw fit" (Judges 17:6).

ISRAEL CRIES OUT FOR A KING

Four hundred years later, Israel cries out for a king like all of the surrounding nations. Of course, they don't need a king because they have God, but God accommodates them anyway. For a while the plan goes beautifully, with David ascending to the throne and leading Israel to unprecedented power and influence. Solomon follows with wisdom never before seen and builds a glorious temple, only to see God's people go to war again—only this time it's with each other. Only days after Solomon's death, civil war breaks out. It would be easy to blame this division on political conflict, but the Bible makes it clear these problems can be traced to Solomon's unfaithfulness to God (1 Kings 11). The ten northern tribes form their own confederacy, calling themselves "Israel," while the two southern tribes take the name "Judah," making Jerusalem their capitol.

It's a mess and the days get increasingly dark. More idolatry, increasing sinfulness, and a departure from God's truth leads to exile at the hands of the great secular powers of the time. Once again God's people live in captivity. The prophet Jeremiah speaks for his people after Jerusalem is destroyed: "So I say, 'My splendor is gone, and all that I hoped from the LORD'" (Lamentations 3:18). Has God finally given up on Abraham's descendants? Only a person with the ability to look past the despair and see God's hope would have any optimism now. That's just fine with God. He has a few messengers of hope in mind when He calls a series of prophets to speak His truth to His people.

GOD SPEAKS THROUGH THE PROPHETS

God has not forgotten His promise to Abraham to bring a savior to the world through Abraham's descendants. During these years when hope has seemingly died, God speaks through the prophets with a message full of hope: God will send a Messiah—the anointed king who will be a direct descendant of David—to be a suffering servant who will carry the sorrows of God's people, to be a light to the nations, and ultimately to restore Israel (Isaiah 49:6; 52:13–53:12). God will make a new covenant with all people, a covenant placed on their hearts, wherein He will remember their sins no more (Jeremiah 31:31–34).

Meanwhile, God graciously arranges for His people to return to their homeland and rebuild the temple and the city of Jerusalem. It's not long, however, before their lives back home begin to resemble their existence in exile. The Israelites aren't exactly in captivity, but neither are they free. In fact, these people now called Jews are under the thumb of the Romans, one of the most powerful regimes in history. When will their Messiah come to deliver them from their oppressors? Will God send them another Moses to deliver them or another David to lead them to national glory? The prophets have stopped their pronouncing. God isn't talking. As the Old Testament closes, the silence is deafening.

GOD GETS DOWN TO EARTH

How will God break through the silence? With the rumble of chariots coming to the rescue? How about a helpless baby born in obscurity? It certainly isn't what God's people are expecting, but it is in God's plan all along. The almighty, eternal, invisible God Himself comes down to earth in the form of a human being called Immanuel, "God with us," and He is given the name Jesus, "because he will save his people from their sins" (Matthew 1:21).

As predicted by the prophet Isaiah, God's people do not accept Jesus as their Messiah (Isaiah 53:3), nor do they receive Him. But God's plan to bless all the people of the world through this descendant of Abraham is not thwarted. As John writes in his gospel:

He came to that which was his own, but his own did not receive him.
Yet to all who did receive him, to those who believed in his name,
he gave the right to become children of God—children born not of
natural descent, nor of human decision or a husband's will, but born
of God (John 1:11–13).

This is Jesus, God in human form, the light of the world come
to rescue and redeem a wrecked and ruined world, so that all who
believe in Him would not perish but have eternal life. Jesus is the
Good News—the *Gospel*—for a lost and dying world. Eden's gates are
once again open. We can be at peace with God through the life, the
death, and the resurrection of Jesus Christ.

Act 4: All who accept God's redemption plan live forever.

God's plan has always been to be in relationship with us; it's why
He created us in the first place. Sin disrupted that plan, but it didn't
take God by surprise. In fact, we know from Revelation 13:8 that
Jesus is the lamb sacrificed before the foundations of the world. God
had a plan all along. Our rebellion merely triggered the plan He
already had in place, "to be put into effect when the times will have
reached their fulfillment—to bring unity to all things in heaven and
on earth together under one head, even Christ" (Ephesians 1:10).
It's a plan that is not dependent on us or our ability to meet God's
standard of perfection—something that is impossible anyway. Rather,
it is based on God's grace. Our salvation from the penalty of sin is
God's gift to us, made possible by the person and work of Jesus.

For it is by grace you have been saved, through faith—and this is
not from yourselves, it is the gift of God—not by works, so that no
one can boast. For we are God's workmanship, created in Christ
Jesus to do good works, which God prepared in advance for us to do
(Ephesians 2:8–10).

When we receive the gift of salvation by faith, we are spiritually
restored, and not just so we can have eternal life. In the in between
time after Jesus came to earth the first time and the time He comes
again, we are required and empowered by God to "do good works." If
there's ever a sense in which heaven is brought to earth, it's because
God is working through His people—now including *all* people, men

and women, slave and free (Galatians 3:28)—to illuminate the dark corners of the world and the human heart with the light of Jesus.

Then, at some time in the future that no one knows, Jesus will come to earth a second time to gather all who have called on Him for salvation. Living in God's story means our death isn't the end of our lives. As Mike Erre writes:

> God will not abandon this world; He will redeem it. When He restores and renews it, He will raise His people (those in Christ) to live in it in physical resurrection bodies. He is present with us now, but we see Him only partially and dimly. One day this veil will be lifted, heaven and earth will be rejoined, Jesus will be fully revealed and present with us, and every knee will bow and every tongue will praise Him. The universe will be renewed, the dead will be raised, and all that God intended for His world will come to pass.[9]

HOW DOES THE BIBLE AFFECT YOUR GODQUEST?

GodQuest is both the title and the theme of this book. So far it's been about you on a quest to discover God: the truth of His existence, the clues of His reality through the natural world, and now the revelation of God through His Word. You're on a quest for God, both to know Him and to have a relationship with Him.

Maybe you've already thought about this, but we'd like to suggest another way to look at the title of this book: God is on a quest for you. When you examine God's story as we have done in this chapter, it's clear that God is the one who pursues a fallen and rebellious humanity. If God truly exists and the Bible is an accurate written record of His story, then there's something amazing about the way the story unfolds. In other stories, the characters can't interact with the author. For example, it would be futile, as C. S. Lewis once suggested, for Hamlet to look for Shakespeare in the attic of his castle.

GODQUEST

THE MAN I MET IN THE ATTIC

I (Stan) can relate to this. My father died when I was very young. My mother soon remarried and we moved to another state. We were a happy family, and I didn't have much of a desire to know about my birth father. It wasn't until many years later when I was an adult that I decided to learn more about him. Traveling back to the place of my father's birth, I connected with his older brother (my uncle) who had a box full of letters and photos of my dad. After dinner one evening, the two of us climbed into his attic where the memories were stored. My uncle pulled a string to turn on the light, and we sat there on boxes in that musty attic for several hours, reading letters and looking at fading photos.

That's how I met my father. In that attic, through the letters and photos and my uncle's stories, I got a very good picture of the kind of man my dad was. I saw myself in a different light as well because I discovered that we shared many physical features and personality traits. For the first time in my life, I knew what it meant to say, "I am my father's son."

As much as I learned about my father that night, there was no way I could interact with him. Not so with my heavenly Father. Unlike my earthly father, my heavenly Father is very much alive, and He has taken very deliberate steps to enter my world in the person of His own Son. In this way, as Tim Keller observes, God is not a man in the attic, and the Bible is more than a collection of letters and photos written by someone who no longer exists. God is very much alive and very real, and as the author of this grand story we have just reviewed, He has done something quite extraordinary: God has written himself into the plot. Consequently, as characters in this same story we have the opportunity to relate to Him personally because He became the central character in history's greatest story when He became a human and lived among us.

So how does the Bible affect your GodQuest? May we suggest that it affects it significantly—as long as you know you can trust it to be God's very Word. That's what we're going to talk about in the next chapter.

CHAPTER 8

CAN YOU BELIEVE GOD'S STORY?

No one disputes that the Bible is a popular book. In every year since the Bible was first published on Johannes Gutenberg's now-famous printing press in the mid fifteenth century, it has been the number one best-selling book in the world. As impressive as that is, the Bible's sales records don't begin to tell the whole story. The Bible truly is a global phenomenon—it has been translated into more than twenty-four hundred languages—and no book is more popular online. Just one smartphone app, the YouVersion of the Bible, has been downloaded more than ten million times. Countless numbers of small groups and classes study the Bible on a regular basis. Pastors in churches around the world teach from its pages every week. There's absolutely no question that the Bible is the most popular book in the world.

At the same time, the Bible is also the world's most controversial book. Even though there are many people who believe the Bible they have and read is the complete Word of God, there are many who think there are missing books that should have been included. For every person who trusts the Bible to be the completely trustworthy and accurate Word of God, there is another who finds it to be full of errors and contradictions. In other words, everybody has an opinion about the Bible.

Just because the Bible is popular doesn't mean it deserves to be read. There are many books filled with half-baked ideas that crowd the bestsellers' lists. But the controversies surrounding the Bible shouldn't automatically disqualify it as a credible source either. The key to accepting or rejecting the Bible goes beyond public scrutiny to the core of what the Bible claims to be: God's Word. When you think about it, this is an astounding claim, that a written book contains the very message of the invisible God. Here's how the Apostle Paul puts it:

When you received the word of God, which you heard from us, you accepted it not as the word of men, but as it actually is, the word of God, which is at work in you who believe (1 Thessalonians 2:13).

Given this claim that the Bible comes from God, there are basically three questions any thoughtful person should ask about the Bible:

- *How do we know the Bible comes from God?* This question has to do with inspiration or how the Bible was written. The answer to this question reflects the trustworthiness and *reliability* of Scripture.

- *How do we know the Bible really is God's Word?* This question has to do with canonicity, or how the Bible was put together. The answer to this question involves the *authority* of God's Word.

- *How do we know the Bible we have today is the Bible God wanted us to have?* This question has to do with *transmission,* or how the Bible was passed down from the original writers to us. The answer relates to the *accuracy* of the Bible.

If we can answer these questions in a way that gives you more confidence in the Bible, or at the very least encourages you to investigate the issues on a deeper level, we believe you will have the tools you need to continue on your faith journey. And here's one more thing to keep in mind. As important as the Bible is, the Bible should never be the object of your faith. That may sound rather obvious, but it's easy to place the Bible in the same category as God—mainly because it has the word *holy* in front of it. While the Bible is God's special revelation to us, it is not God. Just as God is distinct from all He created, God is distinct from all He has said.

GODQUEST

THE WORLD'S MOST AMAZING BOOK

Before we get to the task of answering those three questions about the Bible, we want to remind you just how amazing and unique the Bible really is:

- *The Bible is made up of sixty-six books written by forty different authors.* There are thirty-nine books in the Old Testament and twenty-seven in the New Testament. The subject matter of this anthology includes thousands of topics, many of them controversial, yet the authors wrote in complete harmony with each other, even though most of them didn't know each other and didn't live at the same time.

- *The Bible was written on three continents over a span of centuries.* Starting with Moses and Job, and ending with the Apostle John, the Bible was written over a period of fifteen hundred years on the continents of Asia, Africa, and Europe.

- *The Bible was written in three languages.* Hebrew is the original language of the Old Testament, while the New Testament was written primarily in Greek (with just a little bit of Aramaic thrown in for good measure).

The Bible has one theme and one message throughout. You would think that with all the writers involved, the vast time span when it was written, and the different locations and languages involved, the Bible would be one mixed-up book. But just the opposite is true. From Genesis to Revelation, the books of the Bible record one internally consistent theme and message: God is on a rescue mission to bring fallen humanity back into an eternal relationship with Him through the life, death, and resurrection of His Son, Jesus Christ. What this means for you is that God wants a relationship with you. It's just that simple.

The Bible's theme and message don't stand alone but are wrapped in the events of human history. And just in case you wonder if the general narrative we gave you in the last chapter stands up to objective scrutiny, you can be sure it does. Reflecting the consensus among historians, researchers Kenneth Boa and Robert Bowman point out, from a strictly historical point of view, "the general outline of events narrated in the Bible, broadly speaking, has never been in serious doubt."[11] According to historical and archaeological records, the nation of Israel really did exist, their slavery in Egypt and escape to the Promised Land is a credible story, and the rise of Israel as a major power under David and Solomon is not in dispute. That the divided kingdoms of Israel and Judah were conquered by the Assyrians and the Babylonians, respectively, is corroborated by historical records. History also shows that Jesus of Nazareth really did exist in Palestine in the first century, and His execution and subsequent resurrection are recorded by nonbiblical sources. The events recorded in the Bible are not myth, but real historical occurrences.

What all of this means is that on one level, reading the Bible is not like reading a book of fairy tales. You can trust the Bible as an accurate historical document because the Bible fits into history the way it really happened. Of course, there's much more to the Bible than history. On another level, the Bible contains supernatural phenomena—otherwise known as *miracles*—that make it much more interesting, and for some, much more problematic. No less an American luminary than Thomas Jefferson was so troubled by the supernatural elements of the New Testament that he took it upon himself to produce a Bible stripped of all miracles, including the resurrection of Jesus.[2]

But why should the presence of the supernatural in the Bible be a problem? After all, isn't that what you would expect in a book written by a supernatural being?

HOW DO WE KNOW THE BIBLE COMES FROM GOD?

This question goes to the heart of how the Bible was written, a process known as *inspiration*. It's a term that comes from 2 Timothy 3:16, which says, "All Scripture is inspired by God and is useful to teach us what is true and to make us realize what is wrong in our lives. It corrects us when we are wrong and teaches us to do what is right" (NLT). The phrase "inspired by God" literally means "God-breathed."

What this tells us is that the message of the Bible begins with a revelation from God given to a prophet. Inspiration also speaks to the inherent *trustworthiness* and *reliability* of the Bible because it comes directly from God.

The Apostle Peter further explains the process of inspiration when he writes, "For prophecy never had its origin in the will of man, but men spoke from God as they were carried along by the Holy Spirit" (2 Peter 1:21). This kind of inspiration is more than we think of when we're inspired to do something. This is divine influence, given to a select group of prophets over a period of many centuries, for the purpose of providing a written record of God's message to all of humanity. When Peter writes that these prophets were "carried along," he means they were moved "like a ship is carried by the wind. God carried each writer along as he wrote so the message was kept intact."[3]

THE BREATH OF GOD

God's breath gives *life*. When God breathed into the human authors, He gave life to His Word. Does this remind of you another amazing act of God breathing in life for the benefit of humanity? How about when God formed Adam's body from the dust of the ground? The Bible says He "breathed into his nostrils the breath of life, and the man became a living being" (Genesis 2:7). Think about this amazing truth: The same breath God used to give life to the human race gave life to His Word, the very Word you can read and study any time you like!

Bible scholars don't know exactly how this breathing in business worked on a practical level, but they are convinced it was not like dictation. The prophets, acting as spokesmen for God, were not secretaries. The individual personalities and writing styles of the different authors can be clearly seen in their respective books. But neither was the process of inspiration a matter of the writers interpreting what God moved them to record. Biblical scholars Norm Geisler and Ron Brooks explain it this way:

The only adequate view [of inspiration] incorporates both divine and human factors; it is the prophet model. In this process, the human writer is seen as one who has received a revelation and actively participates in its writing, while God gives the revelation and oversees the writing. Hence, the message is wholly from God, but the humanity of the writer is included to enhance the message. Both the divine and human concur in the same words.[4]

As for the role of the Holy Spirit in the process of inspiration, theologian R. C. Sproul writes, "The word *inspiration* also calls attention to the process by which the Holy Spirit *superintended* the production of Scripture. The Holy Spirit guided the human authors so that their words would be nothing less than the word of God."[5]

The reason we know the Bible comes from God is because it was written by men of God who were inspired by God to express the very concepts God wanted them to communicate. As Geisler and Brooks assert, the Bible is "not simply a record of revelation, but a revelation itself. It is God's message in written form."[6]

HOW DO WE KNOW THE BIBLE REALLY IS GOD'S WORD?

In 2003, a novel by Dan Brown, an unheralded author whose first three books generated little attention, was published for the first time. Following the adventures of "symbologist" Robert Langdon on his mission to uncover the meaning of a mysterious murder in Paris' Louvre Museum, *The Da Vinci Code* created an international sensation because of its central theme—that the Bible we have today isn't accurate and truthful, but is the result of intentional manipulation by the Church to insure its political and ecclesiastical power. The truth, according to Brown, is that Jesus never died, was never resurrected, but instead married Mary Magdalene. In particular, the four biographies of Jesus—also known as the four Gospels—are inaccurate and incomplete, presenting as they do the wrong view of Jesus and Christianity. According to Brown, the truth lies in the "hidden" eyewitness accounts buried by the Church, a group of books Bible scholars refer to as the "Gnostic gospels." The word *Gnostic* means "hidden."

GODQUEST

Since its publication, *The Da Vinci Code* has sold more than eighty million copies worldwide and was made into a major motion picture featuring American acting legend Tom Hanks, so its influence cannot be underestimated. Many Christians were rattled by the assertions of this fictional tale, while unbelievers looking for a reason to discredit the Bible were emboldened by its theme. If true, the book's accusations could seriously undermine not just the credibility of the Bible, but its central message as well.

A few years have passed since the peak popularity of *The Da Vinci Code*, and most Christians who were stirred up by the book have come to realize that it was a clever, poorly researched, fictional account of the history of Christianity and the Church. If there was a silver lining to the whole affair, it was that many Christians were compelled to look at the facts concerning the Bible and how it was put together. In a negative, but ultimately beneficial way, *The Da Vinci Code* forced Christians to answer the question, "How do we know the Bible really is God's Word?"

THE QUESTION OF CANONICITY AND AUTHORITY

This question goes to the heart of *canonicity*, or how the Bible was put together. How do we know the sixty-six books of the Bible are the only ones that should be included? What about the Gnostic gospels? What about the books referred to as the Apocrypha? The answer, found in the concept of canonicity, should give you the confidence you need to know that the books in your Bible are the ones God intended to be there—nothing more and nothing less. Because of the process of canonicity, they are stamped with the *authority* of God.

The word *canon* comes from a root word translated as "reed." Reeds were used as measuring sticks in ancient times, so when applied to the Bible, canon indicates the measure or the standard used to evaluate which books were inspired and which ones were not. Part of the confusion comes from an incorrect perception of canonicity, that somehow it was the responsibility of various groups of people meeting together (they were called church councils) to determine which writings were from God and which ones weren't. This is a false assumption that puts the authority in the wrong place.

Since God is the one who initiated the writings of Scripture through the divine superintendence of the Holy Spirit, God is the one who knows the writings that truly come from Him. Getting back to the notion of you writing your biography, let's say that your book was about to be published, but first you needed to read through the manuscript to make sure everything you said and everything said about you were true. Nobody but you would be in a position to know what should stay in the book and what should be eliminated.

Same goes for God, the author of the Bible. When it comes to His Word, no one besides Him is in a position to know everything He said and everything said about Him. So when it came time to put the Bible together in the decades and centuries following the writing of the final book in the New Testament (the book of Revelation late in the first century), the church councils in charge of putting the New Testament together had just one task: to *recognize* the divine influence that was already there.

Geisler and Brooks list five questions these church councils asked as a way of recognizing God's divine voice in the books they were asked to consider:[7]

1. *Was it written by a prophet of God?* This followed the protocol set forth in Deuteronomy 18:18 and 2 Peter 1:20–21 that God reveals himself only through the prophets. As the writer of Hebrews says in the opening verse of his book, "In the past God spoke to our forefathers through the prophets at many times and in various ways."

2. *Was the writer/prophet confirmed by an act of God?* Hebrews 2:2–4 states that there should be some kind of miraculous confirmation that the prophet claiming to speak for God is the real deal.

3. *Does it tell the truth about God?* Any writing that contradicted other writings about God were considered false. The same thing applied to false prophecies made in the name of God (Deuteronomy 18:22).

4. *Does it have the power of God?* Any writing that did not display the transforming power of God was rejected. Again, from Hebrews we read: "For the word of God is living and active. Sharper than any double-edged sword, it penetrates even to dividing soul and spirit, joints and marrow; it judges the thoughts and attitudes of the heart" (Hebrews 4:12).

5. *Was it accepted by the people of God?* That some books were rejected shows that there were books that didn't resonate with God's people. Because God speaks to His people with the same Holy Spirit who inspired the prophets to record His message, we should expect a high level of discernment regarding true versus false writings.

The bottom line is that the Bible you have in your home, in your backpack, on your smartphone or tablet—wherever you have the Bible available to read—is the true and trustworthy Word of God. It's the message God wants you to know. There's nothing He left out, so you don't have to wonder if there are some secret or hidden writings waiting for discovery. In summarizing the process of canonicity, Talbot School of Theology New Testament professor Ken Berding writes:

> The teachings of the Lord and his apostles were considered self-authenticating and authoritative from the days they were first spoken/written. As the apostles died off, orthodox Christians continued to use the writings of the apostles as authoritative. The church did not establish a canon of its choosing; it is more proper to speak of the church recognizing the books that Christians had always considered to be an authoritative Word from God.[8]

WHAT ABOUT THE APOCRYPHA AND THE GNOSTIC GOSPELS?

Even though the Apocrypha, books written between the close of the Old Testament canon and the opening of the New Testament canon, and the Gnostic gospels, books written after the close of the New Testament canon, were all rejected by the church councils, they were rejected for different reasons. The books of the Apocrypha, which you will find in some Bibles, have historical value and are not considered to be in error, but they were never recognized as inspired.

The Gnostic gospels, on the other hand, weren't just about history. They presented a different story and a different view of Jesus than the four canonical Gospels. Scholars from the Jesus Seminar, a group that disputes the portait of Jesus as found in the four canonical Gospels, claim the Gnostic gospels of Thomas, Judas, Philip, Peter, and Mary (among a total of twenty) reveal a view of Jesus that is just as valid, if not more so, than the four Gospels. In light of the claims made by these noncanonical books and their proponents, Josh McDowell poses this question in his book *More Than a Carpenter,* "Are these recently discovered gospels transforming our understanding of Christianity?"[9] Some scholars believe they are.

Elaine Pagels, a professor of religious history and the chief promoter of the best-known Gnostic gospel, "The Gospel of Thomas," believes the correct view of Jesus is not presented in the four canonical Gospels, in particular the gospel of John. For Pagels, who influenced the writing of Dan Brown, in order to know God we must move beyond belief to find what lies hidden in each one of us. "The divine light Jesus embodied is shared by humanity."[10]

In fact, "The Gospel of Thomas" and all of the "lost" gospels are "obviously inferior theologically and historically to the four accounts that eventually came to be regarded as the only canonical Gospels," writes New Testament scholar Bruce Metzger.[11] The primary reason scholars like Metzger, historian Philip Jenkins, and a host of others reject the Gnostic gospels is their late dating. "While the four Gospels were all written within the first century, all evidence points to these other gospels being composed between AD 120 and 250, at least three generations removed from the life of Christ."[12] Only the four Gospels writers, who wrote as eyewitnesses to the person of Jesus Christ and who were under the influence of the Holy Spirit, correctly understand the gospel—or good news—message of Christ, because only those eyewitness writers portray Jesus as He really is: the embodied and living God who speaks with divine authority.

GODQUEST

HOW DO WE KNOW THE BIBLE WE HAVE TODAY IS THE BIBLE GOD WANTED US TO HAVE?

So far we've talked about the *trustworthiness* and *reliability* of God's Word, qualities that depend on the way God wrote the Bible—*inspiration*. We've also discussed the authority of God's Word, which deals with the way the inspired books of the Bible were recognized as God-inspired—*canonicity*. Now we want to touch on a third area that should be very important to you as you continue your GodQuest. If the Bible is going to be your primary guide book, your map, your instruction manual, you need to be confident that the Bible you are reading is the one God wanted you to have, that it is *accurate* in all that it says. This has to do with the way the Bible was *transmitted* or copied from the early centuries to the present time.

It is correct to say that the original inspired writings that make up the canon of Scripture are infallible or inerrant. That means they are without error, which is a logical conclusion since God the author is incapable of error. However, it is not correct to say that the Bible translations we use today are completely without error. Only the original manuscripts were absolutely correct. But that doesn't mean the Bible you use is full of errors. To the contrary, your Bible is completely accurate. Does that sound like double-talk? Hang on and we'll explain.

BIBLE TRANSMISSION HAS NOTHING TO DO WITH CHANGING GEARS

As we said before, God inspired forty different authors over a period of fifteen hundred years to write the Bible. With all of the materials and people involved, how did God make sure His Word was transmitted accurately from one person to the next, from one generation to the next, and from one century to the next. Since there were no copy machines, printing presses, or digital scanners back then, there had to be a reliable way to copy the Scriptures so God's Word could be accurately transmitted and preserved.

From the earliest times, Jewish scribes (read as "professional human copiers") had to follow detailed procedures and rules for copying Scripture. These rules helped ensure complete concentration and accuracy. Their meticulous approach set the standard for monks and other scholars who transcribed the Bible through the ages. Here are just three rules for scribes (Jewish scholar Samuel Davidson lists dozens) that will give you some idea as to the painstaking detail involved in copying God's Word:

1. No word or letter or any other mark may be written from memory. The scribe must look directly at the original scroll for every stroke.

2. Between every letter, the space of a hair or thread must intervene.

3. Should a king address him while writing the name of God, the scribe must take no notice of the king until finished.

So how accurate were these transmissions? In *The Unshakable Truth*, a book that I (Sean) wrote with my father, Josh, we point out that there was no way of knowing just how accurate these transmissions were until recently when the Dead Sea Scrolls were discovered in a cave near Qumran in Israel. Prior to this discovery, the oldest complete Hebrew manuscript dated to AD 900. But with the discovery of the Dead Sea Scrolls, scholars had manuscripts dated around 125 BC. Amazingly, they found that nearly eleven hundred years of copying the Old Testament "had produced only excruciatingly minor variations, none of which altered the clear meaning of the text or brought the manuscript's fundamental integrity into question."[13]

What does that mean to you? Where the Old Testament is concerned, you can be confident that what you are reading is the trustworthy, reliable, authoritative, accurate Word of God.

WHAT ABOUT THE NEW TESTAMENT?

As you would expect, the Jewish scribes did not employ their meticulous methods to the New Testament documents. Why should they? The New Testament is all about God's new covenant with Jews and Gentiles alike through Jesus; and since the Jewish leadership did not embrace Christianity, there was no reason to copy the Gospels, the book of Acts, or the letters of the apostles. So what about those twenty-seven New Testament books in our Bibles? How accurate are they?

Scholars have a way of determining if ancient documents are accurate. First, how many copies exist of a document? The more copies there are, the more chance you have to compare the copies and test the accuracy. So concerning the New Testament documents, archaeologists have uncovered more copies of ancient Bible manuscripts than any other document of antiquity. There are more than twenty-five thousand various manuscript fragments of the New Testament Scriptures alone!

MISQUOTING JESUS

Many Bible scholars see this abundance of New Testament manuscript fragments to be a positive factor in determining the accuracy of the texts we have in our Bibles. Other scholars don't see it that way at all. In 2005 textual critic Bart Ehrman wrote a book, *Misquoting Jesus,* in which he claimed that the New Testament we have today cannot be trusted precisely because there are so many manuscript fragments. With so many fingers in the pie, so to speak, the chance of some copiers making mistakes and others making intentional errors is just too high for the New Testament to have any credibility. Specifically, Ehrman calls into question the truthfulness of the very words of Jesus as recorded in the four Gospels. If Ehrman is right, this is a big problem indeed.

Ehrman points out that there are 300,000 to 400,000 textual variants among New Testament manuscripts. A variant occurs any time the manuscripts have alternate wordings. He is troubled by the fact that there are more than twice as many variants as there are words (138,000) in the Greek New Testament. On the surface, Ehrman seems to have a point, but when you look at what those variants are about, a logical explanation emerges. When all the variants are analyzed, it is clear to even the most skeptical scholar that 75 to 80 percent of them involve spelling differences and the use of synonyms. In other words, differences that have nothing to do with the *meaning* of the text. And even in those instances where the meaning may be impacted, there are no discrepancies that jeopardize the central theological truths of the New Testament.

In addition to the abundance of manuscript fragments, there is a second factor that gives the New Testament tremendous credibility. It's a question scholars ask of any ancient text: How close to the date of the original manuscript are the copies? The New Testament shines in this area as well. The earliest manuscript fragment has been dated to within fifty years of the time when the Apostle John wrote the original. The longest time span for manuscript fragments of the complete New Testament from the original date is 225 years. As with the Old Testament, what this abundance of evidence means is that you can trust the New Testament to be accurate in all that it says.

WHAT ABOUT THOSE MIRACLES?

Even with all of this evidence for the reliability, authority, and accuracy of the Bible, there's another lingering issue that bothers a lot of people, especially those who are strongly influenced by a culture that prizes naturalism and denigrates supernaturalism. The issue, of course, is miracles, something the Bible contains in abundance—from the creation act itself to the events that will occur at the end of the world. The birth of Jesus, and the perfect life He lived are miracles, not to mention all of the miracles He performed while on earth. And then there's the resurrection of Jesus Christ, a supernatural act the Bible considers to be the pivotal event in the history of the world and the hinge of the Christian faith. We will deal with the miracles of Jesus, specifically the resurrection, in Chapter 12 under "Signpost 5: The King." But before we leave this chapter on the Bible and whether or not you can believe it, let's spend a moment on miracles. After all, if miracles are part of God's story, then we can't discount them. Either they are real and happened, or the Bible is telling us a series of lies. The Bible can't be true if miracles are not.

Skeptics will often say they object to miracles because they violate the laws of nature. This is a reasonable question, but it misses the point. We've already defined *supernatural* as being *above* nature. When a miracle occurs, there's no violation of nature because miracles don't originate from a material part of the universe.

GODQUEST

They originate from God or from power given by God, who is an immaterial being. So if belief in God is reasonable, then belief in miracles is also reasonable.

We find it interesting that people who believe in God often get hung up on whether or not Jonah could have been swallowed by a whale, or whether God really did speak through a donkey in the book of Numbers. But think about this for a moment. If God can speak the universe into existence by the power of His word, then having Jonah survive three days in the belly of a big fish is no big deal. Let's put some of the miracles that may be troubling you into perspective. If the clues about the existence of God have compelled you to believe that He is a real, then God is fully capable of doing some smaller and perhaps even some unconventional things, such as speaking through a donkey, to get our attention.

But let's say the skeptic is not compelled by the clues and doesn't yet believe in God. Is there another way to approach miracles? We think there is, and with a little thought experiment, we think you will get our point. Here it is: Are there things in our experience that are not natural in the sense that they are not "real"? For example: Your physical person is real, but what about your personhood? Is the concept of your personhood—the qualities that make you unique completely you—a real thing, or is it immaterial? Of course, you know the answer, and so does the skeptic. In fact, you could list five other immaterial things right now that aren't real in the sense that they are not natural or material, but they are real and exist just as surely as a physical object exists.

Following this thought experiment, doesn't it seem likely that there are two kinds of realities in the universe—material and immaterial? It would take a hardened skeptic—or someone in denial of reality—to deny that only material things exist.

WHAT DOES IT MEAN IN YOUR LIFE TO TRUST (OR NOT TRUST) THE BIBLE?

In his book A Reason for God, Tim Keller makes an excellent point about the trustworthiness of the Bible. Many people like you who are on a serious GodQuest often let their disagreements with the Bible stand in the way of their trusting the Bible. For example, someone may disagree with what the Bible says about a particular moral issue (such as the Bible's view on marriage), so they let that disagreement prevent them from trusting the Bible completely. But this is totally backward. You have to begin with trusting the Bible before you can deal with your disagreements. Keller frames this issue in the context of a relationship:

If you don't trust the Bible enough to let it challenge and correct your thinking, how could you ever have a *personal* relationship with God? In any truly personal relationship, the other person has to be able to contradict you. For example, if a wife is not allowed to contradict her husband, they won't have an intimate relationship.[14]

What Keller is saying is that the quality and the depth of your relationship with God stand in direct proportion to your level of trust of His Word. To put it another way, if you don't trust God's Word, you can't have a vital and growing relationship with Him. It would be like a wife saying to a husband, "I trust you, but I don't believe anything you say." Trust is based on belief, even if there's disagreement.

Does this mean you have to agree with everything the Bible says? Of course not. Disagreements will happen, as they do in any relationship. But because you trust God and His Word, you won't let those disagreements stand in the way of your relationship., You will be open to the possibility that as you mature in your understanding of God and His Word, your disagreements will decrease, or at least become less bothersome.

As your GodQuest continues, we have one more chapter before we leave "Signpost 3: The Word." This is a chapter dealing with the way you interpret what you read in the Bible and how the meaning you discover can completely change the way you live.

CHAPTER 9

FINDING YOUR PLACE
IN GOD'S WORD

When we talk about finding your place in God's Word, we mean
this in two ways. First, there's the sense of knowing where you are in
terms of the story of the Bible. The Bible describes God's involvement
in human history from the time He created humanity up to the first
century, when the New Testament was written. Yet, despite the fact
that the Bible's narrative ends in Revelation, the story doesn't stop
there. Even though God hasn't written anything in the past two
thousand years, He is still very involved in human history. And we
know from what the Bible tells us about the future that God is going to
get even more involved when Jesus returns to earth a second time.

So here we are living in the "in between time"—between Jesus'
first appearance on earth when He lived, died, and was resurrected,
and the unknown future time when He will be coming back to earth
in what is known as the Second Coming. How are we supposed to
live? What are we supposed to do? How do we find our place in God's
Word in terms of the flow of history and God's plans for the future?
More specific to your GodQuest, how do you find meaning and a
greater purpose for your life, and is it possible to find that meaning and
purpose in the pages of the Bible? The quick answer to this important
question is simple: It's possible, but only if we fit our lives into God's
story rather than trying to fit God's story into our lives.

IT'S NOT ABOUT YOU

We humans are such a self-centered bunch. We're always looking out for our own best interests, doing things that make us feel better, and basically orienting everything we do around us, including the Bible. But this is backward. If God exists, and the Bible is His Word, and the story of God found in the Bible is true, then we have to realize that our individual stories—as important as they are to us—are nothing apart from the larger story of God. It's only through God that we find ultimate meaning and purpose in this life, and the assurance that there is a life after this life where we will be with God forever.

Knowing and believing this affects how you approach the Bible. If you're the center of the universe, then the Bible will be just one more thing to add to your life, like a self-help book. But if God is the center of the universe, then the Bible becomes something you will want to read, study, and know. By doing this, you can find out what God has said throughout history and what He is saying to you right now so you can orient your life—your habits, your behaviors, your morality, and your beliefs—around the Bible.

Make no mistake. Approaching the Bible this way will put you in direct conflict with the story of the world. You see, the story of the Bible features an immortal, immaterial, eternal, and perfectly just and holy God who has reached out to a fallen humanity through the person and work of Jesus Christ. By contrast, the story of the world is self-focused and human centered. Meaning and fulfillment is found in individual effort and achievement. Salvation isn't needed because we aren't that bad off. The meaning of life hinges on the meaning you bring to it through your own deeds.

Because this way of thinking has so permeated the mindset of humanity, including many Christians, our default setting is to bring all of our interests, passions, and skills to our relationship with God and our reading of the Bible. We are so caught up in what we want to achieve and become that we hope God will bless what we are doing. But again, this is backward. Mike Erre explains the right way of approaching our relationship with God: "We exist to discover how to get on board with God's program, not the other way around. Your life will never be a success if you spend all your time and energy trying to figure out how Christianity can help you."[1]

The same principle applies to reading the Bible. If we want to find ourselves in God's Word, the most important thing we can do is to fit into God's plan. Walt Russell, professor of New Testament at Talbot School of Theology, emphasizes this point: "The focus of both the Old and New Testaments is on the fulfillment of God's plan, not on our individual plans."[2]

If you have found the Bible to be boring and irrelevant to your life, it's likely that you have been trying to fit the grand story of the Bible into your own world. Don't get us wrong. Your world is meaningful and important, and it's important to God. But rather than wondering why God doesn't pay more attention to you, try taking on the attitude of King David, who had every reason to brag about his accomplishments, but instead saw himself correctly in comparison to the great creator God who formed the universe with the power of His Word:

> O LORD, our Lord,
>> how majestic is your name in all the earth!
> You have set your glory in the heavens.
> From the lips of children and infants
>> you have ordained praise because of your enemies,
>> to silence the foe and the avenger.
> When I consider your heavens, the work of your fingers,
>> the moon and the stars,
>> which you have set in place,
>> what is man that you are mindful of him,
>> the son of man that you care for him?
> You made them an little lower than the heavenly beings
>> and crowned him with glory and honor.
> You made him rulers over the works of your hands;
>> you put everything under his feet:
> All flocks and herds,
>> and the beasts of the field,
>> the birds of the air,
>> and the fish in the sea,
>> all that swim in the paths of the seas.
> O LORD, our Lord,
>> how majestic is you name in all the earth! (Psalm 8)

Just like the universe is not about you, The Bible is not about you. The Bible is about God. But it was written by God for you, that you may understand who God is, believe that He wants to have a relationship with you, and trust Him with your life—both now and forever. Furthermore, the Bible was written to show you how to live and to give you hope. This is the message the Apostle Paul delivers to the Christians in Rome:

For everything that was written in the past was written to teach us, so that through the endurance and the encouragement of the Scriptures we might have hope (Romans 15:4).

WHY YOU NEED TO READ AND STUDY THE BIBLE

The second way to find yourself in God's Word is to develop a lifelong habit of reading and studying the Bible. But before you even think about starting this process, there's something you need to know. Reading and studying the Bible isn't like reading and studying an ordinary book, where you go through it once and then, satisfied that you know the contents, put it on the shelf. This is God's Word, and when you connect with it, when you dive into its story and discover how God works in the world, you are quite literally connecting with God. When you read and study the Bible with this in mind, you take what He says from front to back quite seriously.

Because the Bible is "living and active" (Hebrews 4:12), it has the power to influence you—and your life—in a way that other books or readings could not possibly duplicate, simply because no other book has been inspired by God Himself.

We can't see God, and Jesus isn't walking the earth at the present time. But we have the presence of God's "living and active" Word that puts us in touch with God on a personal level. Furthermore, because God exists as a Trinity (God in three persons), we have the Holy Spirit, who is the presence of Christ in each Christian, given by God as a gift and guarantee that God is with us (Ephesians 1:13–14).

Jesus is very clear about this when He explains the purpose of the Holy Spirit in the life of the believer:

> *But when he, the Spirit of truth, comes, he will guide you into all the truth. He will not speak on his own; he will speak only what he hears, and he will tell you what is yet to come. He will bring glory to me by taking from what is mine and making it known to you (John 16:13–14).*

Do you see what's going on here? If you have a relationship with God through Jesus Christ, you also have the Holy Spirit—the Spirit of truth—who will help you understand the truth of God's Word. Because of the Holy Spirit, the Bible comes alive, and when you read it, whether for a few minutes or an hour, it's as if you are hearing God's voice. This doesn't mean the Holy Spirit will do the work of interpreting the Bible for you. But as you are intentional, systematic, and consistent in your Bible reading and study, the Holy Spirit will help you understand and apply God's Word to your life. Walt Russell summarizes the dynamics of what happens when you, as a Christian, read and study the Bible:

> We are not alone as we read the Bible! Jesus Christ manifests Himself to us through the person of the Holy Spirit during the process. As we read, Jesus brings about the changes He wants in our lives through the Holy Spirit driving home the truths from Scripture. Jesus transforms us as our will directs our mind to interact with the thoughts of God's Word while our spirit submits to the person of the Holy Spirit. The Holy Spirit then teaches us "the things freely given to us by God." These things re-form our souls and cause our hearts to burn with renewed love for our God.[3]

As you continue on your GodQuest, what do those words mean to you? Do you believe them? Do you think your mind can literally interact with the thoughts of God's Word? Not only is it possible, but it is what God wants for you. As much as you want to have a relationship with God, He wants it even more. As much as you desire to connect with God on an intimate level, God has an even greater desire to connect with you.

But as we said, the connection doesn't happen automatically. Even with the best of intentions, you will never experience God's Word in this way on a consistent basis unless you first learn the discipline of Bible study. Like anything else in life that's worthwhile, the *benefits* you receive from reading the Bible—not to mention the real life change that goes with it—will be in direct proportion to the effort you put into *understanding* the Bible and then applying it to your life. This is what the Apostle James means when he warns us to "not merely listen to the word, and so deceive yourselves" but to "do what it says" (James 1:22). It's what the Apostle Paul intends to convey when he tells his protégé, Timothy:

> Do your best to present yourself to God as one approved, a workman who does not need to be ashamed and who correctly handles the word of truth (2 Timothy 2:15).

This is huge! God approves when you "correctly handle" His Word. The Greek word for "correctly handle" in this verse is the same word used for drawing a straight line or making a straight cut in a piece of wood. God doesn't want you to half-heartedly attempt to understand His Word. He is pleased when you follow a straight and true path as you read and study the Bible.

Becoming skilled at determining the meaning of what the Bible is saying and how this applies to your life is what is known as *hermeneutics*, which is from the Greek word meaning "to interpret." Whenever you approach the Bible, whether you're reading a few verses in the morning or studying a chapter in preparation for a Bible study, your goal should always be to correctly handle, or interpret, God's Word.

GETTING THE BIG PICTURE

There's no question that the Bible is an incredibly complex book. As we've already stated, it was written over a period of fifteen hundred years by at least forty writers on three continents and in three languages. The history covered by the Bible spans ten to fifteen millennia, and there are a dizzying array of characters and places included in its pages. The Bible is also written in a number of literary genres: history, poetry, prophecy, and biography. Because of its complexity, many people who attempt to study the Bible end up picking a favorite book—maybe the Psalms or the Gospel of John or one of Paul's letters—and study that. Or because they have a hard time understanding much of what the Old Testament has to say, they stay primarily in the New Testament. Or they simply pick and choose those verses they like and skip the ones that are harder to understand.

Certainly there is value in studying any part of the Bible, but "picking and choosing" what you want to read and study based on personal preference will ultimately leave you unsatisfied for a simple reason emphasized by Mike Erre: You will miss the point that the Bible "presents a unified story, the individual pieces of which are best understood in light of the whole."[4]

Okay, so let's assume that in the course of your GodQuest, you have decided to study the Bible in a way that increases your understanding of what God is saying so you can become a skilled interpreter of His Word. Where do you start? Well, the first thing we would suggest is to get the big picture.

A few years ago my wife and I (Stan) visited the Louvre in Paris, the most famous art museum in the world. It's a huge place, with hundreds of thousands of art objects on display in a series of buildings that cover several acres. Most people visit the Louvre the way most people study the Bible. They rush in and make a mad dash past the vast majority of the paintings and sculptures, looking for the most famous ones, such as the *Mona Lisa*—the "John 3:16" of the Louvre. At the end of the day, their mind is a blur and their feet are aching.

Do these mad dashers appreciate what the Louvre has to offer? Probably a little, if for no other reason than they are impressed with how big it is. Do they get anything out of their experience? Perhaps, but not as much as they could if they took a different approach, like my wife and I did.

Before our trip to Paris, we read a book about art history and appreciation. When we got to Paris, we bought a Louvre guidebook to study before we actually went to the museum. Then, on the day we set aside for our Louvre adventure, we each rented one of those audio headphone sets museums offer for a self-guided tour, where docents and experts explain the backgrounds and the meaning of many of the art pieces. We took our time and purposely walked to the areas containing the art we thought would best represent what the Louvre had to offer. At the end of the day, we were a bit weary, but at the same time we felt exhilarated, because the "homework" we had done prior to our visit greatly enhanced our appreciation for the Louvre and its magnificent art.

Think of your own Bible study in those terms. Dashing through the Bible from one famous "Mona Lisa" verse to another without any preparation, plan, or purpose can be exciting and temporarily fulfilling, but it won't give you a lasting appreciation or a useful understanding of the Bible's story and what God is trying to tell you. On the other hand, a deliberate, disciplined, informed approach to Bible study will give you a greater appreciation for, and greater insights into, God's Word. And ultimately that will lead you to a greater appreciation for who God is and what He wants for you.

Remember, there's nothing in the Bible that doesn't have meaning for your life in one way or another. Here, again, is Paul instructing his protégé, the young pastor Timothy, on the way the Bible was written and the power it has in every area of our lives:

> *All Scripture is inspired by God and is useful to teach us what is true and to make us realize what is wrong in our lives. It corrects us when we are wrong and teaches us to do what is right. God uses it to prepare and equip his people to do every good work* (2 Timothy 3:16–17, NLT).

So let's take a look at the various sections of the Bible and see how each one contributes to the overall message of the Bible. There is a definite chronological flow to the story of the Bible, but there are also different parts that require some careful study in order to understand the whole. We'll do this in a survey style that gives you a bird's eye view of each one.

GODQUEST

THE LAW

The first five books of the Bible, sometimes called the Pentateuch (because there are five books) or the Books of Moses (because he wrote them), cover a lot of human history—from creation to the death of Moses. If there's one central theme in these books, it's the Law, epitomized by the Ten Commandments, given to Moses by God on Mt. Sinai. Don't get stuck in a preconceived notion of these famous laws, which have done more to influence the human legal system than any other set of standards, as a mere list of regulations. Essentially, the Law was given by God to His people to show them how to relate to Him. Even more, the Law points to the glaring difference between God's holiness and the sinfulness of humankind.

Even though these five books of the Law contain many familiar stories, it's common for students of the Bible to skip these books because they contain more than six hundred commandments. While that may seem excessive, we can't just shrug off this section of the Bible, mainly because the Law always shows us our need for God's grace. As New Testament scholar Robert Stein points out, "the attempt to keep the commandments perfectly will always fail and can never lead to salvation. Due to our fallen nature and sin, we do not and cannot keep the commandments (Romans 3:1–20)."[5]

God's grace means we aren't held accountable to the Law, but to Jesus Christ, who is "the end of the law so that there may be righteousness for everyone who believes" (Romans 10:4). Here are three principles to remember about the first five books of the Bible as they relate to Jesus:

- *Jesus helps us see the continuing relevance of the principles behind the Law.* When asked to name "the greatest commandment in the Law," Jesus responded by summarizing the entire Law into two commands: "'Love the Lord your God with all your heart and with all your soul and with all your mind.' This is the first and greatest commandment. And the second is like it: 'Love your neighbor as yourself.' All the Law and the Prophets hang on these two commandments" (Matthew 22:37–40). For your GodQuest, those are the most important priorities you can have, and they come from the Law: Love God and love others.

- *The incarnation, message, and atonement of Jesus are best understood in the context of the Law.* The Law came through Moses, and God's unfailing love came through Jesus (John 1:17). The Law could not save us, so God put into effect a different plan to save us (Romans 8:3). Christ rescued us from the curse pronounced by the Law (Galatians 3:13). In other words, Christ has fulfilled the Law through his sinless life and sacrificial death so our salvation is not dependent on perfectly keeping the Law. We are saved by faith in Jesus Christ, not our own efforts.

- *The Law leads to Christ.* It makes us aware of our sin and shows us that we are guilty before God (Romans 3:19–20). It also leads us to Christ as the only one who can justify us before God (Galatians 3:24).

NARRATIVE

The Bible is many things—God's inerrant Word, your guidebook for life, a roadmap for your GodQuest—but at its simplest and most basic level the Bible is a storybook. Of course, within that story are hundreds of plots and subplots told through a literary device called *narrative*, defined as "an account of particular events and characters having a beginning and an end, taking place in specific points in time and location." Because narrative makes up a good chunk of both the Old and New Testaments, it's important to understand how it works in order to be an effective Bible interpreter. In fact, it has been estimated that more than 70 percent of the Bible is narrative.[6] Here are some key points to remember whenever you read narrative:

- Don't let the story become an end in itself. Narrative always points to a bigger story.

- Avoid the tendency to focus on the characters as heroes. God is always the hero.

- Be careful about using narrative as a proof for various points of view.

- Remember that the story does not create the event. The event creates the story.

- Don't pull out more application from the text than is there. Let the story drive your study not the other way around.

- Keep in mind that you are not the original audience for the narrative. Know who the audience is in each case.

After the five books of the Law, the next twelve books are mostly narrative. These books tell the story of God's people from the time they entered the Promised Land (Joshua) to the time they were allowed to return to their homeland after spending many years in captivity (Nehemiah and Esther). As you read these books, appreciate the fact that the Bible is honest in its portrayals of real-life people. You see the good, the bad, and the ugly! Also, keep in mind that although the Bible is a reliable history book, the narrative doesn't cover all of history. Like any reliable storyteller, the authors of these books present particular selections and unique perspectives of events, people, and locations, always pointing to God as the ultimate object.

POETRY

Poetry has been called the purest form of literary expression. Through the ages, poets have expressed majestic—as well as intimate—thoughts about life, love, and heaven, and earth in a way that captures the imagination like nothing else. It's no wonder that the Bible, the greatest piece of literature ever written, should contain some of the most magnificent poetry ever composed. God, who inspired the biblical writers, is the source of all creativity and imagination.

When you read the Psalms, where most of the Bible's poetry is found, it doesn't take long to realize that the imagery of these beautifully evocative words can have a greater impact on your life than any narrative. That's because this poetry reminds us of our relationship to God (Psalm 27), awakens our praise to God (Psalm 66) and stimulates us to have a passion for God (Psalm 23).

WISDOM

The Bible has three books devoted to wisdom—Proverbs, Job, and Ecclesiastes—but there are bits of wisdom in other parts of the Bible as well. Wisdom literature is like poetry in that it uses unique and creative sound and speech, but it takes a step further by connecting wisdom to action. And there's no greater action than obeying God! The verse we cited earlier from the book of James (considered the Proverbs of the New Testament), encapsulates the importance of turning wisdom into obedience: "Do not merely listen to the word, and so deceive yourselves. Do what it says" (James 1:22).

When you read the books of wisdom, think about how God is teaching you to live life skillfully, with your heart open to the Spirit of God so your mind can be engaged with the Word of God.

PROPHECY

During the period of the Old Testament, God spoke to His people through men and women who were chosen by God to communicate His messages. The messengers were called prophets, and their job was to be God's mouthpieces (Hebrews 1:1). While the circumstances of each prophet were different, they all spoke about God's holiness. Whether they were speaking directly to a king or to the people at large, the prophets fearlessly condemned sin and spiritual indifference. As you would expect, they weren't always popular, and they were often ignored.

It's easy to avoid reading the seventeen books of Prophecy in the Old Testament because their messages aren't always easy to understand. You have to work to uncover the historical background, the intended audience, and the core message. But once you learn to skillfully read and interpret Old Testament prophetic literature, you will be richly rewarded.

THE GOSPELS

If all the verses of the Bible were puzzle pieces, then the cover of the puzzle box would be a picture of Jesus. He is what the Bible is all about. Jesus is the predominant theme of the Bible, and there's no better place to learn about Jesus than in the first four books of the New Testament—Matthew, Mark, Luke, and John—commonly known as the Gospels. These four historical biographies were written exclusively about Jesus. The word *gospel* means "good news," and that's exactly what these books and the message of the gospel are all about—that our relationship with God can be restored through Jesus.

Because you will likely spend a lot of time in the Gospels, here are a few things to keep in mind when you read and study these amazing books. In particular, you should note the way they present the life and teachings of Jesus:

- Many of Jesus' sayings and teachings are presented in the Gospels without context. That means the writers didn't always tell you what happened before or after.

- His teachings were circulated in small groups of believers for years without organization. In other words, the writings weren't organized into verses and chapters like we have in our Bibles.

- The sayings of Jesus are interwoven with the stories about Jesus.

- Keep in mind that the writers had *historical* concerns, which led them to report the facts about the life of Jesus. They also had *existential* concerns, which led them to record the teachings of Jesus.

- When quoting the words of Jesus, the Gospel writers used two methods: actual word-for-word quotes, known as *ipsima verba*, and an accurate summary of what Christ said, known as *ipsima vox*. Both of these methods were common and acceptable in the first century.

- The Gospel writers selected their material differently based on their intent and the direction of the Holy Spirit. For example, Matthew wrote his biography primarily for Jews and therefore emphasizes Jesus as the Messiah. Mark wrote his biography for a Roman audience, so there's lots of action and Jesus is always on the move. Luke, a Greek physician, writes with precision for a Greek and non-Jewish audience and he emphasizes the human side of Christ's nature. John's Gospel is very personal and quite different from the other three. John's intent is to prove that Jesus was God.

ACTS

Are you looking for renewal in your life? Do you want a stronger sense of God's presence? Do you want to do something incredibly significant in your life? Then learn all you can about the book of Acts, which tells the story of the beginning, the flourishing, the persecuting, and the scattering of the Church. Because this book is a narrative written by Luke, you may be tempted to see it as a story rather than a set of instructions. But don't miss these incredibly important principles that will prove to be important components of your GodQuest:

- The place of God's Word in the Church and the believer's life.

- The role of the Holy Spirit in the Church and the believer's life.

- The importance of prayer in the Church and the believer's life.

- The need to share the gospel with a lost and dying world.

- The need to reach out to society's outcasts.

LETTERS

After the four Gospels and the book of Acts, the New Testament contains twenty-one books which are really letters, sometimes called the *Epistles*, written to churches or individuals in the first century following the resurrection and ascension of Jesus. These are not biographies of Jesus like the Gospels, nor are they a historical account of the growth of Christianity as found in Acts. The letters were written primarily by Paul, a former persecutor of the Church who was dramatically transformed into the greatest missionary the Church has ever seen.

Paul started many churches in various cities throughout the Mediterranean region on a series of missionary journeys detailed in the book of Acts. To stay in touch with these fledgling churches, Paul wrote letters to them. He used his letters as a way to give them further instructions about God and godly living. As a result, some of these letters are a little like written sermons, which is the meaning of the word *epistle*. When the church received a letter from Paul (or Peter, James, or John), it would be read to the entire congregation.

The letter would then be passed on to another church so all the Christians could benefit from the instruction.

The key to understanding and interpreting these letters is to remember that they were not written to us. It's important to know the original writers and audience, who were on the same wavelength and shared a common understanding of the issues. Pay careful attention to key doctrines, which have formed much of the basis for the way we understand the Gospel and live the Christian life. The doctrines found in the epistles clarify what character and attitudes a follower of Christ should have. Keep in mind that the letters were written primarily to new Christians, so all of the basics of the Christian faith are explained: *sin* (James 1:15), *salvation* (1 Peter 1:18–19), *faith* (Ephesians 2:8-9), the *Holy Spirit* (Romans 8:11), and *Christ's return* (1 Thessalonians 5:1–11).

REVELATION

Reading and studying the book of Revelation takes you to another world. It's like watching the greatest science fiction book ever— only this isn't science and it's not fiction. While we may not fully understand what all the imagery and symbolism mean, we can be sure that the events described in Revelation are very real. Even through we don't know when these events will happen, we can be assured that they will occur because the same God who created the universe and got everything going in the first place has a plan for how it's going to end.

People usually refer to this book as the Revelation of John, and it's true that the Apostle John received the visions while exiled on the Isle of Patmos. But more accurately, this is the Revelation of Jesus Christ. It opens by telling about the Second Coming of Jesus (1:7–8) and then gives us a vision of Jesus (1:9–16) before showing us the power of Jesus (1:17–20). Jesus is God, He is alive, He has power over sin, and He holds the keys to death and the grave.

In a dramatic way, Revelation finishes what Genesis began. "Revelation is a wonderful way to finish the story which began in Genesis," writes Henrietta Mears. "All that was begun in the book of beginnings is consummated in Revelation."[7] In Genesis, sin is born; in Revelation, sin is destroyed. In Genesis, Satan makes his entrance; in Revelation, Satan makes his exit. In Genesis, death comes to humankind; in Revelation, death dies.

SEVEN HABITS OF HIGHLY EFFECTIVE INTERPRETERS

As you begin the process of intentional, systematic, and consistent Bible study, there are a couple of things you should know. First, the Bible is understandable, but some parts are harder to understand than others. The primary "good news" message of the Bible is clear and plain to all, but there are some parts of the Bible that are just plain difficult. The Apostle Peter makes this point when he writes about some of Paul's teaching: "His letters contain some things that are hard to understand, which ignorant and unstable people distort, as they do the other Scriptures, to their own destruction" (2 Peter 3:16).

Kevin DeYoung, a pastor and popular blogger, points out that this verse tells us a couple of things. First, "the hard parts of the Bible still have right and wrong interpretations."[8] We need to be diligent to "correctly handle" God's Word so we aren't caught with wrong interpretations. Second, according the DeYoung, some wrong interpretations can be damaging. Yes, there is room for disagreement among Christians about some issues in the Bible. "We don't have to be lockstep on every debatable matter," DeYoung continues. "But on some issues errant interpretations are not just wrong, they are dead wrong. The false teachers in Peter's midst were twisting the Scriptures to their own destruction."[9]

The bottom line is that it's important to develop skilled Bible study habits. In order to help you know where to start and how to continue being a diligent student of God's Word, here are seven habits of highly skilled Bible interpreters:

1. *Remember that context rules.* Whenever you read a chapter, a verse, or even a word of Scripture, always take it in *context*, which means, "that which goes with the text." Start with this test of

context: Is your interpretation of a particular section of Scripture consistent with the theme, purpose, and structure of the book?

2. *Always seek the full counsel of God's Word.* Don't develop an idea on just one or two isolated verses. R. C. Sproul writes, "What is obscure in one part of Scripture may be made clear in another."[10]

3. *Remember that Scripture will never contradict Scripture.* The Bible never contradicts itself because God is the author and God cannot lie or contradict Himself. If two passages of Scripture seem to be in contradiction, keep digging until you have a fuller understanding.

4. *Don't base your doctrine on an obscure passage of Scripture.* As we said, some verses and passages in the Bible are difficult to understand. Don't build your faith on these. Base your faith on the clear and repeated messages of the Bible. Here's a good phrase to remember: The plain thing is the main thing.

5. *Interpret Scripture literally.* What this means is that you should interpret the Bible *as it is written.* "To interpret the Bible literally is to interpret it as *literature*,"[11] Sproul writes. This means you first have to look at literary form (known as *genre*), such as poetry, prophecy, and narrative.

6. *Look for the author's intended meaning.* It's easy for any student of the Bible to read something and jump to the conclusion, "What does it mean to me?" We need to determine what the author meant to say to the original audience by first asking, "What does it mean?" before we can move on to personal application.

7. *Check your conclusions by using outside sources.* When you read and study a passage, you should always start with your own observations. We're going to illustrate this soon. Get up close and personal with the Bible by directly studying it without the notes in your study Bible or a commentary. Once you've encountered Scripture for yourself, then it's entirely appropriate and useful to consult with a reliable Bible commentary or a skilled Bible teacher.

HOW TO GET STARTED: A CASE STUDY

If you're felling a little overwhelmed at this point, we don't blame you. This chapter has been filled with an enormous amount of information and advice. The last thing we want to do is make the process of Bible study seem unattainable and overly complicated. And we would never want to leave the impression that simply by following certain protocol and procedures, you are suddenly going to understand everything in the Bible. At the same time, we are convinced that your GodQuest and your life will take on new meaning and importance once you decide to become a diligent student of God's Word.

To help you get started, I (Sean) thought it would be helpful to share a recent experience that I had with my students. I wanted to help them overcome the common obstacles to Bible study—not enough time and not enough understanding—so they would see how rewarding it can be to study God's Word. So I decided to try a new approach. Taking cues from my friend Brett Kunkle of Stand to Reason, I took my students on a two-week journey of the book of Ephesians to see how much they could garner from a guided expedition.

Rather than reading from our Bibles, I printed out the entire book of Ephesians with the chapters, verses, and headings removed. Ephesians was written as a letter from Paul to the church at Ephesus and, quite obviously, did not originally contain these divisions. With the divisions gone, the students could see the letter in a much closer form to the original and come to their own conclusions about its structure and meaning. While chapters and verses are helpful in some respects, they often cause us to focus on the particulars and miss the larger point.

The first thing I had my students do was read the entire book in one setting without taking any notes. It took about twenty minutes the first time. This was the first time some of them had ever read an entire book of the Bible straight through. I told them to focus on the big picture of Ephesians and not get lost in the details. Then we briefly discussed the central ideas of Ephesians. I asked them what they learned by reading the book straight through.

GODQUEST

The next day we began class by reading Ephesians again in its entirety. I told them to focus on what is repeated throughout the book so they could pick up on important themes and trends. This time I let them take notes. Afterward, I asked them what they learned about the church at Ephesus just by reading the book. They observed that the people were having trouble with *both* their beliefs and behaviors.

The third day we read it through out loud, popcorn style. Then I asked what they learned by hearing it instead of reading it. I also pressed them to share what big ideas they see in both the structure of Ephesians and the ideas of Ephesians.

The fourth day they read it again silently. Then I put them in groups to work out a summary statement for the whole book. They came back with lengthy sentences strung together, which should have been broken down into three to four separate sentences. But they were starting to get the idea that an entire book of the Bible has a central theme that ties it all together.

The fifth day I had them read the entire book again silently for the last time. Now it took about fifteen minutes rather than twenty minutes. Then they worked again in groups to try to simplify their summaries to one punchy statement. I wrote them on the board, and as a group, we evaluated them. After about twenty minutes we came up with a summary statement for all of Ephesians: *By God's grace and truth, live like Christ in unity.* Those of you familiar with the book of Ephesians will realize rather quickly that they did a great job. The class cheered when we came up with it.

All of this took one week of class, which is five periods of forty-five minutes each. For the second week, I had them work in groups to break the book down into chapters and subchapters and to come up with a heading for each of them. Rather than simply accepting the existing divisions of Ephesians, they came up with their own analysis of the structure of the book. Once they broke the book down into their own divisions, they used the existing chapters and verses to communicate how they believed it should be organized. The outline they came up was very similar to the existing outline in the Bible.

For the last step we took three verses, Ephesians 2:8–10, and analyzed them in-depth. I had them work in groups and come up with at least twenty-five observations of those two verses. Yes, twenty-five observations! We wrote many of their observations on the board and talked about them. The next day I put them in groups again and made them come up with ten more. Here are some of the observations they came up with:

- Good works are the result of salvation, not the cause.

- Part of the reason we were created is to do good works.

- Salvation is a gift from God, not from our efforts.

These observations are simple, but profound. In fact, both Mormonism and Jehovah's Witnesses miss the relationship between works and salvation that these verses so clearly lay out. We talked about this so they would see how critical the details are. This also helped them see how much depth can be found in a single verse. And yet they also realized that individual verses only made sense with an understanding of the whole book. This experience highlights a few key truths about youth and Bible study:

1. Many people want to study the Bible, if they can just have a simple, understandable, practical plan.

2. Dictionaries, commentaries, and Bible atlases are all critical, but understanding of the Bible can be mostly attained by simply reading it with a purposeful plan.

3. Repetition is one of the most important Bible study principles. This is true in two ways. First, reading the same passages continually brings out certain truths we often miss on initial reading. Second, important truths in the Bible are often repeated for emphasis. For example, the word *Jordan* is repeated twenty-four times in Joshua 3–4, because the crossing of the Jordan was a monumental period in the life of Joshua and the Israelites.

4. The best Bible study plan is to start from the big picture and then work down to the details. As I said earlier, *the particulars only make sense in light of the whole.* The chapters and verses in our Bible are helpful, but they predispose us to read the Bible in a

way not intentioned by the original authors. Sometimes it's best to take them out.

The Bible is an understandable book. We don't have to speak Greek or have a doctorate in theology to study the Bible effectively, as helpful as these may be. We just have to be willing to put in a little thought and effort. Are you willing?

SIGNP⊙ST

④

THE QUESTION

WHAT YOU BELIEVE ABOUT
GOD'S GOODNESS DEFINES YOUR
RELATIONSHIP WITH HIM.

In this life, there are times of pain and suffering that can be very difficult to understand and accept. During those times, you can choose to trust God even when you don't understand, or you can turn your back on Him and walk away.

CHAPTER 10

DEALING WITH DOUBT AND QUESTIONS ABOUT GOD

There's a little prayer that children have been reciting before meals for generations. Maybe you were taught this prayer:

God is great, God is good,
Let us thank Him for our food.

Besides the fact that "good" and "food" don't actually rhyme, there may be something else that bothers you about that childlike prayer now that you're grown up and thinking for yourself. You may agree that God is great, but the "good" part may be a bit of a problem for you. It isn't that God isn't good with respect to His *holiness*. But how about God being good with respect to His *goodness*? It's difficult for us to relate to God's perfection, but goodness is another matter. We have a hard time trying to be holy, but we can conceive of being good—if by good we mean decent, fair, and helpful. We all try to live good lives by exhibiting those qualities, and if we're being honest, we like to think that God is doing the same thing. We want Him to be decent, fair, and helpful. Yet when we look around and notice all of the injustice, suffering, and just plain evil in our world, we wonder: How can God be good if there's so much bad?

If this question has caused you to have doubts about God, don't feel guilty. Doubt is a natural part of human existence, and doubt about God and His ways is perfectly natural. So don't worry if you have doubt in the course of your GodQuest. In fact, we would be worried if you didn't have any doubt, because that would likely be an indication that you're not thinking deeply enough about God.

THE BENEFITS OF DOUBT

Fuller Theological Seminary recently conducted a study of young adults who left the church after high school. The researchers came to this conclusion: "The more college students felt they had the opportunity to express their doubt while they were in high school, the higher [their] levels of faith maturity and spiritual maturity."[11]

In this chapter, we're going to struggle with three tough questions about the goodness of God, but first we want to spend some time on doubt. When it comes to God, doubt can be both good and bad. It's a good thing when you doubt or question something you hear or read about God that just doesn't seem right, and when you take it upon yourself to verify the truthfulness of the statement. When the Apostle Paul and his ministry partner came to the region of Berea to do some teaching, the people "received the message with great eagerness." But they had some doubts, so they "examined the Scriptures every day to see if what Paul said was true" (Acts 17:11). Rather than take offense, Paul commended them. Just because someone claims to have the truth doesn't mean they do. Doubt motivates you to sort truth from error.

But doubt can also play a negative role if it keeps you from doing an investigation into the claims of Christianity. If the Bereans had simply said to Paul, "We don't believe you," and then failed to do their due diligence, their doubt would have been counterproductive.

REASONS FOR DOUBTING GOD

Why do you have doubts about God in the first place? We can think of a few reasons. Here are some common doubts in two categories: intellectual and emotional.

GODQUEST

INTELLECTUAL DOUBTS

- *You have doubts because you don't know God.* Very often your doubts about God or something God has said in His Word are there because you don't have enough information or knowledge. You haven't studied enough and you haven't done your due diligence, so you form opinions rather than doing your homework. Doubting something you don't know anything about isn't doubt—it's ignorance.

- *You have doubts because you don't understand God.* You may have knowledge about God, but there are certain things you don't understand, such as how a loving God could allow suffering and evil. This kind of doubt is healthy and can lead to fruitful investigation. You may not get all of your questions answered and all of your doubts resolved, but in the process of discovery you will come to know and understand God better than you did before.

- *You have doubts because you don't believe God.* This was Adam and Eve's problem. They doubted that God's Word was true. The same may be true for you. You may doubt something in God's Word because you don't believe it, or because you don't think it applies to you. Before you can work your way through this kind of doubt, you need to come to grips with the crucial distinction between merely believing *in* God and believing God. In the first case you believe God exists, but in the second you believe what He says is true.

EMOTIONAL DOUBTS

- *You have doubts because you are disillusioned or disappointed.* Sometimes other people let you down (it's inevitable), and you feel deeply hurt or wounded. When this happens, you may choose doubt rather than facing the possibility of being disappointed again. This is perfectly natural, but if you continue to live in the realm of disappointment, you will find yourself going backward in your GodQuest rather than forward.

- *You have doubts because you are disheartened or afraid.* You may have a tendency to focus on your own weakness rather than God's strength. The problems around you may be so great that you doubt God is capable of providing a way out. This kind of doubt comes from an inadequate or incomplete view of God.

- *You have doubts because you are discouraged.* You may be weary from the cares and pressures of life, so you get to a place where you doubt the very one who can help you overcome your problems.

- *You have doubts because you are living immorally.* Let's face it, if we are doing wrong things, we need to justify them intellectually so we aren't living in tension. I (Sean) once had a student come to me with deep questions about intelligent design, the historical Jesus, and the problem of evil. We worked through these issues for weeks. Yet much later he confessed that he was struggling with sexual issues and he'd secretly hoped Christianity was not true so he could pursue that lifestyle wholeheartedly. The bottom line is that our moral state deeply influences our analysis of truth.

OVERCOMING DOUBT

If the issue is a *lack of information* or knowledge, you need to do some study, which is what you are doing by going on a GodQuest. You may not be able to resolve every problem or answer every question, but you will make progress if you persist and gain knowledge about God and your faith. There's more to faith than knowledge, but without knowledge, your faith will be overly dependent on your feelings.

If the issue is a *lack of understanding*, ask God to give you wisdom. Guess what? He will do it (James 1:5). Spiritual understanding is a little different than knowledge in that you don't get it by cracking open a book or doing a search on the Internet. It comes through the Holy Spirit, and that means we have to ask for it (Colossians 1:9).

If the issue is *unbelief*, then you need to ask God for help. Once a man brought his son to Jesus for healing. He wanted so much for Jesus to heal his son, but he struggled to believe it was possible.

"Everything is possible for one who believes," Jesus told him. And the man replied, "I do believe; help me overcome my unbelief!" (Mark 9:23–24).

If the issues are *disillusionment, fear,* or *discouragement,* you may need spiritual refreshment. Often a spiritual retreat or conference can be just what you need when your spiritual gas tank is low. Or you may need to simply ask some stronger and more mature Christians to help you. Whatever you do to bolster your faith, make sure you include the Word of God. As the psalmist David writes, "The law of the LORD is perfect, reviving the soul" (Psalm 19:7).

If the issue is *moral,* you may need to make some decisions to get your life right. Do you need to confess your sins? Is there some behavior you need to stop? The Scriptures tell us, "If we confess our sins, he is faithful and just and will forgive us our sins and purify us from all unrighteousness." (1 John 1:9).

Most of all—and we can't emphasize this enough—ask God for help. He is the ultimate encourager, prayer partner, teacher, and mentor. When you have doubts about God, seek Him all the more. As James writes:

If any of you lacks wisdom, you should ask God, who gives generously to all without finding fault, and it will be given to him (James 1:5).

Okay, it's time to move to three questions about God's goodness.

QUESTION #1:

IF GOD IS REALLY GOOD, WHY IS THERE EVIL AND SUFFERING?

The questions about evil and God are no longer confined to theology. The problem of evil today is philosophical, political, moral, and spiritual. And people are no longer content to focus only on ways we can *stop* evil and suffering, although that remains an important issue. Today the bigger focus is on trying to figure out why God doesn't stop evil and suffering. It's a question everybody is asking—atheists, skeptics, and Christians alike. *New York Times* columnist Ross Douthat provides some context:

> As our lives have grown longer and more comfortable, our sense of outrage at human suffering—its scope, and its apparent randomness—has grown sharper as well. The argument that a good deity couldn't have made the world so rife with cruelty is a staple of atheist polemic, and every natural disaster inspires a round of soul-searching over how to reconcile with God's omnipotence with human anguish.[2]

The "atheist polemic" Douthat references takes the positive attributes of God and uses them to make a case for the nonexistence of God. Here's a classic argument that's been offered by atheists for many years:

An all-powerful God would be able to eliminate evil.

An all-good God would want to eliminate evil.

An all-knowing God would know how to eliminate evil.

But evil exists.

Therefore, God is not all-powerful, all-good, nor all-knowing.

Therefore, the God of Christianity does not exist.

On the surface, that logical sequence sounds rather convincing: Because there's so much evil in the world, God doesn't exist. The problem with this argument is that the first three statements, upon which this argument rises or falls, are fundamentally flawed. Let's take a look at each one to see if it holds water:

First, an all-powerful God would be able to eliminate evil. This statement assumes that God can do anything, but that's a false premise. To say "God is all-powerful" doesn't mean He can do something that violates His character or a defining quality. For example, God can't lie because He is holy. God can't make a mistake because He is perfect. And God can't cease to exist because He is eternal.

Here's something else God can't do: *God cannot make free moral agents and guarantee they always choose right.* This statement is

GODQUEST

part of a relatively recent argument, called the "free will" defense, developed by the philosopher Alvin Plantinga. It goes like this:

A world with moral good is better than a world with no moral good.

Only free agents can do moral good.

Even God cannot create free moral agents who can never go wrong.

Therefore, it is not within God's power to create a world with moral good but no moral evil.

At the heart of this argument is the idea that God cannot create truly free moral agents who do not have the freedom to do wrong. If they didn't have that freedom, they wouldn't be free moral agents. To put it another way, even an all-powerful God "cannot forcibly prevent sin without removing our freedom."[3]

Second, an all-good God would want to eliminate evil. This statement fails to recognize the true definition of good as it relates to God. Goodness is more than kindness. It's more than trying to make people happy. As Wayne Grudem defines it, "The goodness of God is the final standard of good, and all that God is and does is worthy of approval."[4] When God created the universe, He pronounced it "good" at every stage (Genesis 1:31).

This goodness includes God's creation of free moral agents, people who have the freedom to do wrong along with the freedom to do good. And what is the highest good for all free beings? It's love (Matthew 22:36–39, which is impossible without freedom, whether we freely love God or our fellow human beings. Peter Kreeft puts it this way:

Why didn't God create a world without human freedom? Because that would have been a world without humans. Would it have been a place without hate? Yes. A place without suffering? Yes. But it also would have been a world without love, which is the highest value in the universe. That highest good never could have been experienced. Real love—our love of God and our love of each other—must involve a choice. But with the granting of that choice comes the possibility that people would choose instead to hate.[5]

Third, an all-knowing God would know how to eliminate evil. This statement assumes that God doesn't know how to stop evil. Isn't that a bit arrogant of someone to think that they know what God knows or doesn't know? Think about yourself for a moment. Just because you don't do something doesn't mean you don't know *how* to do something. The same principle applies to God. Just because He doesn't eliminate evil doesn't mean He doesn't know how.

GOD IS BEING PATIENT

Is it possible that God, who knows how to eliminate evil, is holding off for our sake? That's exactly what the Apostle Peter says:

> *The Lord is not slow in keeping his promise, as some understand slowness. He is patient with you, not wanting anyone to perish, but everyone to come to repentance* (2 Peter 3:9).

Here's the deal. God knows how to deal with evil, but He is being patient with us. He is choosing not to act on His knowledge of how to destroy evil because He loves us, and He knows that destroying evil would mean destroying us. Best-selling author Joni Eareckson Tada, a quadraplegic who is also fighting cancer, expresses this truth with understanding and eloquence:

> The rule of thumb is that we experience much suffering because we live in a fallen world, and it is groaning under the weight of a heavy curse. If God being good means he has to get rid of sin, it means he would have to get rid of sinners. God is a God of great generosity and great mercy, so he is keeping the execution of suffering. He's not closing the curtain on suffering until there is more time to gather more people into the fold of Christ's fellowship.[6]

Just because God isn't eliminating evil now doesn't mean He never will. At some point in the future, God will deal with evil once and for all. "If we restate the argument to correct this oversight in temporal perspective," write Norm Geisler and Ron Brooks, "it turns out to be an argument that vindicates God."[7] Here's what that argument looks like:

If God is all-good, He *will* defeat evil.

If God is all-powerful, He *can* defeat evil.

Evil is not *yet* defeated.

Therefore, God *can* and *will one day* defeat evil.

Can you live with that future promise? Admittedly, it takes faith because you can't yet see when that will happen. But it will happen. Evil will be defeated. Geisler and Brooks conclude:

There is no question here that if it has not yet happened and God is as we suppose Him to be, that we simply haven't waited long enough. God isn't finished yet. The final chapter has not been written. Apparently God would rather wrestle with our rebellious wills than reign supreme over rocks and trees. Those who want a quicker resolution to the conflict will have to wait.[8]

DOES GOD HAVE A PURPOSE WHEN WE SUFFER?

Believing that God will someday deal with evil doesn't offer much comfort to those who are hurting right now. How do we deal with our own suffering? What purpose could God possibly have in our accidents, medical issues, and the loss of friends and loved ones?

This was exactly the experience of Job, one of the most famous characters in the Old Testament. Job is described as a man who "was blameless and upright" and someone who "feared God and shunned evil" (Job 1:1). And yet within a small window of time Job lost his possessions, children, home, and even his own health. He was in so much pain that he cursed the day he was born. Job demanded his right to a hearing before the Creator of the universe.

To the disappointment of some, God never says *why* He allowed Job to suffer. Instead, He instructs Job about his place in the universe, asking him a series of questions: "Where were you when I laid the earth's foundation? Tell me, if you understand?" (Job 38:4). "Have you ever given orders to the morning, or shown the dawn its place, that it might take the earth by the edges and shake the wicked out of it?" (Job 38:12–13).

If you are familiar with the story of Job, you may have wondered how different the outcome would have been if God had simply told Job why he suffered. After all, that is what Job asked for. But would Job have really cared? If God had given Job a philosophical justification for evil, would he have been satisfied? It's doubtful. Explanations are rarely what we need when we're hurting. What we need is comfort.

This may be *one reason* why God allows us to suffer. Maybe God allows us to go through pain so we will reach out to others in their pain and comfort them. Maybe God allows us to go through evil to soften our hearts and give us a vision to reach a broken and hurting world.

ALL WILL BE WELL

A few years ago I (Stan) joined several others to pray earnestly for a dear friend who had a deadly brain tumor and was about to have surgery. The surgery was performed, and the outlook was grim. We continued to pray, hoping for a miracle, but it was not to be. Within months, our friend passed into eternity, but not before I had a chance to visit him. When I walked into his room, I was shocked at his appearance. Physically, he was deteriorating, but there was a sparkle in his eye. As we talked, I asked if he was disappointed that God had not healed him. "Oh, but God has healed me," my friend replied. "God has healed me in ways you can't imagine. I don't want you to worry about me. God is in control. All will be well."

I didn't know what to say. I didn't understand until my friend explained. "This is how God has healed me. He is using my life to touch others with His love. As long as I live, I want God to use me." In fact, God used my friend to shine on hundreds of people who visited him in the last weeks of his life. God had healed him in the most profound way, in his spirit, and through that healing,

God showed a great many people just how much He cares for us all, especially in the middle of our pain and suffering.

GOD KNOWS WHAT IT'S LIKE TO SUFFER

We may feel like blaming God for our pain, and it's perfectly natural to ask where God is when we suffer. We want to know if God really cares. Yes, God cares, and He showed us how much He cares when He sent Jesus to take on human flesh and become one of us, subjected to every kind of suffering and humiliation that any of us could ever experience.

When we think that God neither cares about us nor identifies with us when we suffer, we cannot forget that Jesus suffered on our behalf. From the beginning of His life on earth, Jesus knew what He had to do: bear the cumulative sin, sickness, evil, disease, and pain of the entire human race. This was the astounding burden Jesus carried. It was His mission, and He knew it (Matthew 16:21).

QUESTION #2:

IF GOD IS REALLY GOOD, WHY DOESN'T HE ACCEPT US FOR WHO WE ARE?

The answer to this question has to do with something most people don't like to hear about: human depravity. The meaning of human depravity is summed up in just a few words by the Apostle Paul in his letter to the first-century church in Rome: "For all have sinned and fall short of the glory of God" (Romans 3:23).

The idea that we are all sinners goes against the dominant idea in our culture that sin and evil are, as R. C. Sproul observes, "something peripheral or tangential to our nature."[9] We think evil resides in other people, not in us. "Basically, it is assumed, people are inherently good."[10]

When Osama bin Laden was killed by U.S. special forces, people across America erupted in joyful celebration. Indeed, there's nothing wrong with rejoicing when "the wicked perish" (Proverbs 11:10). The problem is when we see the evil in others and fail to see the corruption in our own hearts. Sproul provides a good perspective on just how deep the corruption goes, making an important distinction in the process:

> The Bible teaches the total depravity of the human race. Total depravity means radical corruption. We must be careful to note the difference between *total* depravity and utter depravity. To be utterly depraved is to be as wicked as one could possibly be. Hitler was extremely depraved, but he could have been worse than he was. I am a sinner. Yet I could sin more often and more severely than I actually do. I am not utterly depraved, but I am totally depraved. For total depravity means that I and everyone else are depraved or corrupt in the totality of our being. There is no part of us that is left untouched by sin. Our minds, our wills, and our bodies are affected by evil. We speak sinful words, do sinful deeds, have impure thoughts. Our very bodies suffer from the ravages of sin.[11]

Clay Jones, who teaches in the Christian Apologetics program at Biola University, has become an expert in the topic of human depravity. His research into the theology of evil as measured against the reality of evil in our world has led him to a radical conclusion: "We prefer to think that great evil is limited to a few depraved individuals, but that's not true. Large populations commit heinous crimes."[12]

Jones cites example after example of unspeakable atrocities being committed, not just by crazed evil doers, but by many otherwise sane and normal individuals who assisted the megalomaniacs in charge—from Hitler to Stalin to Mao Tse Tung—in torturing and murdering tens of millions of people in the twentieth century alone. And that doesn't even take into account the estimated fifty million unborn babies that have been aborted in the United States since 1973. Jones' startling conclusion is that these unthinkable horrors weren't "inhuman" (as we like to label things that turn our stomachs). "No," writes Jones. "Humans did these things." He continues:

> Humans have an amazing capacity for evil, and for each person who pulled the trigger or scalded the unborn, there are family,

friends, and even majority parties who knew of the slaughter and did nothing to stop it. We cannot argue that unusually depraved people perpetrate these evils. Difficulties may encourage their actions, but otherwise they're just ordinary folk—sons and daughters, brothers and sisters, mothers and fathers.[13]

How Does This Knowledge Help Us?

Clay Jones gives us two possible answers to the condition of human depravity. A third answer summarizes our thoughts as related to the question at hand: *If God is good, why doesn't He accept us for who we are?*

1. *Understanding the depths of human depravity shows us that we are blaming the wrong person for the problem of evil.* We are the ones who do evil, not God. Therefore, it's our problem, not God's. As C. S. Lewis wryly observes, "It is men, not God, who have produced racks, whips, prisons, slavery, guns, bayonets, and bombs; it is by human avarice or human stupidity, not by the churlishness of nature, that we have poverty and overwork."[14]

2. *Understanding the depths of human depravity justifies God's judgment and even hell.* Jones observes that God's judgment seems barbaric if humans are basically good. But once we understand how depraved we are, God's wrath, as C. S. Lewis puts it, appears "inevitable, a mere corollary from God's goodness."[15]

3. *Understanding the depths of human depravity helps us appreciate God's mercy and grace.* If we have the view that human nature is basically good, what need do we have of God's mercy—not giving us what we deserve, which is death (Romans 6:23a)—or God's grace—giving us what we don't deserve, which is life (Romans 6:23b)? Thank goodness, God knows us better than we know ourselves. He knows we are depraved. Our sins are offensive to Him. Even so, God has offered us mercy and grace if we are willing to accept His solution to our sin problem.

GOD'S FINAL SOLUTION

Motivated by His absolute and unconditional love, God's solution to our sin problem is centered in the person and work of Jesus Christ:

> You see, at just the right time, when we were still powerless, Christ died for the ungodly. Very rarely will anyone die for a righteous man, though for a good man someone might possibly dare to die. But God demonstrates his own love for us in this: While we were still sinners, Christ died for us. Since we have now been justified by his blood, how much more shall we be saved from God's wrath through him! (Romans 5:6–9)

The bottom line is that God loves us too much to leave us the way we are. And He has demonstrated that love by providing a way for our sinful natures to be regenerated—literally, made new—by Christ's death and resurrection. But God doesn't stop there. He loves us too much to let us continue to behave according to our sinful natures. If we surrender our lives to His plan to save us from our sins, He will lovingly provide the means and the power for us to live in a manner that pleases Him and benefits others, as long as we live for Him and not for ourselves. The Apostle Paul summarizes this process in a way that we can all understand:

> So I say, walk by the Spirit, and you will not gratify the desires of the sinful nature. For the sinful nature desires what is contrary to the Spirit, and the Spirit what is contrary to the sinful nature. They are in conflict with each other, so that you are not to do whatever you want. But if you are led by the Spirit, you are not under the law. The acts of the sinful nature are obvious: sexual immorality, impurity and debauchery; idolatry and witchcraft; hatred, discord, jealousy, fits of rage, selfish ambition, dissensions, factions and envy; drunkenness, orgies, and the like. I warn you, as I did before, that those who live like this will not inherit the kingdom of God. But the fruit of the Spirit is love, joy, peace, patience, kindness, goodness, faithfulness, gentleness and self-control. Against such things there is no law. Those who belong to Christ Jesus have crucified the sinful nature with its passions and desires (Galatians 5:16–24).

GODQUEST

IF GOD IS REALLY GOOD, HOW COULD HE SEND ANYONE TO HELL?

Not long ago, I (Sean) wrote an article for *Clear Horizon* magazine.[16] Little did I know the thoughts I presented in that piece would have special relevance for this chapter and, I hope, your GodQuest.

THE IDEA OF HELL BOTHERS ME

To think that some of my loved ones could spend eternity in a place where there is "weeping and gnashing of teeth" and eternal torment is deeply troubling, to say the least (Matthew 8:12; Revelation 20:10). The prophet Isaiah painted a particularly graphic picture of hell as a place where the "worm will not die, nor will the fire be quenched" (Isaiah 66:24). Hell is compared to a bottomless pit (Revelation 20:1), an unquenchable fire (Mark 9:43-48), a perpetually burning dump (1 Peter 3:10), and a place of anguish and regret (Luke 16:28).

Given such terrifying images, I can understand why people are troubled by the concept of hell. Despite my emotional reservations, however, I have come to believe, like Jesus, that hell is a very real place that God had good reasons for creating. For that reason, I would like to offer you some *humble* thoughts on why a loving God might allow someone to go to hell. Perhaps I might even help equip you with a good answer for those who argue that a loving God could not allow someone to go to hell. If this issue is troubling you, I hope what I say will help you deal with your own doubts. Even more, as you come to grips with this difficult issue, my prayer is that you will be motivated with a deeper sense of compassion for those who don't have a personal relationship with God.

WHAT IS HELL REALLY LIKE?

Throughout this book we've been talking about having a personal relationship with God. Because that is the highest priority God has for you, it should not surprise you that relational separation from God, characterized by utter agony and despair, is the root of hell. Hell is truly the greatest loss imaginable. To be in hell is to be excluded from the very source of life, goodness, and hope—God Himself. The idea of partying in hell is completely mistaken. Partying implies joy and goodness, but neither of these is experienced in hell. As my friend Dale Fincher says in his book *Living with Questions,* "Hanging out with your friends won't happen in hell because there is joy and goodness in that, and those feelings are only found in God."[17]

So that's it? After all, separation from God doesn't sound all that bad. Whenever my students offer up that question, I often ask them if they would prefer a broken arm or a broken heart. Most prefer the broken arm. Why? Because they realize *emotional* pain can sometimes be even greater than *physical* pain. The Bible uses physical imagery such as flames to help us grasp the horrors of hell. Hell is the worst possible situation that could ever happen to a person. It is the absence of everything that is good.

WHY DOES GOD SEND PEOPLE TO HELL?

The popular question asked in reference to hell is, "How could a loving God send someone to hell?" This question is flawed by its very nature, for God does not "send" anyone to hell. Rather, people *freely* choose to reject God's gift of salvation. God has given people freedom of will, which means some may choose to resist the Holy Spirit forever (Acts 7:51). While God desires that everyone believe in Him (2 Peter 3:9), the sad reality is many people do not want to submit their lives to their Creator.

God gives people permission to live their lives as they please. If they don't want to form a relationship with Him, God won't shackle their freedom. Matthew 23:37 makes it clear that those who reject God do so because they are unwilling to turn to Him. Christ longed to gather the people of Jerusalem together as a hen gathers her chicks under her wings, but they were unwilling to allow themselves to be drawn to Him.

Heaven and hell are not surprise outcomes; God does not draw names out of a hat or roll dice when each person dies. Hell is the natural outcome for people who reject God in this life, just as heaven is the natural outcome for those who embrace Him. Our eternal destiny logically and naturally flows from how we live and operate on earth.

Hell is a punishment for sin, but it is also the natural result of a mind set against God. As C. S. Lewis puts it:

> There are only two kinds of people in the end: those who say to God, "Thy will be done," and those to whom God says, in the end, "Thy will be done." All that are in hell, choose it.[18]

Ironically, heaven would be a living hell for those who do not want to be in God's presence. Since heaven involves continual worship of God, unbelievers who do not find God worthy of praise would find the experience intolerable. This is where God's gift of free will, once again, comes into play. He ultimately gives each person the choice to choose heaven or hell.

IS HELL UNJUST?

One common objection to the justness of hell is that the penalty is disproportionate to the crime. As some might put it, finite wrongs in this life surely do not merit an eternal punishment. One response is simply to admit the logic behind this objection, but realize that those in hell might be punished for eternity nonetheless. How can this be fair?

A second response might state it as actually false that sins committed in this life merit only a temporary penalty. The weight of an offense depends on the nature of the offended. Plants, animals, and humans all warrant different punishments for crimes committed against them. Injury to a human deserves a greater penalty than injury to a cat. Since God is infinite in His knowledge, goodness, and being, any human offense against Him merits an infinite penalty.

This is why the deity of Christ is necessary for human salvation. If Jesus wasn't God, then how could His sacrifice cover all the sins of humankind committed against an infinite God? The answer is very simple: it couldn't. No mere human being can pay an infinite price. The sacrifice required a divine being. This is a stark contrast to the animal sacrifices of the Old Testament, which were only temporary coverings until the death of Christ could wipe away sin for all time (Genesis 3:15; Jeremiah 31:31–34).

DOES GOD SEND CHILDREN TO HELL?

Perhaps one of the most troubling aspects of hell is the prospect that children might populate it. Would God really send a child to hell? Given Jesus' tender affection for children, not to mention the lack of any biblical support that there are children in hell, it's almost inconceivable that this could be the case. Jesus regularly went out of His way to bless children and to lift them up as an example of faith for others to emulate. In Luke 18:16 Jesus permitted the children to come to Him, and He said the kingdom of God belongs to such children. Since God is good, loving, and just, we can trust Him to do the right thing regarding children.

There is a biblical precedent to believe in an "age of accountability," in which children who die go directly to God's presence. Isaiah 7:16 mentions a period before a child is morally accountable to God. It seems likely that people are not held accountable for their sins until they are old enough to embrace either right or wrong. If so, then children who die before this stage go directly to be with God in heaven.

WHY DOESN'T GOD FORCE PEOPLE TO GO TO HEAVEN?

God created human beings to have a meaningful relationship with Him, even though He knew some would reject Him. God doesn't want robots; He desires a relationship with beings who *freely* choose to love Him. Exodus 34:14 describes God as a jealous God. He wants his relationship with you to be personal and unique.

Since God is just, He must punish sin (Habakkuk 1:13). But God is also love (1 John 4:8), so He cannot force people to love Him. Love cannot coerce, or it ceases to be love. Coerced love is a contradiction in terms. God can persuade us and woo us, but he cannot force us to love Him. God's love demands that there be a place such as hell. While it may seem ironic, the presence of hell is due to God's love; it is where persons who do not want to be in His presence can experience complete separation, where God can say to them, "*Thy will be done.*

SIGNPOST

5

THE KING
WHAT YOU BELIEVE ABOUT JESUS' IDENTITY DETERMINES YOUR PATH IN LIFE.

Jesus made claims about His identity unlike any other major religious figure. He didn't just claim to know the truth—He claimed to be the truth—to be God in human flesh! You can either choose to believe Jesus and follow Him, or you can trek out on your own. Which path will you follow?

GODQUEST

CHAPTER 11

THE PERSON OF JESUS

A few years ago, I (Stan) was doing research for a book about science and religion. Part of my research included interviews with a number of well-known scientists to get their view of how the universe came into existence. I traveled to the University of California at Berkeley, home of more than a few Nobel Prize winners in the field of science. I will never forget one interview in particular that caught me off guard, not because of the scientist's view of origins, but because of his question about Jesus Christ.

The credentials of the scientist I talked with were impressive. For starters, he had led a team of astrophysicists who developed the Cosmic Background Explorer (COBE) satellite that measured the heat from the first creation event, otherwise known as the Big Bang. Stephen Hawking called their development "the discovery of the century, if not of all time." As our interview came to a close, I thanked this eminent astrophysicist and was literally on my out the door when he posed a question for me.

"Can you help me with something," he asked "Why is that someone can live a really bad life, and then on his death bed say he believes in Jesus, and he goes to heaven? And why is it that someone else can live a really good life, but die without believing in Jesus, and go to hell? I've never understood."

As I said, the question caught me off guard. It wasn't that it was a spiritual question. We had already talked about whether or not the Big Bang pointed to God, and this scientist said it was obvious there was meaning and purpose to life that went beyond mere physical existence. No, I was surprised at the question because it was about Jesus. Why was this scientist so interested in Jesus, and whether or not belief in Him meant you got into heaven?

HE IS THE MOST INTERESTING MAN IN THE WORLD

Truth is, all kinds of people are curious about Jesus—scientists, artists, entrepreneurs, teachers, social-justice activists, students, religious people, agnostics, even atheists. Because of what He did and who He claimed to be when he lived on earth nearly two thousand years ago, and because of the miracles the Bible says He performed—most of all the miracle of coming back from the dead—Jesus instantly became, and has ever since been, the most interesting man in the world.

Jesus Christ is the centerpiece of human history and the key figure in the religion that bears His name. Yet virtually every other world religion claims Him to some degree or another. Muslims respect Jesus as a prophet and someone who lived a sinless life. Jews call Jesus "one of us," a rabbi who preached love and tolerance. Hindus have a god named Vishnu, who has the qualities of grace and love. Like many people, Hindus may not know Jesus by name, but they long for a God who can love them and relate to them on a personal level, perhaps even live among them.

In fact, isn't that what all people desire? Isn't that what you desire? If God truly exists, if He created the universe and everything in it, including you, and if God made the effort to tell you something about Himself in a remarkable book, wouldn't you like to know Him "up close and personal"?

THE FATHER YOU NEVER KNEW

Suppose you had a father you had never met. You knew he existed and from the day you were born he had cared for you and provided everything you needed. And let's say your father wrote to you on a regular basis, telling you things about him and the other people he knew. And let's say he expressed a desire to one day have a personal relationship with you. Would you not want to meet your father? Of course you would. Not only that, but you would do everything you could to track him down so you could meet him and get to know him better.

Obviously, our point is that if you had such a strong desire to meet and become acquainted with your earthly father, now much more would you be interested in meeting your heavenly Father. There's only one problem. Unlike your earthly father, who is a lot like you, your heavenly Father is very different from you. For one thing, He's God and you're not. Simply put, that means He is infinite, immortal, invisible, all-wise, all-powerful, and perfect. You, on the other hand, are finite, mortal, very visible, kind of smart, sometimes frail, and far from perfect. So how do you relate to God? How do you approach Him?

There was a time when all of humanity had a personal, intimate relationship with God. Okay, humanity was only two people, but the promise was that the relationship with God and His human creation would always be perfect—as long as they obeyed God. But the humans rebelled, breaking the relationship and effectively pitting themselves against the most powerful and most holy being inside and outside the universe.

We can't possibly imagine the awesome power and utter holiness of God. Sinful people approaching almighty God is a little like Dorothy, Scarecrow, Tin Man, and the Cowardly Lion fearfully approaching the Wizard of Oz for the first time, their knees shaking and their hands trembling. Only God isn't Oz. God is real, and He isn't using tricks to scare us.

Approaching God is like coming "to a mountain that can be touched and that is burning with fire; to darkness, gloom and storm;

to a trumpet blast or to such a voice speaking words that those who heard it begged that no further word be spoken to them" (Hebrews 12:18–19). When Moses approach God, the Bible says, "the sight was so terrifying that Moses said, 'I am trembling with fear'" (Hebrews 12:21).

Without this picture of God as incredibly powerful, thoroughly holy, all-knowing and all-consuming, we can't possibly begin to appreciate Jesus. But now that we're here, at this stage in your GodQuest, it's time to introduce Jesus, the answer to the question, "How do you approach God?" He's also the answer to the question, "How can you know God?" Even more, Jesus makes it possible for us to approach and know God without fear. In fact, Jesus was announced to the world with the words, "Do not be afraid" (Luke 2:10).

You might be wondering why we waited until now to talk about Jesus. Why not start with Him? Why did you have to go through four Signposts before you arrived at "Signpost 5: The King"? That's actually a very good question. because it goes to the heart of why God waited so long before sending Jesus into the world. It was all about timing and God's plan to bring fallen humanity back into a personal relationship with Him. And before you can understand how Jesus fits into your GodQuest, you need to know something about Jesus the King.

THE STORY OF THE KING

The crucifixion of Jesus is one of history's best-known stories. People who know anything about the Bible and the life of Christ know that Jesus was crucified by the Romans in response to the Jewish leaders calling for His execution. What you may not know is that there was a "tipping point" on the day of the crucifixion, something that so infuriated the religious leaders that they would demand the execution of Jesus by the Roman state, even though Pontius Pilate, the Roman ruler in Palestine, was unable to find Him guilty.

Of course, there were many things about Jesus that frustrated the religious leaders. His claim to be the Son of God and, therefore, equal to God, made them mad. And Jesus had this habit of calling them hypocrites, something that didn't exactly endear Him to the leaders. But ultimately the claim that precipitated the death of Jesus on a Roman cross was very clear and simple: Jesus came to earth as a king, but not the kind of king the Jews were expecting. He came "to seek and to save what was lost" (Luke 19:10).

In fact Pilate asked Jesus this very pointed question when Jesus stood trial before him on the morning of his crucifixion: "Are you the king of the Jews?" (John 18:33). Jesus affirmed that He was, but He clarified that He wasn't an earthly king. "My kingdom is not of this world," Jesus told Pilate. "So you are a king, then!" Pilate replied. And Jesus answered him:

> "You are right in saying I am a king. In fact, for this reason I was born, and for this I came into the world, to testify to the truth. Everyone on the side of truth listens to me" (John 18:37).

Wow! Talk about coming full circle. You began your GodQuest with a comprehensive look at truth and why it's important to determine what is truly true. And here you have Jesus the King telling the earthly ruler who thinks he holds the fate of Jesus in his hands, "I am the truth." On the night before, in a private dinner with His closest followers, Jesus had declared, "I am the way and the truth and the life. No one comes to the Father except through me" (John 14:6). And now Jesus is telling the world that He is the ultimate truth. And He is a king, but His kingdom is not like Rome's. As New Testament scholar Edwin Blum writes, "It is a kingdom of truth which overshadows all kingdoms."[1] This is bold. This is significant. This is who Jesus is.

Perhaps frustrated that the populace was asking him to condemn to death an innocent man, Pilate offered to release "the King of the Jews." But the people would have none of it. They asked for Barabbas, a common criminal, to be released instead. Pilate decided to have Jesus flogged, a brutal and inhumane procedure, and then summoned Jesus to once again stand before him. Again he tried to let Jesus go, but the Jewish leaders told him that if they released this man whom Pilate called a king, he would be rebelling against Caesar. Finally Pilate relented and told the crowd, "Here is your king!" (John 19:14).

And that was the tipping point. Enraged by this Jesus who claimed to be God and king, the crowd cried out, "Away with him—crucify him!" And so it happened, but not before Pilate, that shrewd and cowardly ruler, had a sign placed above the cross on which Jesus hung. Written in three languages—Hebrew, Latin, and Greek—the sign read, "Jesus of Nazareth, the King of the Jews." The Jews objected, but Pilate insisted the sign remained, saying "What I have written, I have written." Of course, it should not be lost on us that Pilate may have written the words, but "God wanted His Son to die with this proclamation on the cross."[2] Why? The answer can be found in the Garden of Eden.

GOD'S RESCUE PLAN

In the Garden of Eden, the great rebellion of the human race against God occurred, breaking the intimate relationship between God and humanity. But as we saw in Chapter 7, God was not about to give up. When hope had seemingly died, God set into motion His rescue plan for all humankind, a plan centered in Jesus Christ (Ephesians 1:9–10). God's promise of a Savior who would bridge the gap between Himself and sinful humanity was first announced in Genesis 3:15:

> "And I will put enmity between you and the woman, and between your offspring and hers; he will crush your head, and you will strike his heel."

Jesus would be the one who would crush Satan's head at the cross, but it would be thousands of years before that would occur. What happened in the meantime? Throughout the Old Testament, God promised that He would send a king who would establish God's kingdom on earth. This king was referred to as the Messiah. In the New Testament, Jesus is often called "Jesus Christ." *Jesus* is a personal name, meaning "one who saves" (Matthew 1:21), but *Christ* is a title, meaning "Anointed One." This is a title fit for a king. In fact, in the Old Testament, kings were anointed as representatives of God to the people (1 Samuel 24:6).

When hope had seemingly died, God spoke through the prophets with a message full of hope: God would send a Messiah, the anointed King who would be a suffering servant to carry the sorrows of God's people, be a light to the nations, and ultimately restore Israel (Isaiah 49:6; 52:13–53:12). Here are just a few verses in the Old Testament that show how God carefully and with great precision arranged for Jesus the Messiah to be born exactly as the prophets predicted:

- Through the seed of the woman (Genesis 3:15)
- Through the line of Seth (Genesis 4:25)
- Through Noah (Genesis 6–9)
- A descendant of Abraham (Genesis 12:1–3)
- Through Isaac, Jacob, and Judah (Genesis 17:19; 28:14; 49:10)
- Through Boaz, Obed, Jesse, and David (2 Samuel 7:12–13)

Even though God was carefully guiding the royal lineage from which Jesus the King would come, there was a big mystery surrounding the Messiah. Although they knew He was coming because God had promised them, the Jews weren't sure how they would know who He was, and they didn't know when He would arrive. But through the predictions in the Old Testament, the Jews had some very specific clues about this Messiah. Here is a checklist they had from their own prophets:

- *City of birth.* The Messiah was going to be born in the town of Bethlehem (Micah 5:2).
- *Parentage.* He would be a direct descendent of the famous King David (Isaiah 11:1).
- *Distinguishing characteristics.* As strange as it seems, the Messiah would be born to a virgin (Isaiah 7:14).
- *Childhood.* Although born in Bethlehem, He would spend His childhood in Egypt (Hosea 11:1).

- *Notoriety.* He would have a ceremonial entrance into Jerusalem on a donkey (Zechariah 9:9). A rather humble and inauspicious ceremony for a king, don't you think?

- *Death.* The Messiah would die by crucifixion, the method of death reserved for the most heinous criminals (Psalm 22:16).

- *Famous last words.* Even the Messiah's dying words were predicted (Psalm 22:1).

- *Resurrection from the dead.* The Messiah was predicted to come back to life after His death (Psalm 16:9–10).

Over the centuries, as the list of prophecies about the Messiah become longer, the pool of potential candidates got smaller. That doesn't mean there weren't imposter Messiahs. In fact, by the time Jesus was born, there were all kinds of people claiming to be the Anointed One the prophets had spoken about. But there was only one true Messiah, only one king who was qualified, both by His human heritage and also by His divine nature, to be the Savior God promised in the Garden. And only one who fulfilled every one of the prophecies concerning the Messiah King:

- He was born in Bethlehem (Luke 2:4, 6–7).

- He was a descendant of King David (Luke 1:31–33).

- He was born of a virgin (Matthew 1:18, 22–23).

- He was raised in Egypt (Matthew 2:13–21).

- He rode into Jerusalem on a donkey (Matthew 21:1–11).

- He uttered the last words the prophets predicted (Mark 15:34).

- He died on a cross (Matthew 27:32–35)

- He came back to life (John 20–21).

His Own Did Not Accept Him

One of the great mysteries of the Bible is why, after all the anticipation and precise foretelling, the very people King Jesus came to save rejected Him. The quick answer is that the Jews in first-century Palestine were an oppressed people, and there were zealots among them who were calling for a full-blown revolution. If they were to follow a king, he would have to be a king like David, a warrior and a political deliverer. But that wasn't God's plan. God's plan for redemption has never been about saving people from earthly powers and oppression, but about freeing them from the bondage of sin and its effects.

Jesus knew exactly what His mission was about. Once, while in the synagogue on the Sabbath with the religious leaders watching and listening, Jesus read from the scroll of the prophet Isaiah:

> "The Spirit of the Lord is on me, because he has anointed me to preach good news to the poor. He has sent me to proclaim freedom for the prisoners and recovery of sight for the blind, to release the oppressed, to proclaim the year of the Lord's favor." Then he rolled up the scroll, gave it back to the attendant and sat down. The eyes of everyone in the synagogue were fastened on him, and he began by saying to them, "Today this scripture is fulfilled in your hearing" (Luke 4:18–21).

This is Jesus the Christ, Jesus the Messiah, Jesus the King: God in human form, the light of the world who came to rescue and redeem a wrecked and ruined world, so that all who believe in Him would not perish but have eternal life. Jesus is the Good News—the gospel—for a lost and dying world. Eden's gates are once again open. We can be at peace with God through the life, the death, and the resurrection of Jesus Christ.

As predicted by the prophet Isaiah, however, God's people—the descendants of Abraham—did not accept or receive Jesus as their Messiah (Isaiah 53:3). But God's plan to bless all the people of the world through this descendant of Abraham was not thwarted. As John writes in his Gospel:

> He came to that which was his own, but his own did not receive him. Yet to all who received him, to those who believed in his name, he gave the right to become children of God—children born not of natural descent, nor of human decision or a husband's will, but born of God (John 1:11–13).

So rather than a select group of people welcoming Jesus the Messiah King, all people—Jews and Gentiles, slave and free, men and women—can approach God and become His spiritual children through the person and work of Jesus. Does that mean all people have accepted Him for who He is and what He came to do, or is something else going on?

THE JESUS WE WANT

Remember when we talked about the God we want and the God who is? You can apply the same principle to Jesus. There is the Jesus who is (we'll talk about Him in a minute), and there is the Jesus people want—a great teacher, a rabbi who taught love and tolerance, a nonjudgmental religious leader who didn't condemn sinners. This Jesus is more human than divine. In fact, he's not divine at all, but more like the Jesus in Dan Brown's *The Da Vinci Code*, who didn't die but instead got married and raised a family.

And it isn't just writers of popular literature who believe in this kind of Jesus. According to members of the Jesus Seminar, Jesus didn't perform miracles, but was simply a Jewish peasant "spirit person" like Buddha, combining qualities of sage and prophet, who tried to reform Jewish society and was killed for it. Jesus Seminar scholars discount the Gospel of Mark (the first of the four Gospels to be written), asserting that Mark created a myth based on the beliefs of first-century members of the "Christ cult," which reinvented Jesus as a divine being.

The Jesus Seminar even published its own version of the Gospels called The Five Gospels, given that title because it includes the gospel of Thomas along with Matthew, Mark, Luke, and John. The words of Jesus in The Five Gospels are in red (as they are in many Bibles). But as it turns out, less than 20 percent of the sayings traditionally attributed to Jesus are in red. That's because the Jesus Seminar scholars have determined that the other 80 percent aren't authentic.

When you take a composite snapshot of the popular portraits of Jesus based on popular literature, Jesus Seminar scholars, and uninformed people who have never studied the life of Christ and considered the evidence for who He really is, here's what you get:

- Jesus was an itinerant social critic and Jewish philosopher.
- He never claimed to be the Son of God.
- Jesus never claimed to forgive sins.
- He never claimed to be the only way to God.
- The crucifixion of Jesus was an accident.
- His corpse was thrown into a shallow grave, where it rotted away or was eaten by wild animals.

BUT THAT'S NOT MY JESUS!

In the course of your GodQuest, you may look at this list and the motivations behind it and vehemently deny that this is the Jesus you follow. You would be correct to object. No less a scholar than William Lane Craig has written that such a Jesus would never have upset the authorities of His day to the point where they wanted Him dead.[3] Only the Jesus as portrayed in the Bible could have engendered such fierce opposition.

Scholars like Craig are not the only ones who have rejected this revisionist portrait of Jesus. In his book *The Case for the Real Jesus*, investigative reporter Lee Strobel conducted exhaustive interviews with today's top Bible and historical scholars on the attacks against the identity of Christ. The responses he received were overwhelmingly in favor of the four Gospels of the Bible being accurate and trustworthy, with the other phony gospels, such as the gospel of Thomas, being highly suspect. Strobel offers this assessment on Thomas from Craig Evans, a respected scholar who earned his doctorate from Claremont Graduate University, which also produced several members of the Jesus Seminar:

If you are biblically illiterate and don't care about history or what really occurred with Jesus, if you're not interested in the organized church, then Thomas would be interesting. Let's face it: we're in a postmodern era that is interested in oddball, eclectic, in some cases downright spooky aspects of spiritually, and Thomas kind of fits in.[4]

The Jesus Seminar Jesus may not be your Jesus, but what about the Jesus of popular culture? This is the Jesus who caters to our needs, accommodates our desires, and makes us happy rather than uncomfortable. This is the Jesus who doesn't challenge or offend us. As Mike Erre writes in his excellent book The Jesus of Suburbia, this is "the gift shop, swimming pool Jesus who exists to provide us with health, wealth, comfort, and happiness."[5]

This "Jesus of Suburbia" is also politically correct, fitting into whatever political position you happen to hold. Are you a liberally-minded, social-justice Christian? No problem! Jesus can be a social activist, calling you to feed the poor and free the oppressed. Are you someone who favors the values of the religious right? Jesus can fit into your agenda as well, giving you support for your particular moral positions.

There's only one problem with this politically correct Jesus. He doesn't exist! That may be the Jesus we want, but He's the not the Jesus who is. William Lane Craig says it best:

> If you insist on being politically correct, then somehow you have to get Jesus out of the way. For his radical, personal claims to be the unique Son of God, the absolute revelation of God the Father, the sole mediator between God and man, are frankly embarrassing and offensive to the politically correct mindset.[6]

SO WHO IS JESUS?

People who come up with their own ideas as to who Jesus was and what He represents to our culture overlook something very important and very obvious: Jesus wasn't shy about telling people who He was and why He came to earth. The writers of the four Gospels, who were eyewitnesses to or were told about all Jesus said and did, are generous and harmonious in their recording of Jesus' own words and His understanding of why He came to earth.

GODQUEST

JESUS KNEW HIS MISSION

New Testament scholar Scot McKnight lists several places in the Gospels where Jesus responded to comments and criticisms about His life and ministry by saying, "I have come ..."[7] In reading these quotes, it's clear that Jesus knew what his mission was about:

> "Do not think that I have come to abolish the Law or the Prophets; I have not come to abolish them but to fulfill them" (Matthew 5:17).

> "It is not the healthy who need a doctor, but the sick. I have not come to call the righteous, but sinners" (Mark 2:17).

> "Do not suppose that I have come to bring peace to the earth. I did not come to bring peace, but a sword" (Matthew 10:34).

> "The Son of Man came eating and drinking, and they say, 'Here is a glutton and a drunkard, a friend of tax collectors and "sinners."' But wisdom is proved right by her actions" (Matthew 11:19).

> "For even the Son of Man did not come to be served, but to serve, and to give his life as a ransom for many" (Mark 10:45).

> "For the Son of Man came to seek and to save what was lost" (Luke 19:10).

JESUS KNEW WHO HE WAS

Whenever people reduce Jesus to a mere human with great ideas, accommodate Him to whatever is popular in the culture, or take the edge off of Jesus in order to make Him politically correct, they completely miss the real Jesus. And it doesn't take a lot of research or soul-searching to find out who the real Jesus was, mainly because Jesus knew who He was! Again, the four Gospels are a treasure trove of quotes and observations by those who knew Him intimately and recorded His every word and activity. Scot McKnight lists three of the "self-claims" of Jesus that give us clarity on who Jesus was:[8]

- Jesus demanded that others follow Him. Early in his public ministry, Jesus called people to follow Him, and it wasn't something that could be done out of convenience. Jesus asked His disciples to give up their income, leave their homes and friends, and follow Him (Matthew 4:18–22). He criticized those who looked back after they had started to follow Him (Luke 9:61–62). Even more radically, Jesus told His followers that if they loved others, including family, more than Him, they weren't fit for the kingdom of God (Matthew 10:34–36).

- Jesus claimed that if people didn't confess Him before others, they would not be accepted by God. Jesus demanded that His followers show their true colors. Either they would tell the world they believed in Jesus, or make it clear they didn't. Jesus had no room for followers who said one thing and then did another. In fact, Jesus made a deal with His followers: If they acknowledged Him before others, He would acknowledge them before His Father in heaven; but if they disowned Jesus before others, Jesus would disown them before His Father (Matthew 10:32–33).

- Jesus claimed to be the Son of God. In doing so, Jesus wasn't just making a claim to sonship, but to equality. In other words, by claiming to be the Son of God, Jesus claimed to be equal to God in nature, something John records in his Gospel: "I and the Father are one" (John 10:30). No doubt this is why John could write this about Jesus the Word: "In the beginning was the Word, and the Word was with God, and the Word was God" (John 1:1).

There's no denying that these claims of Jesus are unique and radical. Not only do they separate Jesus Christ apart from any other religious figure in history, but they also separate Christianity apart from all other religions. To say that all religions are basically the same is to be ignorant of the radical claims of Jesus. To say that Jesus is just another moral teacher is to be completely oblivious to what Jesus said He was. C. S. Lewis famously said it best in response to those who want a safe, moral, predictable Jesus:

> I am trying here to prevent anyone saying the really foolish thing that people often say about Him: "I am ready to accept Jesus as a great moral teacher, but I don't accept his claim to be God." That is the one thing we must not say. A man who was merely a man and said the sorts of things Jesus said would not be a great moral

teacher. He would either be a lunatic—on the level with the man
who says he is a poached egg—or else he would be the Devil of
Hell. You must make your choice. Either this man was, and is,
the Son of God: or else a madman or something worse. You can
shut Him up for a fool, you can spit at Him and kill Him as a
demon; or you can fall at His feet and call Him Lord and God.
But let us not come with any patronising nonsense about His
being a great human teacher. He has not left that open to us. He
did not intend to.[9]

SHOULD JESUS BE PART OF
YOUR GODQUEST?

This is a question only you can answer, but before you do, you need
to carefully consider the options. You can believe in a Jesus who will
enhance your life and your GodQuest. This is the Jesus you add
to your life: Jesus the great teacher, Jesus the religious genius, and
Jesus the social activist. Or you can believe in and follow the real
Jesus. This is the Jesus who adds you to His life: He invites you to
follow Him and then, once you've taken that step, requires complete
devotion. This is the Jesus who is the answer to the question "How
do you approach God?" This is Jesus the King, who asks that you
follow Him fully and worship Him only.

As you think about this, here's something else to consider. Which
Jesus—the cultural Jesus or King Jesus—has changed history and
inspired His followers to cling to Him with such devotion that they
would rather die than deny Him? Which Jesus intrigues people of
all stripes, including world famous scientists? In the next chapter
we're going to take a look at many different people who knew Jesus
personally, and we're going to see that the life, the death, and the
resurrection of Jesus are more than historical facts; they are the
reason Jesus is worthy of our own radical devotion.

CHAPTER 12

THE UNIQUENESS OF JESUS

Two things about the person and life of Jesus are incontrovertible: He is the most significant figure in history, and He is the most controversial. If you're more comfortable with Jesus as a quiet, gentle man and wise teacher who taught us how to love our neighbors and forgive our enemies, but didn't make any claims to deity, then the significance and popularity of Jesus is easy to understand. As we said in the last chapter, everybody wants a piece of this Jesus. Martha Woodroof, an award-winning broadcast reporter, speaks for many people when she says this about Jesus: "Personally, I admire and wish to admire him, without having any urge to deify him."[1]

What people aren't as interested in is the deified Jesus, the controversial Jesus. This is the Jesus who is, in the words of Mike Erre, "a threat to everything, for he turns all things upside down."[2] And it wasn't just the things Jesus said that were and remain controversial. It was His life. Consider these seven highlights of His life, which are so unique and so outrageous that they continue to spark controversy nearly two thousand years after Jesus lived on the earth:

1. *Jesus was born of a virgin.* The Bible tells us that Mary was a virgin when she became pregnant with Jesus by the Holy Spirit. Therefore, Jesus had parentage that was both human and divine (Matthew 1–2, Luke 1–2). Besides the controversy of a woman becoming pregnant without having sex, there is the rather

extraordinary implication of this act known as the incarnation: God becoming a human being.

2. *Jesus lived a human but perfect life.* Jesus never committed a sin. He never had to ask for forgiveness because, as Paul explains, He "had no sin" (2 Corinthians 5:21). So what's so controversial about this? For starters, Jesus is the only person in history who lived a sinless life. Not even the prophet Mohammed was sinless. The other issue is that just because Jesus didn't sin doesn't mean He wasn't tempted. His God nature didn't make him immune to temptations, but He was able to resist.

3. *Jesus performed miracles.* The Bible reports about thirty-five miracles performed by Jesus during his three-year public ministry. We're going to deal specifically with the topic of miracles later in this chapter, but in the context of controversy, it's enough to point out that the miracles of Jesus were supernatural acts because they cannot be explained within the confines of the natural world, something that makes many people uncomfortable.

4. *Jesus died by crucifixion.* After three years of public ministry, Jesus went to Jerusalem for the last time. Here the real reason for His life was revealed: He came to die. In the week leading up to Jesus' death, great numbers of people began to acknowledge Jesus as the Messiah. Recognizing that the popularity of Jesus was becoming an insurmountable problem, the religious leaders plotted to put Him to death. Jesus threatened their system of rules and regulations. Jesus taught that what was in the heart mattered most, and that a person's relationship with God was more important than any religious ritual—something that should be very important in your GodQuest.

5. *Jesus came back to life from the dead.* Three days after the crucifixion, just as He had predicted, Jesus rose from the dead in what is known as the resurrection. An angel greeted some women who had come to mourn at the tomb that first Easter morning. The stone covering Jesus' grave had been miraculously rolled away. "He is not here; he is risen" the angel said—and it was true. The tomb was empty. Gripping accounts in Luke 24 and John 20

show that Jesus did not just rise from the dead in spirit. He came back to life in bodily form as well.

6. *Jesus ascended into heaven.* Forty days after the resurrection, Jesus went to a hillside with a group of followers. After giving them some instructions, He ascended into the sky until He was out of sight. This is referred to as Christ's "ascension." Even though the disciples seemed surprised at Jesus' disappearance, He was carrying out exactly what He had told them earlier would happen (Acts 1:1–11).

7. *Jesus has promised to return to earth.* Someday Jesus Christ will come to earth a second time. He won't appear as a helpless baby but as a triumphant King. The angels who appeared immediately after Christ's ascension said it this way:

"Men of Galilee," they said, "why do you stand here looking into the sky? This same Jesus, who has been taken from you into heaven, will come back in the same way you have seen him to into heaven" (Acts 1:11).

The controversy about Jesus started immediately after the resurrection. Even though there were more than five hundred eyewitnesses who saw Jesus in the weeks following His death (1 Corinthians 15:6), the critics planted seeds of doubt. He hadn't really died but merely fainted, they said. They questioned His teachings, the miracles, His claim to be God, and His ability to prophesy. Following the ascension of Christ, the followers of Christ did their part to tell the truth about Jesus as they carried out his command to take the good news of His life throughout the world (Acts 1:8). But one by one many were arrested, imprisoned, and put to death for their faith in the one they called Savior and Lord.

And that's the way it's been in the two thousand years since Jesus walked on this planet. His followers have spread the news about Jesus' love and forgiveness as well as the truth that Jesus is God in human form. On the other side, many scholars and those in authority have done their best to discount, discredit, and destroy the message of Jesus as well as deny His divine nature. We're twenty centuries removed from Jesus' actual life on earth, so you would think that the critics and the controversy would die down. But if anything, the criticism has intensified, because Jesus and His teachings and claims continue to impact every area of life.

CAN WE GET A WITNESS?

Whenever there are polarizing opinions and feelings about someone they are usually based on "hear say" and emotion, and it's always a good idea to get the facts. One of the ways to get the facts about any person is to talk to the people who know him or her. The testimony of these "character witnesses" can go a long way in determining whether or not a particular person lived a life of integrity. In other words, did the actions of that person match his or her words?

In the case of Jesus, there is no shortage of character witnesses who can attest to His life and verify whether or not He lived a life that was consistent with what He taught. We know from the Gospels that Jesus was an eloquent and persuasive teacher, who employed a variety of techniques to get His message across:

He frequently spoke in parables, using a common object or experience from daily life to illustrate a spiritual truth (Matthew 13:3–23).

- Sometimes He would use epigrams—short, wise statements sometimes built around a paradox (Matthew 10:39).

- Other times Jesus used object lessons or some nearby item or event to illustrate His point (Luke 21:1–4).

- Often Jesus would ask questions to draw out the opinions of others and to prompt reflective thinking (Mark 8:27, 29).

But what about His own life? Did Jesus really do the things the Bible says He did? Did He actually heal the sick, raise the dead, calm the seas, claim to be God, die on a cross, and come back to life again? How do we know it's all true and not made up? And if it's true, what difference does it make? That's where the character witnesses come into play. They can help us establish a profile for Jesus. If you know anything about Jesus, you know that He knew, interacted with, and had a profound influence on a wide variety of people. Let's look at four different types of people who knew Jesus well.

THE DISCIPLES

The people who knew Jesus best were His disciples (the word *disciple* means "learner" or "follower"). All but one of these twelve handpicked men followed Jesus wholeheartedly. Jesus recruited "the Twelve" after his baptism, at the beginning of His public ministry. For the next three years—up until the time He ascended into heaven—Jesus taught this ragtag group, and gradually they learned.

A complete list of these twelve men can be found in three of the four Gospels (Matthew 10:2–4; Mark 3:16–19; Luke 6:14–16) and in Acts 1:13. Peter, James, and John—who accompanied Jesus at the Transfiguration (Mark 9:2), on the Mount of Olives (Mark 13:3), and in the Garden of Gethsemane (Mark 14:33)—were closer to Jesus than the others. You could say they were in the "inner circle."

One disciple, Judas Iscariot, was the traitor who handed himself over to Satan (John 6:70–71) and betrayed Jesus. However, Judas could not have done this if Jesus had not allowed it (John 13:27). The other seven disciples were Andrew, Philip, Bartholomew, Matthew, Thomas, James (the son of Alphaeus), Thaddeus, and Simon the Zealot. Matthias was added to the group after Judas hanged himself and Jesus ascended into heaven (Act 1:15–26).

These disciples said and wrote things about Jesus that clearly showed they accepted Him, not just as a charismatic leader, but as the person He said He was: the Son of God. Matthew wrote that the name of Jesus is "Immanuel," which means "God with us" (Matthew 1:23). John opened his biography with the statement that "the Word [Jesus] was God" (John 1:1). When Jesus asked Peter, "Who do you say that I am?" Peter answered, "You are the Christ, the Son of the living God" (Matthew 16:1516). And Thomas, who would not believe that Jesus had come back from the dead until he saw Him with his own eyes, uttered these immortal words when he came face to face with the risen Lord: "My Lord and my God!" (John 20:28).

There's no question the disciples knew who Jesus was. They declared their belief and allegiance to Him in their words and their writings, and perhaps most telling of all, these disciples gave up everything to follow Him. Had any one of them detected that Jesus was not who He said He was, they would have abandoned Him. But none of them did. No mere man claiming to be the Messiah could have had such a profound influence on the disciples. Only Jesus could have transformed these ordinary men into bold and persuasive proclaimers who turned the world upside down with the message that Jesus was the only way to be saved (Acts 4:12). If Jesus had not been who He claimed to be—if He had been a fake—the disciples would have deserted Him or buckled under the pressure of persecution. But they didn't.

In the years following the resurrection and ascension of Christ, all but one of the Twelve was executed for believing in Jesus. They believed He was who He said He was, the Savior who came to take away the sins of the world, and they were willing to die for Him.

THE BIOGRAPHERS

Two of Jesus' disciples, Matthew and John, were also biographers of Jesus. Each of the four biographers wrote from a different viewpoint because each one had a different background and each told the story of Jesus to a different audience:

- Matthew, a Jewish tax collector, wrote his Gospel to prove to his fellow Jews that Jesus was the Messiah.

- Mark wrote his biography to the Romans, who had little interest in the Old Testament prophecies. The Roman mind liked to get to the bottom line, so the Gospel of Mark is short and to the point.

- Luke was a physician and probably a Greek, so he wrote to the Greeks and emphasized the human side of Christ's nature.

- Because John was one of the inner circle, his Gospel is much more personal. By the time John wrote his biography, the other three had already been written, so John didn't retell the same details of the life of Jesus. Instead, he chose to focus on seven events and seven sayings of Jesus to prove that He was God.

In his outstanding book *The Case for Christ*, Lee Strobel interviewed a number of scholars on the life of Christ and the validity of His life and story. Regarding the integrity of the biographers of Jesus, Craig Blomberg, one of the world's foremost authorities on the Gospels and their writers, has this to say: "In terms of honesty, in terms of truthfulness, in terms of virtue and morality, these people had a track record that should be envied."[3]

THE OPPOSITION

It's one thing for the friends and biographers of Jesus to talk and write favorably about Him. You would expect that. But what about those who opposed Jesus, such as the religious leaders? Jesus confronted them and warned His disciples to beware of their false teaching (Matthew 16:11–12). He told the Pharisees and Sadducees that they wouldn't get into the kingdom of God because of their hypocrisy (Matthew 23:13). If anyone had reason to discredit Jesus, it was these people. If there had been any doubts that Jesus spoke with authority, or that His followers were exaggerating His claims, the religious leaders would have jumped on the opportunity to expose Him as a fraud. But that never happened.

No one ever contradicted the claims and teachings of Jesus. No one ever successfully argued with Jesus and proved Him wrong. All His enemies could do is silence Jesus by putting Him to death, which only served to validate the prophecies concerning the Messiah and accomplish what Jesus came to do.

And what about the demons, those supernatural beings pledged to follow Satan, who stands supreme in opposition to God? There were plenty of demons around when Jesus walked the earth, and any one of them could have overpowered Jesus if He had not been the Son of God. (Read a story of how some demons beat up a family of charlatans in Acts 19:13–16.) Yet in every single instance when Jesus was confronted by a demon or a swarm of demons, they obeyed

Jesus as one who had authority over them (Mark 1:27), and they recognized Jesus as "the Holy One of God" (Luke 4:34).

THE HISTORIANS

Even though the Bible is the most reliable and trustworthy ancient document ever written, some people want extra-biblical evidence for the existence of Jesus. If they are willing to look, there are more than enough credible historical writings that show Jesus not only existed, but also did the things He said. Edwin Yamauchi, professor emeritus of history at Miami University in Oxford, Ohio, has compiled an impressive list of non-Christian writers who can attest to the reality of Jesus.

The most often quoted writer is Josephus, a Jewish historian who wrote extensively about Jewish history and life. His most famous observation about Jesus is the "Testimonium Flavianum" from *The Antiquities*, a history of the Jews from Adam to the first century. We want you to know that this passage is somewhat controversial. Because Josephus was Jewish, it's unlikely he would have said, "He was the Christ," leading many scholars to believe the passage was tampered with by Christians later on. Still, the essence of what Josephus wrote is genuine:

> About this time there lived Jesus, a wise man, if indeed one ought to call him a man. For he was one who wrought surprising feats and was a teacher of such people as accept the truth gladly. He won over many Jews and many of the Greeks. He was the Christ. When Pilate, upon hearing him accused by men of the highest standing amongst us, had condemned him to be crucified, those who had in the first place some to love him did not give up their affection for him. On the third day he appeared to them restored to life, for the prophets of God had prophesied these and countless other marvelous things about him. And the tribe of the Christians, so called after him, has still to this day not disappeared.[4]

Yamauchi also cites several Roman historians: Suetonius (c. AD
70–c. 160), Tacitus (c. AD 55–c 117), and Pliny the Younger (AD 61
or 61–c. 113), all of whom establish several facts about Jesus and His
followers that are consistent with the New Testament accounts, but
are independent of the New Testament.

WHAT ABOUT THE MIRACLES?

Miracles in the Bible—especially the miracle of the resurrection of
Jesus Christ from the dead—are a problem for many people. To those
who operate within a worldview of naturalism, a miracle is a violation
of natural law (naturalism by definition excludes the supernatural).
They don't believe in miracles of any kind, most of all the resurrection.

The historical records of people seeing Jesus after the resurrection
(1 Corinthians 15:3–8) are meaningless to naturalists, because the
events happened so long ago during a time when people were more
prone to believe myths and fables. Of course, naturalists don't have a
problem believing in the existence of Julius Caesar, probably because
he never performed any miracles.

Deists don't go much for miracles either. Thomas Jefferson
famously removed all the miracles from the New Testament and
published what is known as The Jefferson Bible, or The Life and
Morals of Jesus of Nazareth. His goal was to present Jesus as a
great moral teacher, without the miracles of the resurrection. Even
some theists would rather not bother with any "proofs" for miracles
because they don't consider them convincing. They would rather
accept the miracles and the resurrection of Jesus by faith without any
corroborating evidence.

So what do we do with the miracles in the Bible, particularly the
miracles Jesus did? Can you prove they really happened? And can
we appeal to miracles to argue for the existence of God and Jesus?
We can, but we have to be smart about doing it. According to the
philosopher Doug Geivett, when offering a defense for miracles and
the life of Christ, it's not a good idea to put a lot of weight on just one
kind of evidence (in this case, miracles) for the simple reason that

it's hard to overcome "worldview commitments" people have that exclude supernaturalism.

That's why Geivett offers an approach that may stimulate your own thoughts about miracles and the supernatural. Start with the probability that God—who is supernatural—exists, and then look for anomalies—another word for miracles—that cannot be explained naturalistically, such as the resurrection of Christ. This is not blind probability, but one that is backed up by a lot of evidence, as we indicated in Chapter 6. If you start with the premise that God exists, you can then proceed to the idea that miracles are not only possible, but also exactly what you would expect from a supernatural being. In other words, if God really does exist, and He brought the world into existence from nothing and made life from nonlife, then miracles are child's play for God.

Think about this question: If a supernatural being wanted to reveal Himself to His created beings, would He not do so in the form of miracles, which are by definition supernatural events? When you look at miracles in this way, Geivett writes, they act like a kind of "divine signature, confirming God's actual sponsorship of a particular revelation claim."[5]

What Geivett is saying here is that the miracles of Jesus were more than spectacular occurrences that demonstrated supernatural power. They confirmed that Jesus was God come to earth. He was the Messiah King foretold by the prophets. When Isaiah wrote of the coming Messiah, here's what he said:

> "Be strong and do not fear; your God will come, he will come with vengeance; with divine retribution he will come to save you." Then will the eyes of the blind be opened and the ears of the deaf unstopped. Then will the lame leap like deer, and the mute tongue shout for joy (Isaiah 35:4–6)

Jesus knew this, of course, so He embarked on a campaign to do all of those things and more. Every miracle Jesus did had a purpose. Yes, He had compassion on people. Yes, He wanted to alleviate their suffering. But even more, Jesus wanted to fulfill the Scriptures and prove that He was God in the flesh, able to save humankind spiritually as well as physically.

THE DEITY OF JESUS

Even though the teachings of Jesus about love and salvation are very compelling, it's possible to listen to what Jesus said and put Him on the same level of other great teachers in history. But we can't ignore the miracles of Jesus. Other people in the Bible, such as Elijah and Paul, performed miracles, but Jesus uniquely did the miracles by His own authority and power. His miracles invite us to respond, because they show us that Jesus was no ordinary man. They show us that He was the Son of God, equal to God in every way, whose supernatural power can change us from the inside out.

Jesus knew this, of course. Any claim that Jesus was a miracle worker who didn't know He was God is ignoring the statements Jesus made. Jesus didn't say He was like a god. He said that He was God. When referring to God the Father, Jesus was very straightforward: "I and the Father are one" (John 10:30). As a result, the religious leaders pick up rocks to stone Him, telling Jesus, "We are not stoning you for any good work, but for blasphemy, because you, a mere man, claim to be God" (John 10:33). Jesus was so clear and His life was such a compelling demonstration of His divine nature that nobody around Him failed to capture the message and its implications. John the Baptist recognized the deity of Christ (John 1:29), and the Apostle Paul wrote, "For in Christ all the fullness of the Deity lives in bodily form" (Colossians 2:9). Even His enemies knew exactly what He meant, and they plotted His death because of it (John 5:18).

Besides the miracles that Jesus performed, there was something else Jesus did that only God can do: He forgave sins. One day He was preaching to a standing-room-only crowd when several men lowered their paralyzed friend down through the house's roof, hoping Jesus would heal him. The first thing Jesus did was to tell the man, "Son, your sins are forgiven." Some "teachers of the law" who were in the house knew immediately what this meant. "Why does this fellow talk

like that? He's blaspheming! Who can forgive sins but God alone?"
(Mark 2:1–12)

Besides having supernatural powers, Jesus had supernatural
qualities that only God can possess. Various passages throughout the
New Testament describe Jesus this way:

- Eternal (John 17:5)
- All-knowing (John 16:30
- All-powerful (John 5:19)
- Unchangeable (Hebrews 13:8)
- The Creator of the universe (Colossians 1:16)

THE HUMANITY OF JESUS

Even though Jesus declared Himself to be God and backed it with His
supernatural power, the Bible also describes Jesus Christ as being all
man. Jesus identified His ancestry as human, referring to Himself as
the son of David because He was born into the bloodline of Israel's
famous king.

But the greatest evidence of His humanity is not what He said about
Himself, but what is revealed in His life. When you read about Jesus in
the Gospels, you can see that He had traits that proved His humanity:

- Jesus got hungry (Matthew 4:2)
- He got thirsty (John 19:28)
- Jesus grew weary (John 4:6)
- He experienced human love and compassion (Matthew 9:36)
- Jesus knew what it was like to grieve (John 11:35)

The most significant part of the humanity of Jesus is that He had
a body. Think about it. They couldn't nail a spirit to the cross. Jesus
died a real, physical death on our behalf. It wasn't a symbolic death.
It was as literal a death as we could possibly imagine.

THE DEATH OF JESUS

Why did Jesus have to die? "The central claim of Christianity," writes Robert Bowman, "is that God has acted to restore us to a sound relationship with Him through Jesus Christ. The crucial way in which Jesus does this, according to the New Testament, is by His death on the cross."[6] As sinners alienated from a holy God, we deserve the penalty for sin, which is death (Romans 6:23). Because God is holy and just, He demands a punishment or a penalty for sin, a penalty we aren't capable of paying because we are sinners. The only one who could offer an acceptable payment is Jesus, because only He lived a sinless life. The Bible is clear when it tells us that it was love that caused God to send Jesus to bear our punishment and pay our penalty:

This is love: not that we loved God, but that he loved us and sent his Son as an atoning sacrifice for our sins (1 John 4:10).

The work that Christ did in His life and in His death to earn our salvation is called the atonement. The death of Jesus by crucifixion was the pivotal event that allowed sinful humankind to get back into a right relationship with God. The crucifixion of Jesus wasn't a tragedy. It wasn't a series of events outside of God's control. This is why Jesus is described as "the Lamb that was slain from the creation of the world" (Revelation 13:8). The death of Jesus was the divinely designed plan of God, centered in Jesus Christ on our behalf.

We have talked several times throughout the book about the importance of having a relationship with God. It's essential to your GodQuest, and it would not be possible without the death of Christ. Here's how this works.

The death of Christ was *substitutionary.* Since we can't live up to God's perfect standard, Jesus died instead of us and in our place (Isaiah 53:4–6). Theologian Paul Enns writes that the doctrine of substitution is important "in that through Christ's death the righteous demands of God have been met; it was a legal transaction in which Christ dealt with the sin problem for the human race. He became the substitute for humanity's sin."[7]

- The death of Christ fully satisfied all the righteous demands of God toward the sinner (Romans 3:25). The theological term for this is *propitiation.* God is propitiated—His holiness is vindicated and satisfied by the death of Christ.

- Because we are at odds with God—literally, we are His enemies—we need *reconciliation* so that we can have peace with God. Through His death, Jesus is the great reconciler, or peacemaker, between God and us. He turns us from enemies to friends of God (Romans 5:10–11).

- Finally, through the death of Christ we have *redemption*, from the Greek word that means, "to purchase in the marketplace." In our natural state, we are literally slaves to sin and in bondage to Satan with no way out. God sent Jesus into the world to redeem us— literally, to be a ransom for us (Mark 10:45)—so that we could be set free from sin and Satan (Romans 6:17-18).

From a historical standpoint, the death of Jesus is beyond dispute. Besides the fact that the writers of the New Testament are in full agreement that Jesus actually died, the same extra-biblical sources that affirm His life (such as Josephus and Tacitus) also verify His death. Why is it so important that we know for sure that Jesus died? Because His death means that Jesus is "the only Savior, the only One who can restore us to a relationship with God."[8] Not only that, but if Jesus did not die, then He was never resurrected. And if Jesus were never resurrected, then the Christian faith is useless.

THE RESURRECTION OF JESUS

Our good friend, Craig Hazen, chairman of the Department of Apologetics at Biola University, is fond of saying that the Christian faith hangs on a single thread: Jesus Christ's resurrection from the dead. Seems like a rather risky proposition. Wouldn't it be better to say that the Christian faith hangs on many threads, one of which is the resurrection? Not if you want to be in agreement with the Apostle Paul, who writes, "if Christ has not been raised, your faith is futile; you are still in your sins" (1 Corinthians 15:17). Not only that, but without the resurrection, those who believe in Jesus Christ "are to be pitied more than all men" (1 Corinthians 15:19). Why is Paul so strong in his assessment? Think about it. Without the resurrection of Jesus from the dead, there would be:

- *No Messiah.* The true Messiah must fulfill every single prophecy, including the prophecy that the Messiah would die for the sins of the world (Isaiah 53:7–8) and that God would raise Him from the dead (Psalm 16:9–10).

- *No eternal life.* Jesus didn't just say He would be resurrected. He said we would be resurrected as well (John 11:25–26). If Jesus wasn't raised from the dead, we won't be either, and there's no eternal life.

- *No hope.* People who believe in Jesus as the great moral teacher, but deny His resurrection are, in the words of the Apostle Paul, a bunch of fools. What good is it to follow someone who lied about what He did? There's no point to it, and there's no hope whatsoever that we can have a relationship with God.

So how are you feeling about this "single thread"? Actually, you should be feeling pretty good, because as it turns out, says Dr. Hazen and an impressive array of Bible and historical scholars, it is reasonable to believe the resurrection happened. Here are three "proofs" for the resurrection of Jesus Christ that support what the Bible clearly says.[9]

1. *The proof of the empty tomb.* There's no stronger proof that Jesus rose from the dead than the empty tomb. We know from the Bible and from history that Jesus died. We know that Jesus was buried because a historical character by the name of Joseph of Arimathea put the body of Jesus into his own tomb (Matthew 27:57–60). We know that Joseph had a giant stone rolled in front of the entrance (Matthew 27:60). And we know Pilate sealed the tomb and posted soldiers to guard the tomb at the request of the religious leaders, who were afraid the disciples would steal the body to make it look like Jesus came back from the dead (Matthew 27:62–66).

Given all of this painstaking detail to make sure the dead body of Jesus is safe and secure in a guarded tomb, it stands to reason that if the tomb is empty, Jesus rose from the dead, right? Not so fast.

Ever since the resurrection, people who don't buy into the reality of Jesus as God have disputed the empty tomb. The way they figure it, if you disprove the resurrection by showing that the tomb wasn't really empty—or it was empty for a reason other than the resurrection—then you can discredit Christ and Christianity. We don't disagree. So let's look at the three most popular alternative explanations for the empty tomb and see if they are valid.

Explanation 1: Jesus didn't really die. We've already covered this, so we won't gointo detail here, except to give this theory a name: the "swoon theory." The theory is that Jesus didn't die as a result of his beatings and the torture of the crucifixion, but merely "swooned" and was buried alive. Of course, in order for Jesus to walk out of the tomb on his own power, He would have had to move a gigantic rock and overpower the armed Roman guards. Bottom line: this theory is what's swooning, not Jesus.

Explanation 2: The disciples stole the body. This theory was first proposed by the religious leaders. In fact, they bribed the Roman soldiers assigned to guard the tomb to spread the rumor that the disciples stole the body of Jesus (Matthew 28:12–15). There is a clear reason this theory is weak. Even if the disciples were able to pull off the plan to steal Jesus' body and tell the world Jesus had been resurrected when they knew He wasn't, why would they die for a lie? The noted Anglican minister John Stott writes, " If they had themselves taken the body of Jesus, to preach his resurrection was to spread a known, planned falsehood. They not only preached it; they suffered for it. They were prepared to go to prison, to the flogging port and to death for a fairy tale."[10]

Explanation 3: The disciples were hallucinating. One of the proofs of the empty tomb is that hundreds of people saw the resurrected Christ. Contrary to this, one of the theories proposed by those who don't believe in the resurrection is that the followers of Jesus wanted so much to believe Jesus was alive that they saw something that wasn't there. This theory has two problems. First, the disciples weren't expecting Jesus to rise from the dead. When reports of the resurrection first came to them, they didn't believe it (Mark 16:11). Second, the same hallucination could not possibly occur to hundreds of people in several locations over a period of forty days. If anything, such a consistent report from that many people is a proof for the resurrection, not a refutation.

2. *The proof of hundreds of eyewitnesses.* Jesus clearly wanted people to see Him after His resurrection, and hundreds did. The Bible records

ten different appearances from the time He rose from the dead until His ascension, including one appearance to more than five hundred people (1 Corinthians 15:6). Tim Keller points out the obvious to those who say these eyewitnesses were hallucinating, or that there was a giant "conspiracy theory" in place after Jesus died.

> The size of the groups and the number of the sightings make it virtually impossible to conclude that all these people had hallucinations. Either they must have actually seen Jesus, or hundreds of people must have been part of an elaborate conspiracy that lasted for decades.[11]

3. *The proof of transformed believers.* Perhaps the most convincing proof for the reality of the resurrection can be found in the lives of those throughout history who have believed Jesus is alive—from the actual eyewitnesses in the first century, to those in the centuries since who did not see Jesus personally, but have nonetheless experienced His resurrection power in their own lives. There's no question the resurrection was the centerpiece of the early Christian church. Because they had seen the risen Christ firsthand, they believed and told other people. When the religious leaders tried to stop them, Peter and John replied, "As for us, we cannot help speaking about what we have seen and heard" (Acts 4:20). And that's the way it's been in ever since. People can't help talking about the Jesus. The resurrection is more than a myth, and Jesus is more than a man. The resurrection really happened, and Jesus really is the Messiah King, the living, personal, powerful, unparalleled, unrivaled, unmatched Savior of the world who has been transforming lives for two thousand years.

We have one more chapter under "Signpost 5: The King." What we want to do is focus on belief, specifically belief about Jesus. You see, it's possible to believe all of these things we've explained about Jesus—His life, miracles, death, and resurrection—and still not experience His transforming power. And without that power, according to the Bible, it's impossible to have a personal relationship with God. So follow us to the next step in your GodQuest as we consider this question: Is Jesus one of many paths to God, or is He the only one? The answer will help you determine your own path in life.

CHAPTER 13

THE EXCLUSIVITY OF JESUS

Everybody wants a piece of Jesus, but not everyone is willing to accept Him for who He and the Christian faith say He is: the exclusive and unique way to know God. In fact, this claim of exclusivity by Jesus and the belief system that bears His name is a problem for many people, including some Christians. What about you? As you continue on your GodQuest, you have hung in there with us for a dozen chapters: through the Signposts pointing to truth, God, the Bible, questions about God's goodness, and now Jesus. And even if you're tracking with us on just about every aspect of your journey, this last one may make you a little uncomfortable. At the risk of being a little presumptuous, here's where we think you are right now:

- You agree that truth can be known, and that finding the truth is important to any GodQuest.

- God is more than an idea to you; you accept that He is the Creator of the universe who wants a relationship with you.

- You buy into the reality of the Bible as God's written revelation, inspired by God to show you how to live and how to properly relate to the Author of Scripture and the Author of life.

- Based on the evidence from a variety of sources, you believe that Jesus is God in human form—who by His life, death, and resurrection is the way God has arranged for you to relate to Him personally.

Are we close? You may still be working through some questions and doubts—in fact we hope you are—but there's nothing to prevent you from accepting or continuing with God's plan and path for your ultimate destination.

Except for one little stumbling block. How can it be possible that God has designed only one way for people to relate to Him and ultimately go to heaven? And how can that single path travel through just one person?

Pastor Kevin Shrum, adjunct professor of theology for Union University in Jackson, Tennessee, points out the discomfort that people of all stripes feel when confronted with the statement: Jesus is the only way to God.

> Within the church the issue of exclusivity makes some Christians cringe because they do not want to appear to be narrow-minded, unloving, disengaged, arrogant, parochial, and isolated from culture. Outside the church the claim of the exclusivity of Jesus Christ as the only way to know God comes off as prideful, uninformed, and sophomoric. How can the Christian message claim to be "the" exclusive way to know and experience God in a personal, saving way? What hubris! What spiritual bigotry! And yet, this is the historic claim of Christians.[1]

The reason this is the historic claim of Christians is because this is the historic claim of Jesus Christ. William Lane Craig explains it this way:

> The Christian religion stands or falls with the person of Jesus Christ. Judaism could survive without Moses, Buddhism without Buddha, Islam without Mohammed; but Christianity could not survive without Christ. This is because unlike most other world religions, Christianity is belief in a person, a genuine historical individual—but at the same time a special individual, whom the Church regards as not only human, but divine.[2]

WHY SHOULD YOU BELIEVE JESUS IS THE ONLY WAY TO GOD?

Perhaps you grew up in a church where belief in Jesus as the only way to God was assumed to be true, but you never knew why. Although believing something without knowing why isn't necessarily a healthy thing in the long run, it's perfectly normal. Many of the things Christians believe to be true are *a priori* assumptions. That is to say, they are principles or truths that have been passed down from one generation to another and you believe them without prior study or examination.

Now, just because certain principles are passed down doesn't mean they are true. For example, you may have heard the statement, "God helps those who help themselves," and assumed it comes from the Bible. But it's not there. Go ahead, try to find that verse. You won't be able to find it because it doesn't exist, even though most people think it does. On the other hand, just because something is passed down doesn't mean it's not true. It may just be that you don't know why it's true. The statement, "Jesus is the only way to God,' is one of those truths. You may or may not believe it, but you don't know why.

So let's go on a mini journey of discovery to find out if you can believe this statement. Of course, discovery doesn't necessarily lead to belief. Even if you agree with our conclusion about the exclusivity of Jesus Christ, it will still be up to you to accept or reject it.

The place we're going to go with this is straight to Jesus. And why shouldn't we? If Jesus is who He said He was, then we need to take His words seriously. If Jesus made certain claims about Himself, we need to pay attention. Isn't that what you would want if someone was investigating your life? The opinions and insights of others about you are important, but ultimately the things you say about yourself are the most credible of all—as long as your words and actions are consistent with the perceptions of others about you.

Here are six claims Jesus made about Himself:

1. *Jesus claimed to be the only way to God.* Ever since Jesus walked the earth, critics have disputed this claim, saying Jesus never actually said, "I am the only way to God." Evidently they

overlook this direct statement made by Jesus to His followers on the night He was betrayed: "I am the way and the truth and the life. No one comes to the Father except through me" (John 14:6). Another time, when Jesus was teaching His followers, "He told them, 'This is what is written: The Christ will suffer and rise from the dead on the third day, and repentance for the forgiveness of sins will be preached in his name to all nations, beginning in Jerusalem'" (Luke 24:46–47).

Clearly Jesus saw Himself as the only way to God. If you are a follower of Christ, you don't have to "prove" this claim to exclusivity. Jesus does it for you. "Let Jesus bear the weight of this claim," writes Shrum. "He can handle it."[3]

There's no question the followers of Jesus "got it." Following the most dramatic demonstration of His divine nature—His resurrection from the dead—the disciples became bold proclaimers of this singular message: "Salvation is found in no one else, for there is no other name under heaven given to men by which we must be saved" (Acts 4:12).[4]

2. *Jesus claimed to be God.* We showed you in Chapter 11 that Jesus claimed to be the Son of God, but did Jesus ever say, "I am God"? Again, critics maintain that Jesus never uttered those words, and you know what? They are right. Jesus never actually said the words, "I am God." However, Jesus was so clear about His deity in other statements that it's perfectly reasonable to conclude that Jesus indeedclaimed to be God.

A strong statement came right after His claim to exclusivity on the night He was betrayed. Notice in this conversation how one of His disciples doesn't quite get the meaning of His words, so Jesus repeats His claim to deity in a slightly different way:

> *"If you really knew me, you will know my Father as well. From now on, you do know him and have seen him." Philip said, "Lord, show us the Father and that will be enough for us." Jesus answered: "Don't you know me, Philip, even after I have been among you such a long time? Anyone who has seen me has seen the Father. How can you say, 'Show us the Father'?" (John 14:7–9)*

Those who opposed Jesus certainly understood that Jesus was claiming to be God, both in His words and in His actions. John makes this observation:

> For this reason the Jews tried all the more to kill him; not only was he breaking the Sabbath, but he was even calling God his own Father, making himself equal with God (John 5:18).

And let's be clear on another aspect of Jesus' deity: He didn't become God when He was born. Jesus always has been and always will be God. The Apostle Paul states that Jesus, though equal to God, did not hesitate to take on the form of a human servant so He could die for the sins of humanity and therefore make it possible for us to have a relationship with God:

> Your attitude should be the same as that of Christ Jesus: Who, being in very nature God, did not consider equality with God something to be grasped, but made himself nothing. taking the very nature of a servant, being made in human likeness. And being found in appearance as a man, he humbled himself and became obedient to death—even death on a cross! (Philippians 2:5–8).

3. **Jesus claimed to act and speak with divine authority.** By "authority," we don't mean the kind of authority that people earn because of their position, like a law enforcement official. The divine authority of Jesus is found in His very being; it's part of His nature. Therefore, anything Jesus does or says carries the authority of God. William Lane Craig highlights three examples of Jesus' authority in His engagements with others.[5]

The authority of Jesus is evident in His teaching. Whenever Jesus spoke, whether it was to an individual or to a crowd, the people recognized that He was no ordinary teacher. Matthew made this observation after Jesus gave His "Sermon on the Mount"—

> When Jesus had finished saying these things, the crowds were amazed at his teaching, because he taught as one who had authority, and not as their teachers of the law (Matthew 7:28–29).

Whenever Jesus taught, He didn't rely on the wisdom of others like we do. He often quoted Scripture, but more often than not, Jesus would begin a statement with, "Truly, truly I say to you," something unique that established His authority as God, mainly because only God has that kind of authority. Can you imagine a teacher or a pastor using this approach? Our guess is that you would leave that class or church in a heartbeat, because anyone besides Jesus who talks like that is worthy of deep suspicion.

The authority of Jesus is evident in His power over the spirit world. We covered this in a previous chapter, but it bears repeating here. Once when Jesus cast out a demon, He saw it as a sign of His divine authority, saying, "But if I drive out demons by the finger of God, then the kingdom of God has come to you" (Luke 11:20).

The authority of Jesus is expressed in His claim to forgive sins. Craig points out that one of the reasons Jesus made it a practice to relate to prostitutes, tax collectors, and others despised by Jewish society was that He saw them as redeemable. In Jesus' eyes, no one is too big a sinner to be outside the scope of His forgiveness. Only God is capable of such grace and mercy. Aren't you grateful that this is the God who is the object of your GodQuest?

4. *Jesus claimed to perform miracles.* In fact, not only did Jesus claim to perform miracles, but He actually performed miracles as a direct fulfillment of Messianic prophecy (Matthew 11:4–5 and Isaiah 35:5–6). And these were miracles that were truly supernatural, not some parlor trick or illusion often associated with paranormal activity. Furthermore, Jesus didn't need any outside help. He didn't need any medicine or incantations. By the very power of His word Jesus could make the blind see, the lame walk, and the deaf hear.

Once when a centurion, a high-ranking Roman military official, asked Jesus to heal his servant, a paralyzed man who was suffering, Jesus offered to go to his house to heal the servant, but the centurion believed in the authority of Jesus to heal by the power of His word, no matter where He was. "Lord, I do not deserve to have you come under my roof," the centurion said. "But just say the word, and my servant will be healed" (Matthew 8:8). That's the kind of power and authority Jesus has, then and now. Do you believe that? If so, how does it change the way you live your life?

5. **Jesus claimed that He came to replace religion with Himself.**
Tim Keller argues that most religions except Christianity are
based on the principle that the way to have a relationship with
God is to be a good person. He writes:

Some religions are what you might call nationalistic: You connect
to God, they say, by coming into our people group and taking
on the markers of society membership. Other religions are
spiritualistic: You reach God by working your way through certain
transformations of consciousness. Yet other religions are legalistic:
There's a code of conduct, and if you follow it God will look upon
you with favor. But they all have the same logic: If I perform, if I
obey, I'm accepted. The gospel of Jesus is not only different from
that but diametrically opposed to it: I'm fully accepted in Jesus
Christ, and therefore I obey.[6]

What makes Christianity unique among world religions is that
it is based, not on the work of its followers, but on the work of its
leader. In effect, Jesus says, "The law isn't a bad thing; it's just
impossible to keep. So I'll keep it for you." By living a perfect
life on your behalf, and then dying for you so His perfection can
become your perfection, Jesus does something very significant
for you. He makes it possible for you to obey God out of a heart
of gratitude for what He's done for you rather than a burden of
obligation for what you think you should do for Him. That's how
Jesus replaces religion with Himself, and only He is able to do it.

6. *Jesus claimed to determine people's eternal destiny before
God.* This is clearly stated in the most famous verse in the Bible.
These are the words of Jesus about Himself as the Savior of sinful
humanity: "For God so loved the world that he gave his one and
only Son, that whoever believes in him shall not perish but have
eternal life" (John 3:16). In this and other astonishing statements,
William Lane Craig says, "Jesus is claiming that people will be
judged before him on the basis of their response to Jesus. Think
of it: people's eternal destiny is fixed on their response to Jesus."[7]

There's no question that Jesus had a "radical self-concept."[8] He
thought of Himself as the Son of God and He claimed to be God, both
in His words and His actions. When it comes to your GodQuest and

your desire to have a relationship with God, that leaves you with two choices: You can ignore Jesus as God because you just don't buy it, or you can see Jesus for who He is and deal with Him accordingly. Before we consider how to deal with Jesus, let's take a look at some possible reasons you might have for ignoring Him.

REASONS TO BELIEVE JESUS WASN'T WHO HE SAID HE WAS

In his classic book *Mere Christianity*, C. S. Lewis famously proposed that anyone who made the outrageous claims Jesus did would either be a lunatic, a liar, or Lord.[9] Through the years many Christian philosophers and apologists have expanded on these three possible explanations for the person of Jesus.[10] Here are some thoughts on two of these alternatives to the belief that Jesus is who He says He is, plus one more Lewis didn't include.

Jesus was crazy. This is an option that needs to be considered, and I (Stan) have a personal story to back this up. I used to work in a Christian bookstore, which was a wonderful environment because I was constantly around the world's greatest books, including the Bible, as well as some of the nicest customers in the world. From time to time, however, we ran into customers who were, needless to say, a little unusual. Once a man claiming to be Moses came in to our store and began to talk to himself with his arms outstretched, kind of like Charleton Heston about to part the Red Sea. Another time Elijah popped in to say hello. But the most unusual man to come through our doors was Jesus, or at least a man who claimed to have once been Jesus. He didn't talk to anyone, but simply tried to give away a book he had written based on his experiences as a one-time messiah.

The philosopher Peter Kreeft calls this behavior the "divinity complex." It's a recognized form of psychopathology (a variant is the classic "messiah complex"). Is it possible that Jesus was a victim of such a delusion, thinking Himself to be God when in fact He was a crazy person? Kreeft says it's not possible that Jesus had a divinity complex.

Its character traits are well known: egotism, narcissism, inflexibility, dullness, predictability, inability to understand and love others as they really are and creatively relate to others. In other words, this is the polar opposite of the personality of Jesus! More than any other man in history, Jesus had the three essential virtues every human being needs and wants: wisdom, love and creativity. He wisely and cannily saw into people's hearts, behind their words. He solved unsolvable problems. He also gave totally to others, including His very life…. Lunatics are not wonderful, but Jesus the most wonderful person in history. If that were lunacy, lunacy would be more desirable than sanity. [11]

Jesus was a big fat liar. This is certainly an option worth considering. There have been more than a few influential and charismatic leaders who persuaded a great many people by lying to them. But applying this to Jesus just doesn't work. In fact, no one really believes this theory. Again, we like the way Peter Kreeft puts it:

If, on the other hand, Jesus was a liar, then he had to have been the most clever, cunning, Machiavellian, blasphemously wicked, satanic deceiver the world has ever known, successfully seducing billions into giving up their eternal souls into their hands. If orthodox Christianity is a lie, it is by far the biggest and baddest lie ever told, and Jesus is the biggest and baddest liar.[12]

Jesus was a myth. This is probably the most common alternative viewpoint about Jesus. This theory proposes that Jesus existed, but not as the miracle worker, divine Savior, and exclusive way to God that Christianity believes Him to be. All of those ideas about Jesus were added after His lifetime by His disciples and church leaders who desperately wanted Him to be something He never was.

In order for the life of Jesus to be a myth, the four Gospels would have to be mythology or legends, because it's in those four biographies that the life of Christ—including the miracle of the incarnation, the miracle of the resurrection, and every miracle in between—is depicted in careful detail. Here is where Christ's radical claims are recorded. So in order for the life of Jesus to be a myth, the Gospels would have to be legends rather than historical biographies. But that's just not the case.

First of all, the *timing* of the Gospels was too early for them to be legends. At the latest, the four biographies were written forty to sixty years after the resurrection of Jesus. Tim Keller observes, "This means that the Biblical accounts of Jesus's life were circulating within the lifetimes of hundreds who had been present at the events of his ministry."[13] If the stories were made up, there would have been plenty of people around to challenge their truthfulness, in particular those who opposed Jesus.

Second, the *content* of the Gospels is too counterproductive for them to be fiction. Keller makes several great points here. If the writers of the Gospels were making things up to make Jesus look better than He was, why did they depict the disciples of Jesus as "petty and jealous, almost impossibly slow-witted, and in the end as cowards who either actively or passively failed their master?"[14] Why would the writers make up the crucifixion when it was the way criminals were put to death? Why were women recorded as being the first eyewitnesses of the risen Christ, when the testimony of women in the first century was not admissible as evidence in court? And why was Jesus constantly correcting the disciples for misunderstanding His teachings?

Third, the *style* of the Gospels is not the style of myth, but of real eyewitness description. The kind of detailed descriptions that all four biographies feature were unheard of in fictional writing in the first century. "If the events recorded in the Gospels did not really happen," writes Kreeft, "then these authors invented realistic fantasy nineteen centuries ago."[15]

Fourth, the Gospels are backed up by *archaeology*. We know where Jesus was born, grew up, did many miracles, was arrested, put on trial, crucified, buried, and appeared to many of His followers. The idea that Jesus was a myth is simply dismissed in modern-day Israel because the archaeological evidence is too compelling. Even secular humanist, Jewish, and other non-Christian scholars agree on the archaeology surrounding the life of Jesus.

JESUS WAS REAL

If Jesus wasn't crazy, a liar, or a product of myth, then what was He? The only conclusion is that He was real, and everything He said and everything said and written about Him is true. Not only that, but this reality isn't restricted to the first century, when Jesus walked the earth. The reality of Jesus is just as true today as it ever was. How do we know that? Two reasons. One, the Bible tells us that after He ascended into heaven, He sat down at the right hand of God (Hebrews 1:3). What this means is that Jesus is alive in His bodily form. The second reason we know Jesus is alive because He is alive spiritually in our lives, just as He is alive in every other person on the planet who has invited Him into their lives (Colossians 1:27).

Besides being actively involved in our lives and yours if you have made a commitment to trust Him fully, Jesus is engaged in at least three different activities, all of which concern you. First, Jesus is involved in the most spectacular construction project in the history of the universe. He's preparing heaven … for you (John 14:2). Second, Jesus is praying and pleading for you before God (Hebrews 4:15–16). Third, Jesus is keeping the universe going for you. Paul writes that not only was Jesus involved in the creation of the world, but He is also holding all creation together (Colossians 1:16–17).

WHAT ARE YOU SUPPOSED TO DO WITH JESUS?

Before we talk about what you should do with Jesus, we'd like to share what Jesus can do for you. All of these benefits, of course, are based on the resurrection of Jesus. As we said in the last chapter, if Jesus didn't rise from the dead, then everything we're going to tell is nothing but a lie. However, Jesus did rise, so you can count on Him doing at least three things for you.

Jesus can save you. The very name Jesus means "the Lord saves" (Matthew 1:21). The resurrection gives credibility and power to the name. Because Jesus was raised to life, He can save you by bringing you back into a relationship with God. In fact, believing in the resurrection is the prerequisite to your salvation:

> *If you confess with your mouth, "Jesus is Lord," and believe in your heart that God raised him from the dead, you will be saved (Romans 10:9).*

Jesus can conquer death for you. Not only can Jesus save you and restore you to a right relationship with God, but He can also save you from the eternal consequences of sin, which is death (Romans 6:23). The Apostle Paul puts it in language we can all understand:

> *For if, while we were God's enemies, we were reconciled to him through the death of his Son, how much more, having been reconciled, shall we be saved through his life! (Romans 5:10).*

> *Jesus can give you eternal life. If the only hope we have is in this life, then "we are to be pitied more than all men" (1 Corinthians 15:19). But that's not the way it is. The fact that Jesus rose from the dead guarantees God's promise to save you and to give you eternal life (1 Corinthians 15:20).*

Now, knowing all of this about Jesus is fine, but knowledge can take you only so far. As far as your GodQuest is concerned, knowledge is useful but not transforming. It would be like knowing where the Holy Grail is buried, but stopping your quest short of actually putting your hands on it. It would be like Dorothy knowing the way home, but then refusing to do what it takes to get there. A quest is only fulfilled when you've actually found the object you're seeking, or you've taken the steps necessary to follow through on the mission you're striving to complete. A quest left unfulfilled is not a quest, but a means without an end.

So what do you do with Jesus? In our view and the view of Scripture, the next step after knowing about Jesus is trusting Jesus. This is the step of faith. This is not a step of blind faith into the dark, but an intelligent step into the light. As you have seen throughout your GodQuest, there are compelling reasons to believe God exists, that the Bible is His Word, and that Jesus is God's Son. Faith involves personally trusting God because of what you know is true.

In fact, the faith step is inherent in every great quest. Do you remember when Indiana Jones was navigating through the deadly obstacles that were between him and the Holy Grail? The final test was to find a way to cross a great chasm without any bridge. At least it seemed as if there was no bridge. After checking his notes, Indiana realized he had to take a step of faith in order to cross the chasm, even if he couldn't see the bridge. And so he did, and the bridge, which was always there, held him up as he took the step.

In his outstanding book *The Jesus Creed*, Scot McKnight, a professor of New Testament at North Park Theological Seminary, writes that to "believe" is to have "faith" and to "trust." And ultimately to have faith is to have a relationship with a loving God who calls us to love Him and others. McKnight writes:

> If we describe a disciple as one who believes in Jesus ... we also need to remind ourselves that believing is a dimension of love. This is clear if we substitute "trust" for "believing" or "faith." Love and trust are constant friends. The Jesus Creed calls people to love God (by following Jesus) and to love others. To follow Jesus as an act of love means to trust him.[16]

Much more than an action or an agreement to a set of beliefs, faith is a relationship with Jesus. Do you want a relationship with God? Then believe in Jesus. Put your faith and trust in Him so you can have a relationship with the one who died for you and lives today so you can live your life to the fullest, both now and forever.

YOUR GODQUEST AND PERSONAL DECISION

We've thrown a lot at you in this book, and we applaud you for sticking with it to this point. We have a few more things to say in the final chapter, more like some concluding remarks about this relationship we keep talking about. Before we move on, however, we want to put your mind at ease. If you aren't ready to make any kind of decision to truly believe in Jesus, that's okay. We are the last two people who want to rush an important life decision like that.

From the very beginning, we have been assuming that you embarked on your GodQuest so you could find ultimate meaning in your life. If nothing else, we hope that by this stage you have gone from a conception of God as a disinterested being to a personal Creator who is very interested in your GodQuest—after all, it is about Him—and who wants very much to have a personal relationship with you. In other words, you know what God has done and what God wants, but you may not be ready to commit. That's okay. Making a decision to follow God fully by putting your trust in Christ is an enormous decision. Even more, it is the most important decision you could ever make. So you need to make sure this is what you want to do.

Philosopher Doug Geivett has done a beautiful job of articulating this tension between knowing what to do, but not quite being ready to do it, and he makes a wonderful suggestion:

> For those who are impressed by these considerations but still
> have trouble believing, there is something you can do. You can
> put the Christian view of the world to the test in the laboratory of
> your own life. You can do this by performing a kind of devotional
> experiment. If you think the Christian worldview is reasonable,
> but your heart has not caught up with your mind, you need to
> understand that this is a normal part of spiritual development
> in the Christian way. In countless ways, our passions prevent us
> from taking prudent action. But once we recognize this, we are
> in a better position to be led by rational considerations rather
> than impulse. For many, reluctance to embrace Jesus Christ is
> not an intellectual issue at all, though it is often confused for
> one. Even when all of your favorite intellectual questions have
> been answered and your most precious objections rebutted, it is
> still possible to withhold assent to something as momentous as
> Christianity.[17]

Do you have enough gas in the tank for one more chapter? We thought you did. Let's explore what this relationship—the one you've always longed for—looks like in real life.

THE PATH

THE PATH YOU FOLLOW IN YOUR SPIRITUAL JOURNEY DETERMINES YOUR DESTINATION.

During Jesus' ministry, He extended an invitation—to His disciples and to all of us. It was this: "Come follow me." You can either accept God's offer of salvation by believing in and following Jesus, or you can reject God's offer and live without Him.

SIGNPOST

6

GODQUEST

CHAPTER 14

THE RELATIONSHIP YOU'VE ALWAYS LONGED FOR

There comes a realization near the end of every quest that the hero is going to make it, that the hero's journey is going to be successful. If we're reading about a certain quest or watching it in a movie, we witness the exhilarating moment. It's when Indiana Jones chooses the right cup, when Dorothy clicks the heels of her ruby slippers together three times, and when Frodo finally destroys the ring. In each of these examples and more we could give you, the hero comes to that point when he or she is confronted with the final choice in a series of choices that will put them on the path to their ultimate destination.

In your own journey—your GodQuest—that's where you are. In your life to this point you've made a series of choices that have brought you to where you are, and now you're ready to make another choice that will put you on the path to your ultimate destination.

In one way you are at the end of your GodQuest. You've reached the final Signpost and you're at the end of the book. But in another more important way, you're at the beginning of your GodQuest, because the path you will follow has significant implications for the rest of your life.

RETRACING YOUR JOURNEY

It might be a little late to state the obvious, but we're going to anyway. In the previous five Signposts, we've done our best to show you the features of the belief system called Christianity. You may have wondered why we featured only Christianity and didn't present the other great world religions and belief systems. Good question! We have two answers for you.

First, this isn't a book about world religions. It's a book about finding the truth about God. Second, we chose to feature Christianity because among all world religions, it is completely unique. That doesn't make it necessarily true, but it does make the choice of whether or not to believe it very simple: Either Christianity is true or it's not. As C. S. Lewis says:

> Christianity claims to give an account of *facts*—to tell you what the real universe is like. Its account of the universe may be true, or it may not, and once the question is really before you, then your natural inquisitiveness must make you want to know the answer. If Christianity is untrue, then no honest man will want to believe it, however helpful it might be: if it is true, every honest man will want to believe it, even if it gives him no help at all.[1]

We've attempted to show that Christianity is true by presenting its claims at each Signpost. In fact, let's do a little review of the previous five Signposts in order to summarize how the belief system centered in Christ matches up.

SIGNPOST 1:

THE QUEST

WHAT YOU BELIEVE DETERMINES WHERE YOU GO IN LIFE.

At the heart of this Signpost is the importance of getting to the true story. In other words, getting to the heart of the way things really are. Christianity fits this Signpost best for one simple reason: *Christianity is true to the way the world really is.* What we mean by this is that Christianity gives reasonable explanations for the way things are, and it matches what you know instinctively to be true (Ecclesiastes 3:11). That's because the Christian story contains these basic components:

- God exists and is the Creator of the universe.
- God has revealed Himself through His world and His Word.
- God has revealed Himself most fully through Jesus Christ, who is God in human form.
- Jesus lived a perfect life, died and came back to life so that we could have eternal life by believing in Him.

There are many who would deny the Christian story, but in doing so they are simply suppressing the truth, "since what may be known about God is plain to them, because God has made it plain to them" (Romans 1:19). What God has made plain is that He wants a relationship with you, and He has made it possible through Jesus Christ. As you decide what path to follow the rest of your life, pay careful attention to this instinctive knowledge, backed by evidence from our world, the Bible, and the life of Jesus Himself.

SIGNPOST 2:

THE BEGINNING

WHAT YOU BELIEVE ABOUT CREATION DETERMINES
HOW YOU VIEW YOURSELF AND LIFE.

At this signpost we argued from reason, from the real world, and from Scripture for the existence of a God who is both near to us and apart from us and our world. Christianity fits this Signpost because *Christianity is true in what it says about God.* How can we say this? Because the Bible begins with the assumption that the universe had a beginning that was caused by a self-existent, necessary being who by definition must be:

- Independent of the universe
- All-powerful
- Supremely intelligent
- Infinite

- Timeless
- Personal

Christianity is unique in that it describes God in just these terms in a book written centuries before scientists developed a profile for the necessary being. Other religions and belief systems may describe God by using one or more of these descriptions, but some of their accepted beliefs about the nature of God contradict other descriptions. For example, pantheistic religions, such as Hinduism, view God as being one with the universe, not independent of it. Therefore, they are left without an explanation for the creation of the universe. Deism doesn't allow for a purposeful, involved God.

Christianity is also unique among world religions and belief systems in that it portrays God in ways that are consistent with natural revelation. For example, the evidence for an intelligent designer points to the kind of all-knowing, all-powerful, purposeful creator portrayed in the Bible:

The heavens declare the glory of God;
the skies proclaim the work of his hands.

Day after day they pour forth speech;
night after night they reveal knowledge (Psalm 19:1–2).

Again, it's possible to deny the truth about God, but denial is merely a suppression of the truth known by every person. "For since the creation of the world God's invisible qualities—his eternal power and divine nature—have been clearly seen, being understood from what has been made, so that men are without excuse" (Romans 1:20).

SIGNPOST 3:
THE WORD

WHAT YOU BELIEVE ABOUT THE BIBLE DETERMINES HOW YOU LIVE YOUR LIFE.

Here we explored the story of God as told in His personal written revelation, the Bible. We showed that you can believe the Bible because it is rooted in a real story containing real events, people, and places. If the Bible were full of myths, contradictions, and mistakes, you couldn't trust it, and you couldn't trust God, because the Bible comes from God. But you can trust the Bible, not just because it comes from God, but also because its claims are rooted in objective knowledge, not subjective feelings. Craig Hazen puts it this way:

> What I mean by this is that these claims are such that any thinking person can examine the evidence and reasonably determine whether the claims are historically accurate or justified. I think this is one of the primary reasons a thoughtful person sorting through the various religious traditions would obviously start with Christianity. Christianity is unique in that it actually *invites* people to investigate its claims about God, humankind, the universe, and the meaning of life.[2]

For thoughtful people who want to make sure their beliefs are linked to historic, verifiable facts, Christianity as presented in the Word of God stands apart because *Christianity is testable.*

SIGNPOST 4:
THE QUESTION

WHAT YOU BELIEVE ABOUT GOD'S GOODNESS DEFINES YOUR RELATIONSHIP WITH HIM.

As we passed this Signpost, we approached some of the most troubling questions about God and the nature of suffering and evil. We didn't want to dodge these pressing questions because Christianity doesn't dodge them. In fact, *Christianity is unique in that it has an answer to the universal problem of suffering and evil.* According to Hazen, other world religions and belief systems struggle to find a satisfactory answer to the problem of evil. The Eastern religions (Hinduism and Buddhism are the most popular) simply say that evil and suffering are illusions and will fade away as the practitioners of these belief systems gain enlightenment. Atheism makes little or no attempt to explain why there is good and evil in the first place. Where does morality come from if there is no God?

Christianity doesn't minimize evil and suffering. It admits evil exists and doesn't gloss over the tragedy of human suffering. But rather than leaving us with no hope, the Christian story shows us that God, while not necessarily explaining *why* evil exists, has provided a solution that is unique among world religions. Tim Keller explains:

> In no way is the gospel story sentimental or escapist. Indeed, the gospel takes evil and loss with utmost seriousness, because it says that we cannot save ourselves. Nothing short of the death of the very Son of God can save us. But the "happy ending" of the historical resurrection is so enormous that it swallows up even the sorrow of the Cross. It is so great that those who believe it can henceforth fully face the depth of sorrow and brokenness in life.[3]

Christianity alone provides an answer to evil and suffering found in the person and work of Jesus Christ, who knows what it's like to suffer and die. Through His suffering, death, and resurrection, Jesus assures us that our present troubles "are achieving for us an eternal glory that far outweighs them all" (2 Corinthians 4:17).

SIGNPOST 5:

THE KING

WHAT YOU BELIEVE ABOUT JESUS' IDENTITY DETERMINES YOUR PATH IN LIFE.

We made the point in this Signpost that everybody wants a piece of Jesus, including most world religions. As Craig Hazen, an expert in world religions, points out, "Jesus is without a doubt the closest thing the world has to a universal religious figure." Yet, unlike all the other religions and belief systems in the world, *Christianity alone has Jesus at the center.*

The common belief that all religions are basically the same breaks down at this very point. Stephen Prothero, professor of religion at Boston University and the author of the book, *God Is Not One,* makes the observation that all religions begin with the premise that "something is wrong with the world," but they tell very different stories about what can be done about it.

> Religious folk worldwide agree that something has gone wrong. They part company, however, when it comes to stating just what has gone wrong, and they diverge sharply when they move from diagnosing the human problem to prescribing how to solve it. Christians see sin as the problem, and salvation from sin as the religious goal.[4]

When it comes to salvation from sin, the Bible is very clear where this comes from: Jesus Christ (Acts 4:12). Therefore, a Christian is not one who simply believes that God exists. A Christian is someone who accepts Jesus and His claims, which can be summarized as follows:

- *He is God in human form.* Jesus didn't say He was *like* a god; He said He *was* God (John 10:30). Ever since Jesus walked the earth, His followers have understood this without equivocation. The Apostle Paul speaks for two thousand years of Christian tradition when he states, "For in Christ all the fullness of the Deity lives in bodily form" (Colossians 2:9). "Jesus is God" is the foundational premise of Christianity.

- *He rose from the dead and is alive today.* No other world religious leader has made this claim—ever. More crucially, no other world religious leader has made good on this claim. Jesus alone said He would rise from the dead, and Jesus alone did. And because Jesus is alive today, you can count on everything He promised about having a life of meaning and purpose both now and forever.

- *All who follow Jesus can have a relationship with Him.* Jesus doesn't just offer an eternal relationship with God in heaven. He has made it possible for His followers to enjoy an ongoing personal relationship with Him on earth. No other religion offers this sort of intimate connection with the founder. Muslims can't have a relationship with Mohammed; they must follow the Five Pillars of Islam. Followers of Buddha can't relate to their founder personally; all they can do is embrace his teachings. Christianity alone offers the followers of its founder the opportunity to be in a constant, personal, real-time relationship with God Himself through the person of Jesus.

HOW SHOULD CHRISTIANS RELATE TO PEOPLE WHO DON'T BELIEVE THE WAY THEY DO?

Because of the exclusive truth claims of Christianity, which are based on the exclusive truth claims of Jesus Christ, many Christians believe they have the right to disregard and even disrespect the beliefs of others. Consequently, those who believe that Jesus is the only way to God, and that the Bible is the only source of truth, often isolate themselves behind an "I'm right and you're wrong" mentality.

The reality of our world today is that we live in a multicultural, pluralistic culture where there are many competing ideologies and worldviews. In fact, just one-third of the people on planet earth fall into the category of "Christian." Another one-quarter of all people are Muslim. That's nearly sixty percent of the world's population. Just from the standpoint of global stability, Christians and Muslims need to figure out a way to show mutual respect for each other's beliefs. Popular writer and speaker Brian McLaren states the obvious: "If Christians, Muslims, and Jews are at each other's throats, nobody in the world is safe."[5]

Besides doing our best to live at peace with everyone (Romans 12:18), there's another reason why we need to show respect for and do our best to understand other religions and belief systems. By denying that there is truth anywhere outside of the Bible and Christianity, we are in effect denying any opportunity others may have to consider the claims of Jesus. Mike Erre points out that even Jesus didn't isolate Himself in "a fortress of truth."

Jesus clearly met people where they were and engaged them at every level. He was constantly in trouble for hanging out with the wrong people in the wrong places (How else does someone get the reputation for being a drunk and a glutton?) and engaging them with the uncompromising truth of his message.[6]

Christians need to follow Jesus by engaging the culture with God's truth, not being afraid to find out what we have in common with others. As the saying goes, "All truth is God's truth." That means that there is truth in Islam, truth in Hinduism, and in atheistic worldviews that reject God, such as secular humanism and existentialism. However, that doesn't mean that all of these belief systems are equally valid. Rather, as Mike Erre continues, it means, "Christ followers need not be threatened by truth outside the Bible, for all truth is a reflection of the Holy Creator God."[7]

Consider how this would change inter-religious dialogue. We usually approach other faith traditions from an "us versus them" mentality that argues that Christians are right and all other points of view are wrong. What if, instead of leading with the idea that all of Buddhism is wrong, we began from acknowledging that there is truth in Buddhism? When Buddhists begin by saying that life is suffering and out of joint, can't we agree? Wouldn't Paul, Solomon, or Jesus say the same thing? What does it cost us to admit that we agree on the problem but disagree regarding the solution? This is what it means to engage the culture: take it on its own terms. Claim truth wherever you find it and use it to lead others to Jesus—the source of all that is good, true, and beautiful.[8]

SHOW TRUE HUMILITY

Besides acknowledging the similarities, as well as the differences, between Christianity and other religions, there is another way to show respect for other beliefs without coming across as arrogant: *Don't be arrogant.* Talk about a blinding flash of the obvious! Too many Christians offend other people, not by the content of their message, but by the way they deliver it. And often it's the people who are most certain about their beliefs who are the most offensive.

I (Sean) spend a lot of time interacting with people who are totally opposed to the Christian story and its message about God and Jesus Christ. I'm not opposed to debating people who disagree with me, in particular atheists and skeptics. In fact, I enjoy it because I know I have the best arguments for the reality of God's existence. But rather than coming across as absolutely, positively, unequivocally certain of my position, I do my best to show respect by humbly expressing what I believe is true. And then—and this is key in any kind of exchange with someone you disagree with—I try to sincerely listen to what they have to say.

This principle of truly listening was reinforced in a positive way on a night I decided to attend a meeting of the Freethought Alliance of Orange County, a group of skeptics who regularly meet to discount the existence of God. I was an invited guest, so they knew exactly who I was and what I believed. I'm sure they were expecting me to come at them aggressively, but rather than trying to "nail" them with tough apologetic questions, I decided to build common ground and try to understand how they perceive Christians.

Here are some of the questions I asked them and how they responded. I don't necessarily agree with all of their responses, but there are some powerful lessons here that Christians need to take to heart. These are not direct quotes, but it reflects my best reconstructions of the heart of what they said.

What bad impressions do Christians leave?

- Hypocrisy. Christians often focus on particular sins such as homosexuality, while they are committing other egregious sins in their own lives.

- Christians don't take their religion seriously. Why don't they read, study, and follow the Bible if they really believe it is a word from almighty God?

- Christians often criticize us for not having good reasons for what we believe, but when pressed, they can't provide evidence for their beliefs either. They should be at least consistent and admit this.

What blind spots do Christians have?

- Christians are often rational in all areas of their lives, but they leave their brain stems at the door when they enter the church.

- Christians notice the faults in others but not in themselves.

- Christians often discourage questions once they have the truth. In fact, knowing truth tends to silence further inquiry.

How can Christians improve their interactions with skeptics and atheists?

- Listen.

- Have a more open dialogue like tonight.

- Stop looking at atheists as if they are wearing a scarlet letter.

- Don't associate beliefs with the person. Christians often get defensive when they are criticized.

- Stop making slanderous remarks about non-Christians. There are more cheap shots made about atheists than any other group.

What evidence for God would be most compelling to an atheist?

- If "Yahweh" appeared in two hundred-mile-long letters in space, I might be convinced. However, I would still need to investigate it.

- If Christians could actually provide an argument for the existence of God that was not either wrong factually, mistaken logically, or based upon emotion and manipulation.

- If God would eliminate suffering.

I listened to their concerns and did my best to articulate the Christian position as clearly and graciously as I could. We genuinely had a good time. As soon as many of the guests realized that I was not there to attack them and truly wanted to understand what they believed, they quickly dropped their guards. At the end of the evening each of the skeptics expressed how much they enjoyed the evening and hoped it would be only the beginning. Once again I learned that it doesn't matter what I know and how convincingly I argue for my position. If I don't show love and respect to those who disagree with me, they are never going to hear the truth of what I say.

THE ULTIMATE CHRISTIAN APOLOGETIC

With the possible exception of Jesus, nobody encountered more people who disagreed with him than the Apostle Paul. Because his mission was to take the Good News message of Jesus to the Gentiles and to kings (Acts 9:15), he was opposed by Jews and Roman authorities alike. Possessing a brilliant mind and a strong will, Paul was well equipped to confront and debate his opponents. Yet even someone as formidable as Paul knew it was futile to talk about his faith without respecting and even loving his enemies. "If I speak in the tongues of men or of angels, but do not have love," he wrote to the Corinthian believers, "I am only a resounding gong or a clanging cymbal" (1 Corinthians 13:1).

It's one thing to know what you believe and to be convinced that Jesus is the only way to God. And it's critical to know that the only way to have a personal relationship with God is to accept what Jesus has done for you. But unless you follow Jesus by showing love to others, your words—and even your life—will be like a resounding gong or a clanging cymbal, ringing hollow and annoying people wherever you go.

Jesus was very clear that the entire law of Scripture is summarized in just two commands: Love God and love your neighbor (Luke 10:25–28). There's no question who God is, but who is your neighbor? To clarify what He meant, Jesus told the parable of the Good Samaritan, showing that everyone—in particular any person in need—is our neighbor. This means that being a follower of Jesus is more than believing the right things. It's acting on what you believe. It's being an active part of God's story, which has a special purpose and meaning that run contrary to what most people believe.

As sinful and corrupt as this world is, God has not abandoned it. God loves the world. He loves it so much that He sent His only Son to die for every person. Yes, the world is broken, but it's not beyond repair. It's not beyond God's love. Tim Keller puts it this way:

> The world and our hearts are broken. Jesus's life, death, and resurrection was an infinitely costly rescue operation to restore justice to the oppressed and marginalized, physical wholeness to the diseased and dying, community to the isolated and lonely, and

spiritual joy and connection to those alienated from God. To be a Christian today is to become part of that same operation, with the expectation of suffering and hardship *and* the joyful assurance of eventual success.[9]

In your GodQuest, believing the truth about God is imperative, but belief alone won't give your life meaning and purpose. Belief alone won't give you the relationship you've always longed for. Christianity is not about a transaction with God. It's not about checking off a list of correct doctrines, or about passing some sort of theology test. As a wise person once said, when you get to heaven, God isn't going to give you an IQ test. It will be more like an EKG.

Having a personal and purposeful relationship with God is about being transformed by God from a self-centered, sin-infested existence to a life infused with the transforming power of the gospel—the good news that Jesus' life, death, and resurrection have made it possible for you to live a life of meaning and purpose. Of all the paths you could follow in your life, this is the one that leads to a destination that ultimately connects you with the one true God. As Keller concludes:

> The gospel is the ultimate story that shows victory coming out of defeat, strength coming out of weakness, life coming out of death, rescue from abandonment. And because it is the *true* story, it gives us hope because we know life is really like that. It can be your story as well.[10]

FOR THOSE WHO ARE STILL ON THE JOURNEY

Regardless of which path you choose at this stage of your GodQuest, your story is going to continue. If you have determined that Jesus is the path you want to follow, you have made the best choice possible. On the other hand, if you're still not sure, we want encourage you to continue your GodQuest. Don't abandon your quest because God hasn't abandoned you. He is being patient and giving you time because He wants you to come to Him; and He promises to reward you if you continue your journey with faith and sincerity (2 Peter 3:9; Hebrews 11:6).

Continue to ask questions, but don't wait until every question is answered before you choose the path. As important as it is to *know* you're making the right choice, it's more important to *believe by faith* that your choice is the right one. Trust God to give you the confidence you need to follow Him.

Finally, if you truly believe God exists, and the questions you have about God aren't insurmountable, why not give God a try? The psalmist David tells us to "taste and see that the LORD is good" (Psalm 34:8). How do you do that? Spend some time in God's neighborhood: Read the Bible, hang around some Christian friends, read more books like this one, and most important of all, pray and ask God to give you a sense of His presence. If you stay at it, something remarkable is going to happen. You will move from merely believing God exists to personally trusting the path God has made through Jesus. When that happens, your GodQuest will be complete, you will have the relationship you've always longed for, and the journey to your ultimate destination will begin.

CHAPTER 1

[1]Christian Smith and Melinda Lundquist Denton, *Souls in Transition* (New York, NY: Oxford University Press, 2005), 162–163.

[2]Mike Erre, *Why the Bible Matters* (Eugene, OR: Harvest House Publishers, 2010), 27.

[3]Ibid.

[4]Ibid., 28.

[5]Lewis wrote this in a letter in 1931, before he was a Christian, to his friend J. R. R. Tolkein.

[6]C. S. Lewis, *The Lion, the Witch and the Wardrobe* (London: Penguin Books, 1971), 75.

[7]Jon Nielson, "Teens Want More Than Pizza," The Gospel Coalition Blog, August 12, 2010. Available online at http://thegospelcoalition.org/blogs/tgc/2010/08/12/teens-pizza-no-longer-enough/.

CHAPTER 2

[1] Gordon Pennington, "Dr. Pennington on Culture and Identity," thetruthproject.com. Available online at http://www.thetruthproject.org/about/culturefocus/A000000448.cfm

[2] "Truth," wikipedia.org, accessed May 1, 2011. Available online at en.wikipedia.org/wiki/Truth.

[3] Cathy Lynn Grossman, "Pastor Mark Driscoll: Millennials are honest on faith," *USA Today*, April 27, 2010. Available online at http://content.usatoday.com/communities/Religion/post/2010/04/christian-millennials-prayer-church/1.

[4] James Davison Hunter, *To Change the World* (Oxford: Oxford University Press, 2010).

[5] J. P. Moreland and Klaus Issler, *In Search of a Confident Faith* (Downers Grove, IL: IVP Books, 2008), 47–49.

[6] Audrey Barrick, "Thousands Think Orange, Fight 'Surrogate Faith,'" christianpost.com, May 1, 2010. Available online at http://www.

christianpost.com/article/20100501/thousands-think-orange-fight-surrogate-faith/.

[7] Moreland and Issler, *In Search of a Confident Faith*, 52.

[8] Peter Kreeft and Ronald K. Tacelli, *Handbook of Christian Apologetics*, (Downers Grove, IL: InterVarsity Press, 1994), 364–366.

[9] C. S. Lewis, *Christian Reflections* (Grand Rapids, MI: William B. Eerdmans Publishing Company, 1968), 72–81.

[10] Francis J. Beckwith and Gregory Koukl, *Relativism: Feet Firmly Planted in Mid-Air* (Grand Rapids, MI: Baker Books, 2002), 19–20.

[11] Douglas Groothuis, *Truth Decay* (Downers Grove, IL: InterVarsity Press, 2000), 60–82.

[12] Roger Nicole, "The Biblical Concept of Truth," in *Scripture and Truth*, ed. D. A. Carson and John D. Woodbridge (Grand Rapids, MI: Zondervan, 1983), 296.

[13] Timothy Keller, *The Reason for God* (New York: Dutton, 2008), 46.

[14] Josh McDowell and Sean McDowell, *The Unshakable Truth* (Eugene, OR: 2010), 43.

[15] Ibid., 44.

CHAPTER 3

[1] Andy Crouch, "The Gospel of Steve Jobs," ChristianityToday.com, January 21, 2011. Available online at http://www.christianitytoday.com/ct/2011/januaryweb-only/gospelstevejobs.html.

[2] Steve Jobs, "Transcript of Commencement Speech at Stanford University," Freerepublic.com, June 14, 2005. Available online at http://www.freerepublic.com/focus/chat/1422863/posts.

[3] George Barna, "Barna Studies the Research, Offers a Year-in-Review Perspective, Barna.org, accessed January 12, 2010. Available online at http://www.barna.org/barna-update/article/12-faithspirituality/325-barna-studies-the-research-offers-a-year-in-review-perspective.

[4] Ibid.

[5] Cathy Lynn Grossman, "Pastor Mark Driscoll: Millennials are honest on faith."

[6] John Blake, "Are there dangers in being 'spiritual but not religious?'" CNN.com, June 3, 2010. Available online at http://articles.cnn.com/2010-06-03/living/spiritual.but.not.religious_1_spiritual-community-religious-god?_s=PM:LIVING.

[7] Drew Dyck, "Six Kinds of Ex-Christians," ConversantLife.com, October 22, 2010. Available online at http://www.conversantlife.com/belief/six-kinds-of-ex-christians.

[8] Paul Vitz, "The Psychology of Atheism," in A Place for Truth, edited by Dallas Willard (Downers Grove, IL: InterVarsity Press, 2010), 138.

[9] Ibid., 139.

[10] Ibid., 139–140.

[11] Tim Keller, "Reason for God: The Exclusivity of Truth," in A Place for Truth, edited by Dallas Willard (Downers Grove, IL: InterVarsity Press, 2010), 55.

[12] Stephen Prothero, God Is Not One: The Eight Rival Religions That Run the World and Why Their Differences Matter (San Francisco, CA: HarperOne, 2010).

[13] Keller, "Reason for God, The Exclusivity of Truth", 59.

[14] Keller, The Reason for God, 15.

[15] Ibid.

[16] These criteria can be found in Craig Hazen's excellent book, Five Sacred Crossings (Harvest House Publishers, Eugene, OR: 2008).

[17] For more information on this teaching see "2 Nephi 25:23—A Distinctive Mormon Passage on Salvation," by the Mormonism Research Ministry at http://mrm.org/2-nephi-25-23.

CHAPTER 4

[1] A. W. Tozer, The Knowledge of the Holy (San Francisco, CA: Harper & Row Publishers, 1961), 16.

[2] Erwin Lutzer, *Ten Lies About God* (Nashville, TN: Word Publishing, 2000), 3.

[3] R. C. Sproul, *Essential Truths of the Christian Faith* (Wheaton, IL: Tyndale House Publishers, 1992), 32.

[4] James Montgomery Boice, *Foundations of the Christian Faith* (Downers Grove, IL: InterVarsity Press, 1986), 102–103.

[5] Albert Mohler, "The Knowledge of the Self-Revealing God: Starting Point for the Christian Worldview," AlbertMohler.com, December 3, 2010. Available online at http://www.albertmohler.com/2010/12/03/the-knowledge-of-the-self-revealing-god-starting-point-for-the-christian-worldview.

CHAPTER 5

[1] Richard Dawkins, *The God Delusion* (New York, NY: Houghton Mifflin Harcourt, 2006), 31.

[2] Sean has co-written a book responding to the new atheists called *Is God Just a Human Invention* (Grand Rapids, MI: 2010).

[3] Keller, *The Reason for God*, 121.

[4] Bruce Bickel and Stan Jantz, *Evidence for Faith 101* (Eugene, OR: Harvest House Publishers, 2008), 72.

[5] C. S. Lewis, *The Weight of Glory* (Grand Rapids, MI: William B. Eerdmans Publishing Company, 1972).

[6] Keller, 127ff.

[7] Bruce Bickel and Stan Jantz, *World Religions and Cults 101* (Eugene, OR: Harvest House Publishers, 2002), 236.

[8] Thomas Nagel, "The Fear of Religion," review of *The God Delusion* by Richard Dawkins, The New Republic (October 23, 2006).

[9] Bickel and Jantz, *World Religions and Cults 101*, 238.

[10] William Lane Craig, *Reasonable Faith* (Wheaton, IL: Crossway Books, 1994), 31.

[11] Ibid., 48.

[12] This argument is sometimes known as the Kalam Cosmological argument. *Kalam* is an Arabic word that means "speech."

[13] Kreeft, *Handbook of Christian Apologetics*, 37.

[14] Robert Jastrow, *God and the Astronomers* (New York, NY: Norton, 1992), 13.

[15] R. Douglas Geivett, "Two Versions of the Cosmological Argument," in *Passionate Conviction*, ed. Paul Copan and William Lane Craig (Ada, MI: Baker Academic, 2007), 66.

[16] Keller, 141.

[17] C. S. Lewis, *Mere Christianity* (New York, NY: Simon & Schuster, 1996), 30.

[18] Kreeft, 75.

[19] D. A. Carson, *The God Who Is There* (Grand Rapids, MI: Baker Books, 2010), 19.

CHAPTER 6

[1] A. W. Tozer, *The Knowledge of the Holy* (San Francisco, CA: Harper & Row, Publishers, 1961), 10.

[2] C. S. Lewis, "Man or Rabbit?" in *God in the Dock: Essays on Theology and Ethics*, ed. Walter Hooper (Grand Rapids, MI: Eerdmans, 1970), 108–9.

[3] Jay Richards, "The Contemporary Argument for Design: An Overview" in *Passionate Conviction*, ed. Paul Copan and William Lane Craig (Ada, MI: Baker Academic, 2007), 72.

[4] Norman L. Geisler, *Baker Encyclopedia of Christian Apologetics* (Grand Rapids, MI: Baker Books, 2002), 521.

[5] Geisler, 233.

[6] For a thorough treatment of whether or not Darwin's theory of evolution is compatible with belief in God, read *God and Evolution*, ed. Jay Richards (Seattle, WA: Discovery Institute Press, 2010).

[7] Sean McDowell and William A. Dembski, *Understanding Intelligent Design* (Eugene, OR: Harvest House Publishers, 2008), 42.

[8] Some young earth creationists may believe the earth is as old as forty thousand or fifty thousand years old. But what distinguishes all young earth

creationists is that they believe the earth is only thousands, rather than billions of years in age.

[9] Dinesh D'Souza, *What's So Great About Christianity* (Washington, DC: Regnery, 2007), 32.

[10] McDowell and Dembski, 22.

[11] David Berlinski, "The Deniable Darwin," in *Darwinism, Design, and Public Education*, ed. John Angus Campbell and Stephen C. Meyer (East Lansing, MI: Michigan State University Press, 2003), 170.

[12] William Dembski, *The Design Revolution* (Downers Grove, IL: InterVarsity Press, 2004), 63.

[13] Ibid.

[14] Hugh Ross, "Why I Believe in the Miracle of Divine Creation," in *Why I Am a Christian*, ed. Norman L. Geisler and Paul K. Hoffman (Grand Rapids, MI: Baker Books, 2001), 137.

[15] This selected list of fine-tuned characteristics is taken from Hugh Ross, *The Creator and the Cosmos* (Colorado Springs, CO: NavPress, 2001), 154–7.

[16] Francis Collins, *The Language of God* (New York, NY: Free Press, 2006), 74.

[17] Michael Behe, "Irreducible Complexity: Obstacle to Darwinian Evolution," in *Debating Design*, ed. By William A. Dembski and Michael Ruse (New York, NY: Cambridge University Press, 2004), 353.

[18] For a thorough and treatment of irreducible complexity and its influence in the intelligent design movement, see Michael Behe's book *Darwin's Black Box* (New York, NY: Free Press, 2006).

[19] McDowell and Dembski, 128.

[20] For more resources, see the *GodQuest Study Guide*.

[21] Collins, 74–5

CHAPTER 7

[1] Mike Erre, *Why the Bible Matters* (Eugene, OR: Harvest House Publishers, 2010), 20.

[2] Henrietta Mears, *What the Bible Is All About* (Ventura, CA: Regal Books, 1983), 20.

[3] Erre, 27.

[4] Tim Keller, *The Reason for God*, 99.

[5] Robert Jastrow, *God and the Astronomers* (New York, NY: W.W. Norton & Company, 1992), 13.

[6] Don Carson, *The God Who Is There* (Grand Rapids, MI: Baker Books, 2010), 33.

[7] Erre, 69.

[8] Ibid., 84

[9] Ibid., 119.

CHAPTER 8

[1] Kenneth D. Boa and Robert M. Bowman Jr., *Twenty Compelling Evidences That God Exists* (Tulsa, OK: RiverOak Publishing, 2002), 132.

[2] This Bible, known as The Jefferson Bible, or The Life and Morals of Jesus of Nazareth, "gives an account of the events of Jesus' life without references to angels, genealogy, or prophecy. Miracles, references to the Trinity and the divinity of Jesus, and Jesus' resurrection are also absent from the Jefferson Bible in its focus on the physical life and moral teachings of Jesus rather than its spiritual aspects" (from Amazon.com).

[3] Norman Geisler and Ron Brooks, *When Skeptics Ask* (Grand Rapids, MI: Baker Books, 1990), 145.

[4] Ibid., 146.

[5] R. C. Sproul, *Essentials Truths of the Christian Faith* (Wheaton, IL: Tyndale House Publishers, 1992), 15.

[6] Geisler and Brooks, 146.

[7] Ibid., 153–4.

[8] Ken Berding, "How Did the New Testament Canon Come Together?" Sundoulos, Spring 2007, 5.

[9] Josh D. McDowell and Sean McDowell, *More Than a Carpenter* (Wheaton, IL: Living Books, 2009), 68.

[10] Elaine Pagels, *Beyond Belief* (New York, NY: Random House, 2003), 40.

[11] Bruce M. Metzger, *The Canon of the New Testament* (Oxford: Clarendon Press, 1987), 173.

[12] McDowell and McDowell, 69.

[13] Josh McDowell and Sean McDowell, *The Unshakable Truth* (Eugene, OR: Harvest House Publishers, 2010) 96.

[14] Timothy Keller, *The Reason for God* (New York, NY: Dutton, 2008), 113.

CHAPTER 9

[1] Mike Erre, *Why the Bible Matters* (Eugene, OR: Harvest House Publishers, 2010), 133.

[2] Walt Russell, *Playing with Fire* (Colorado Springs, CO: NavPress, 2000), 29.

[3] Ibid., 23–24.

[4] Mike Erre, 169.

[5] Robert H. Stein, *A Basic Guide to Interpreting the Bible* (Grand Rapids, MI: Baker Books, 1994), 195.

[6] Brian Godawa, *Word Pictures: Knowing God Through Story and Imagination* (Downers Grove, IL: InterVarsity Press, 2009).

[7] Henrietta Mears, *What the Bible Is All About* (Ventura, CA: Regal Books, 1983), 624.

[8] Kevin DeYoung, "The Doctrine of Scripture: Four Points from Two Verses," The Gospel Coalition, November 30, 2010. Available online at http://thegospelcoalition.org/blogs/kevindeyoung/2010/11/30/the-doctrine-of-scripture-four-points-from-two-verses.

[9] Ibid.

[10] R.C. Sproul, *Essential Truths of the Christian Faith* (Wheaton, IL: Tyndale House Publishers, 1992), 25.

[11] Ibid.

CHAPTER 10

[1] "Sticky Faith/College Transition," fulleryouthinstitute.org. Available online at http://fulleryouthinstitute.org/college-transition.

[2] Ross Douthat, "A Case for Hell," nytimes.com. Available online at http://www.nytimes.com/2011/04/25/opinion/25douthat.html?scp=5&sq=ross%20douthat&st=cse.

[3] Peter Kreeft and Ronald K. Tacelli, *Handbook of Christian Apologetics* (Downers Grove, IL: InterVarsity Press, 1994), 139.

[4] Wayne Grudem, *Systematic Theology* (Grand Rapids, MI: Zondervan Publishing House, 1994), 197.

[5] Lee Strobel, *A Case For Faith* (Grand Rapids, MI: Zondervan Publishing House, 2000), 37.

[6] Joni Eareckson Tada, "Something Greater Than Healing," www.christianitytoday.com. Available at http://www.christianitytoday.com/ct/2010/october/12.30.html.

[7] Norman Geisler and Ron Brooks, *When Skeptics Ask* (Grand Rapids, MI: Baker Books, 1990), 64–65.

[8] Ibid., 65.

[9] R.C Sproul, *Essential Truths of the Christian Faith* (Wheaton, IL: Tyndale House Publishers, 1992), 147.

[10] Ibid.

[11] Ibid, 147–48

[12] Clay Jones, "Human Nature," presented at Biola University November 18, 2009.

[13] Ibid.

[14] C. S. Lewis, *The Problem of Pain* (New York, NY: The Macmillan Company, 1970), 89

[15] Lewis, 46.

[16] "A Loving God, an Eternal Hell?," *Clear Direction*, June/July/August 2009, 25–27.

[17] Dale Fincher, *Living with Questions* (Grand Rapids, MI: Zondervan/Youth Specialties, 2007),

[18] Lewis, 116.

GODQUEST

CHAPTER 11

[1] Edwin A. Blum, "John," in *The Bible Knowledge Commentary*, New Testament, ed. John F. Walvoord and Roy B. Zuck (Colorado Springs, CO: Victor Books, 2000), 337.

[2] Ibid.

[3] William Lane Craig, *Reasonable Faith* (Wheaton, IL: Crossway Books, 1994), 225.

[4] Lee Strobel, *The Case for the Real Jesus* (Grand Rapids, MI: Zondervan, 2007), 43.

[5] Mike Erre, *The Jesus of Suburbia* (Nashville, TN: W Publishing Group, 2006), 15.

[6] William Lane Craig, "Rediscovering the Historical Jesus: Presuppositions and Pretensions of the Jesus Seminar," www.leaderu.com. Available online at http://www.leaderu.com/offices/billcraig/docs/rediscover1.html

[7] Scot McKnight, "Who Is Jesus?" An Introduction to Jesus Studies," *Jesus Under Fire*, Michael J. Wilkins and J.P. Moreland, eds. (Grand Rapids, MI: Zondervan Publishing House, 1995), 66.

[8] Ibid., 66–67.

[9] C. S. Lewis, *Mere Christianity* (New York, NY: Touchstone, 1996), 56.

CHAPTER 12

[1] Martha Woodruff, "Why Can't We Just Let Jesus Be Jesus?" www.onfaith. washingtonpost.com. Available online at http://onfaith.washingtonpost.com/onfaith/guestvoices/2011/03/why_cant_we_just_let_jesus_be_jesus.html

[2] Mike Err, *The Jesus of Suburbia* (Nashville, TN: W Publishing Group, 2006), 16.

[3] Lee Strobel, *The Case For Christ* (Grand Rapids, MI: Zondervan Publishing House, 1998), 45.

[4] *Jesus Under Fire*, Michael J. Wilkins and J.P. Moreland, eds. (Grand Rapids, MI: Zondervan Publishing House, 1995), 212.

[5] R. Douglas Geivett, "The Evidential Value of Miracles," in *In Defense of Miracles*, ed. by R. Douglas Geivett and Gary Habermas (Downers Grove, IL: InterVarsity Press, 1997), 179.

[6] Kenneth D. Boa and Robert M. Bowman Jr., *20 Compelling Evidences That God Exists* (Tulsa, OK: River Oak Publishing, 2002), 217.

[7] Paul Enns, *The Moody Handbook of Theology* (Chicago, IL: Moody Press, 1989), 323.

[8] Kenneth D. Boa and Robert M. Bowman Jr., 225.

[9] For an in-depth examination of the historical evidence for the resurrection and its significance, see *Evidence for the Resurrection* by Josh and Sean McDowell (Ventura, CA: Regal Books, 1009).

[10] John Stott, *Basic Christianity* (Downers Grove IL: Inter-Varsity Press, 1971), 50.

[11] Tim Keller, *King's Cross* (New York, NY: Dutton, 2011), 218.

CHAPTER 13

[1] Kevin Shrum, "Reclaiming Jesus as the 'Only Way'", www.christianpost.com. Available online at http://www.christianpost.com/article/20110205/reclaiming-jesus-as-the-only-way-48844.

[2] William Lane Craig, *Reasonable Faith* (Wheaton, IL: Crossway Books, 1994), 233.

[3] Shrum, "Reclaiming Jesus as the Only Way."

[4] Greg Koukl, president of Stand to Reason, has written a booklet called "Jesus, the Only Way: 100 Verses." As Greg demonstrates, there are at least one hundred verses in the New Testament where it is claimed that Jesus is the only way to God. This booklet can be purchased from www.str.org.

[5] Craig, 246–249.

[6] King's Cross, 39.

[7] Craig, 251.

[8] Ibid.

[9] C.S. Lewis, *Mere Christianity* (New York, NY: Touchstone, 1996), 56.

[10] One of the best treatments of the Lewis "trilemma" is found in Unbreakable Truth by Josh and Sean McDowell, 160–63.

[11] Peter Kreeft and Ronald K. Tacelli, Handbook of Christian Apologetics (Downers Grove, IL: InterVarsity Press, 1994), 159.

[12] Ibid.

[13] Timothy Keller, A Reason for God (New York, NY: Dutton, 2008), 101.

[14] Ibid., 105.

[15] Kreeft and Tacelli, 163.

[16] Scot McKnight, The Jesus Creed (Brewster, MA: Paraclete Press, 2004), 185.

[17] R. Douglas Geivett, "Is Jesus the Only Way?" in Jesus Under Fire, Michael Wilkins and J. P. Moreland, eds. (Grand Rapids, MI: Zondervan Publishing House, 1995), 199.

CHAPTER 14

[1] C. S. Lewis, God In the Dock (Grand Rapids, MI: William B. Eerdmans Publishing Company, 1972), 108–09.

[2] Craig Hazen, "Christianity in a World of Religions," in Passionate Conviction, ed. By Paul Copan and William Lane Craig (Nashville, TN: Baker Academic, 2007), 143.

[3] Tim Keller, King's Cross (New York, NY: Dutton, 2011), 229.

[4] Stephen Prothero, God Is Not One (San Francisco, CA: HarperOne, 2010), 11.

[5] Brian D. McLaren, A New Kind of Christianity (San Francisco, CA: HarperOne, 2010), 208.

[6] Mike Erre, The Jesus of Suburbia (Nashville, TN: W Publishing, 2006), 163.

[7] Ibid., 167.

[8] Ibid., 167–68.

[9] Timothy Keller, The Reason for God (New York, NY: Dutton, 2008), 224–25.

[10] Keller, King's Cross, 230.

GODQUEST

From Sean McDowell:

What a joy to work with the Outreach team in producing this book. Stan, you were the perfect person to partner with on this project. You brought creativity, passion, and insight. Thanks for coaching us, Jennifer. We definitely could not have done it without you. Scott, thanks for your vision and belief in this project. This has truly been a journey!

From Stan Jantz:

Thanks to Sean and Jennifer and the entire Outreach team for developing the vision for the GodQuest books and resources. I also want to thank Lauren for giving me the inspiration I needed. Working on this book reminded me just how much God loves us and richly rewards those who seek Him.

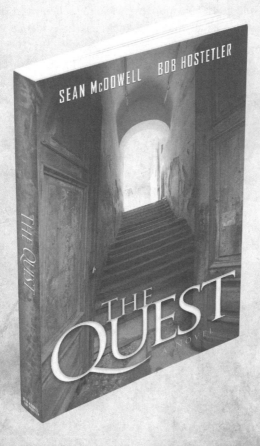

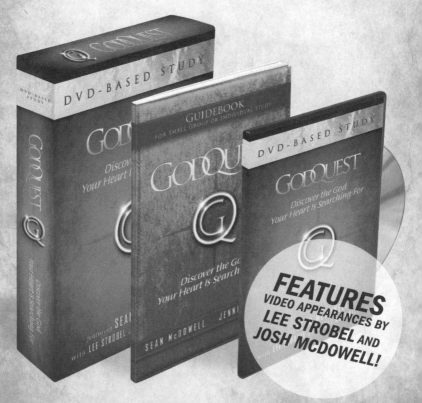

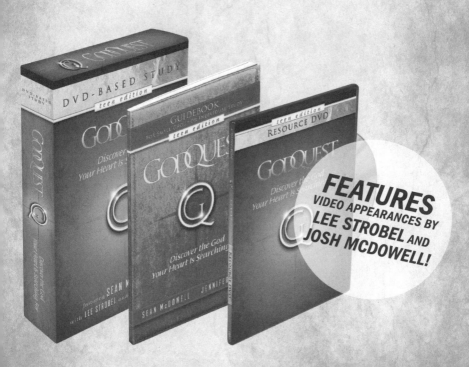